CELEBRATING
THE GREAT MOTHER

CELEBRATING
THE GREAT MOTHER

*A Handbook of Earth-Honoring Activities
for Parents and Children*

CAIT JOHNSON AND MAURA D. SHAW

FOREWORD BY DIANE MARIECHILD

DESTINY BOOKS
ROCHESTER, VERMONT

Destiny Books
One Park Street
Rochester, Vermont 05767
www.InnerTraditions.com

Destiny Books is a division of Inner Traditions International

Library of Congress Cataloging-in-Publication Data

Johnson, Cait.
Celebrating the Great Mother : a handbook of earth-honoring
activities for parents and children / Cait Johnson and Maura D. Shaw.
p.   cm.
Includes bibliographical references and index.
ISBN 978-0-89281-550-0
1. Earth—Religious aspects.   2. Nature—Religious aspects.   3. Seasons—Religious aspects.
4. Goddess religion.   5. Children—Religious life.   6. Parenting—Religious aspects.
7. Rites and ceremonies.   8. New Age movement.   9. Circle—Religious aspects.
I. Shaw, Maura D.   II. Title.
BL438.2.J64   1995
291.4'46—dc20

Printed and bound in India by Replika Press Pvt. Ltd.

10

Illustrations on pages ii, vi, vii, x, 1, 66, 89, 104, 107, 136, 157, 165, 193, and 203 by Lee Lawson
Illustrations on pages v, 23, 32, 33, 44, 93, 97, 116, 120, 131, 137, 144, 146, 147, 154, 159, 162–163,
170, 180, 182, 185, 192, and 200 by Bonnie F. Atwater

Text design by Bonnie F. Atwater
This book was typeset in Minion, Frutiger, and Lucida Sans with Wade Sans Light as a display font.

In honor of the Goddess,
whose rising is our constant inspiration.

For our sons, Reid and Nick,
and our partners, Stu and Joe,
with loving thanks.

If we could strip away the ideologies that separate us,
stop the greedy destruction, and meet by the riverside,
we would discover that we are all children of the same earth
and that our lives are patterned by the ceremonial flow
of the sun, moon, seasons, and tides.
We are all one in the spirit and in the body.

—Sedonia Cahill and Joshua Halpern,
The Ceremonial Circle

CONTENTS

PART 2

THE FESTIVALS

89

PART 3

MAGICAL
ALLIES

203

FOREWORD

You hold in your hands an extraordinary book. With grace and insight emerging from their own deep experience, Cait Johnson and Maura D. Shaw have created a guidebook for parents, teachers, and caregivers to explore earth-based spirituality with their children. While drawing primarily from their roots, a Goddess-based Celtic tradition, they respectfully acknowledge the wisdom of the Native Americans upon whose soil we live. Cait and Maura warmly invite you to join their circle and celebrate the renewal of the Earth and our own inner power. Both authors are the mothers of young sons, and their firsthand knowledge of children shines through their writing. They have provided us with information, rituals, and activities that invite even the most hesitant to joyfully and respectfully reconnect with our home planet.

Parenting is a special commitment and, as parents entering the twenty-first century, we are presented with enormous challenges. One such challenge is how to share a spiritual path with our children in today's glittery and fast-paced world. In preparation for writing this foreword, I called my sons, now in their late twenties, and asked them what they remembered of the rituals and circles we had shared when they were children. What they remembered were not the details of the altar quickly constructed when their pet cat was killed or the candle circle we made during a winter storm when the electricity went out. Instead, they remembered a feeling of kinship and a sensitivity to all life. This pleases me. The world today has too many people who are not afraid to kill. For mutual respect and peace-making, the rituals and practices of the spiritual traditions we share with our young people must have a common foundation of nonharm and loving kindness. We need more people who are not afraid to live fully: to be kind, to have self-respect, to share, to respect others.

The spiritual path is a means to open the heart. The rituals and practices are only guides to the truth. They are not the truth. Spiritual practice is demonstrated by the way we live. Are we kind and respectful? Do we create clear boundaries? Without gentleness there is no room, no freedom. Kindness and clarity create the space where truth can emerge. For us to survive on the spiritual path we have to learn how to deal with obstacles and difficulties, how to process doubts, how to transform our suffering and emotions, how to work with and integrate the practices, how to evoke and enact compassion. Cait and Maura have provided adults and children with a foundation for joining together to mark the changing of the seasons and to connect to the earth, our ancestors, and one another. By celebrating the ancient holy days and cultivating caring, gratitude, and respect for all life, children and adults can learn to embody the clarity, insight, and compassion so needed in the world.

Celebrating the Great Mother is a nourishing and delightful book. I am grateful that it exists, and I am excited by the possibilities it offers to us and to our children. May it be of great benefit to all. May the sound of our children's laughter bring happiness to all that lives.

Diane Mariechild,
author of *Mother Wit*

PREFACE

We are currently in the midst of a great resurgence, a rebirth of earth-honoring community. People everywhere are awakening to the magic of Circles, the ancient, sacred shape of spiritual celebration that gives us such a powerful way to heal the alienation from self and from the earth that the prevailing culture has fostered, with its teachings of domination over nature and separateness from deity. Circles have no hierarchy—they are all-inclusive, the great shape of acceptance and spiritual possibility. In Circles we can celebrate the renewal of the earth, and our own inner power.

For many of us, joining with others to honor the seasons, the ancient holy days that mark the year's progression, is becoming a vital way of life. By celebrating these ancient, powerful festivals together, we make connection to the earth, to our ancestors, and to one another, affirming our own unique place on the ever-turning wheel. And we affirm the return of the Goddess, the feminine value that sanctifies nurturing, creativity, and community-making, rather than exploitation and power-over. The Goddess path celebrates our bodies as wise and holy, and this planet as a living being, calling forth our devotion. It is a path that offers hope for world-healing.

Adults now have a wonderful array of guidebooks to help them as they explore earth-based spirituality. But what if we want to include our children? How can we create meaningful spiritual experiences that will both teach and inspire them? We offer this book as a way for parents, caregivers, teachers, and counselors to involve children in the dance of the seasons—to help them connect with the same sense of earth magic that is so healing and enriching to us.

We are both part of a women's Full Moon group, an energizing place for us to explore our adult issues, heal ourselves and each other, and celebrate the Goddess. By necessity it is an all-adult group. But as we packed our crystals and candles and drums to go to Circle, it gradually began to feel sad and wrong to see our children wistfully watching, left out and eventually left behind. We wrote this book with the children in mind, as a way to include them in this whole wonderful world that we are discovering, to teach them the Goddess's way.

There are so many of us who yearn to inhabit the numinous in our daily lives—who are beginning to recover a sense of oneness with nature—and who long to share the healing and beauty of the earth-based path with our children. This book, filled with Goddess-centered activities and celebrations to inspire and delight children and adults of all ages, helps us to begin. Lots of us could use some ideas and guidance on what to do with our children to celebrate the winter solstice, for instance, or the vernal equinox. And we want to know how to truly honor the spirit of Samhain, the original Halloween, in a way that may include trick-or-treating but that also addresses the spiritual roots of the holiday.

In this book, then, we offer you and your family a gentle and enjoyable way to begin finding your own place on the great wheel, because by giving our children a direct and joyous experience of their oneness with the earth, with other people, and with the divine, we give them the key, not only to personal wholeness and health, but to the health of this planet, which they will one day inherit.

It is also certainly possible to use this book alone or with an adult group of the like-minded: even if you don't have children in your life, there is still a Wild Child in all of us who cries out for nourishment and who responds instantly to the magic and sheer joy of the Great Mother's pattern. It is that pattern we celebrate here.

With great hope for a more life-affirming, earth-honoring, and joy-creating culture, we invite you all to join the ancient, sacred dance that is renewed year after year.

We offer our heartfelt thanks to Robin Dutcher-Bayer, our editor at Inner Traditions, for her enthusiastic support. Her guidance in shaping a deeper and more universal conception of our work made it a stronger book.

It was a pleasure to work with Tami Calliope, our copyeditor, who approached the manuscript with insight and sensitivity. She is a kindred spirit.

We would also like to thank the staff at Inner Traditions, who made this entire book-birthing process such an easy and pleasant one.

PART 1

Earth-Connected Parenting

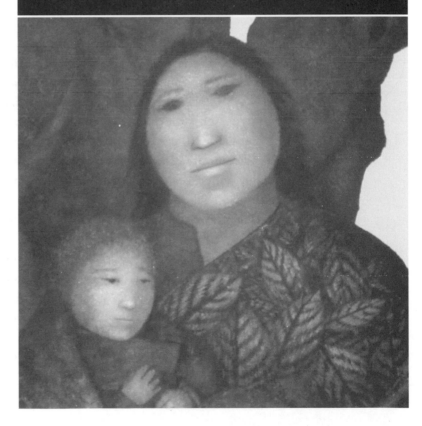

CHAPTER 1

ANCIENT FESTIVALS

A Sense of Coming Home

It is cold and dark. The nights have grown longer and longer—it seems the sun will never return. The earth is barren and the fields are bleak. Huddled together for warmth, the people wait, eyes gleaming in the firelight, telling stories, sharing dreams, honoring the dark time, looking forward to the light. Finally the special night comes. The whole tribe, the adults and the children, meet together—on the hill, or in the square, or in the great hall—because tonight is the longest night of the year. Every person is needed to make the sun rise again. So they build a huge bonfire in honor of the sun, and they dance, and sing, and make noise with rattles and drums and bells, all night long. And when the sun comes up on Yule morning, each person there knows that she or he was actively involved in bringing this about. Joyful, tired, and deeply satisfied, the people greet the dawn. They have shared something that will warm them for the rest of the long winter: a living sense of magic. With their help, the Earth Mother Goddess has labored all night and birthed the sun once more. The days will grow longer now. And in a few months, the fields that are her body will flower. The wheel, the great cosmic circle, has turned itself again.

Once, cultures worldwide held community celebrations to mark the longest night of the year, celebrations that honored each participant—woman, man, and child—as equal sharers in the mystery. Festivals such as these are rooted in prehistory and, although much has been lost, enough has survived to give us a good start if we want to explore and re-experience them. What we are seeing now is a great movement toward doing just that.

For the most part, though, today's movement toward earth-based spirituality and living with a sense of conscious community has focused on the needs and desires of adults. Only adults can buy the books, order the audiotapes, attend the transformative personal-growth workshops, and otherwise nurture their spiritual selves at will. Children have neither the economic power nor the conscious maturity to choose what they need—but they are by nature eager and excited participants in celebrations of any kind. The opportunity to guide that enthusiasm and energy is open to us as teachers, counselors, and parents. In earlier times, the community included children in the rituals of daily life—the songs and stories told by the elders, the traditional ways of planting and harvesting, the creation of beauty in everyday things to honor the Earth Mother for her gifts. But our present Western society, with its isolating segregation of old from young, discourages the inclusion of children in all but the most controlled aspects of spiritual practice. Because so many of us were raised in that culture—where we dressed in our finest clothes each week to sit still without squirming for at least an hour, while grownups at the front of the church or synagogue droned on and on—we may not have many workable ideas about how to bring our own children into spiritual awareness in an enjoyable way. We *want* to include them, to share the joy that connection with a spiritual power greater than oneself can bring, but how can we as individuals learn to reach out to our children while they still retain their innate sense of the mystical?

The simple answer is this: Go back to the beginning. Incorporate into our modern lives the sacred harmony of "living in the present" that our ancestors practiced, and that young children seem to possess so naturally. Create traditions for singing and dancing and celebrating the wonderful gifts of life on our planet. Honor the circle of the seasons, year after year, with activities and rituals that will repeat and also change as the children grow older. In doing these things together, we will begin to reshape the future.

In recent years, pioneering scholars such as Marija Gimbutas and Riane Eisler have uncovered and articulated a body of evidence that suggests the existence of whole societies based on the values of the Earth Mother Goddess—values of community, nurturing, and creativity rather than a hierarchy of power and powerlessness and the desire for gain-at-any-cost of the later sky-god cultures. And while some consider these Goddess cultures to be utopian fantasies, the reality is that we, as a society, are in dire need of transformation, and these values are the very ones we need to encourage and support if our culture is to survive at all.

In remaking our sense of the spiritual, we remake society. This is the work in which many of us, sometimes unconsciously, are involved. In rediscovering the ancient Goddess way, we have found a way to re-member parts of ourselves with which we have been long out of touch and that are waking up at last. The Great Mother offers us healing for ourselves and for our diseased planet. And it is the earth-centered festivals that connect us with her in very real and tangible ways.

We return to these ancient festivals that mark the quarter and cross-quarter days on the great wheel of the year—festivals that our ancestors honored and celebrated with rituals and customs, some of which have survived, more or less recognizably, today. In a sense, renewing our connection to these timeless holy days is a coming home, a way to recover something that we *are,* deeply—but that our society has lost or forgotten. Although our technology has mushroomed past any person's ability to comprehend it all, our inner selves are not much different than they were thousands of years ago. We all share an instinctual, deep self—an inner landscape populated by myth and archetype, nurtured by fairy tales and legends from a distant shared path of consciousness. These ancient celebrations speak to that inner self and its need—the need to take a living, active part in the great drama that nature plays out on our planet year after year.

When we honor the annual cycles of sprouting, growth, fruiting, decaying, dying, and sprouting again, we give ourselves the gift of serenity. There is something deeply satisfying and reassuring about those cycles, a promise of rebirth and renewal while honoring the processes of death and decay. By consciously aligning ourselves with the pattern, we honor our own processes—and we make a deep and powerful connection with our planet. It becomes a kind of sacred trust to share that connection with our children.

These are special events we celebrate here, moments in time created by the sun and earth together. They teach us gently about embracing the moment—and then gracefully letting go. At Mabon, the autumnal equinox, day and night are equal—but only for an instant. Between one breath and the next, our planet has whirled away, and we must wait an entire year for this particular moment of balance and harmony to come again. The festivals mark important pauses and the seasons honor gradual changes. Both have much to teach us about living in the moment and living wisely.

Celebrating the yearly pattern gives us a way to recover our sense of the earth as deeply sacred; the earth becomes the body of the Great Goddess who teaches us so much. She is knowable—we have direct, personal experience of the great mysteries, of a living spirituality—and the world becomes filled with magic. Far from the alienated and alienating views of cultures that teach dominance over nature—giving humanity the license to pollute and destroy the planet—and that make the earth a sterile wasteland devoid of spirit, this ancient way breathes spirit into all things. The very rocks and trees become our guides, the animals our allies. All are sacred and vitally important to the whole.

In exploring and celebrating the ancient ways, we affirm our commitment to healing the planet and each other, since if we see the earth as the body of our sacred Mother, we are much less likely to wound and damage her. And if we honor our own ability to know, to be wise and powerful—if, in fact, we celebrate our own Goddess-essence—we heal the split so many of us have sustained between our daily, conscious selves and our inner, deep selves. Vicki Noble conveys this idea beautifully in her ground-breaking book *Motherpeace:*

> Most of us these days find ourselves less than fully well, physically or mentally—somehow out of balance. We can feel our dis-ease, but don't ordinarily know the solutions to it. If we knew how to make ourselves well, we would almost certainly do so. The great gift of the Goddess is such a healing. To the individual, she brings personal well-being and an experience of fully living. To humanity, she could bring the harmony that comes with a recognition that we are all connected in spirit to this planet. We depend upon it for survival and we owe it the gift of life.

It is vital to emphasize here that following the way of the Goddess is *not* a prerequisite for using the activities in this book. It is meant to be a handbook for everyone, because whatever your religious or spiritual beliefs may be, the one thing we all share is existence on this planet, an existence that is becoming more and more threatened and precarious. For many of you reading this book, the idea that earth-based spirituality offers hope and healing is nothing new. But the idea of actively seeking out ways to involve and teach our children how to walk this path along with us may be very new indeed. And this book is for those of us who want to share our love of the earth with children, who know how important this is for the future of our planet, and who could use some ideas on how to do it.

After all, most families seek to create traditions that teach the values they hold sacred or important and that give continuity, security, closeness, and a sense of magical wonder to their children. The eight festivals celebrated in this book are the traditions of the human family. Before calendars were available to everyone, people looked to the festivals as guideposts for planting and harvesting, for living in ways that would ensure the continuation of human life. Celebration of the great cosmic dance was a celebration of our place on the wheel and of its vast resource for us, as teacher, guide, and nurturing Mother.

Here, then, is an overview of this yearly cycle, a starting point for understanding its impact on us today. We give the festivals their old Celtic names, partly because these reflect our own particular heritage, but also because we have found that the use of an unusual, magical name restores a special significance to these days. So many of them passed us by without our acknowledging their importance; for years, the day may have been just plain old August first—but *now* it's Lughnasad. It makes a difference.

Four of the festivals fall on a different day from year to year, although always within the same three- or four-day period. You will need to check an ephemeris or the trusty *Farmer's Almanac* to see exactly when the solstices and equinoxes will be. There are calendars now available that list the holy days for you, but we enjoy looking them up and marking them on a wall calendar ourselves. In fact, we have made a family tradition of this activity, which we usually perform around New Year's so that we can anticipate the delightful spiral path that we will follow from month to month in the coming year.

We don't advocate trying to recreate the old festivals in any kind of historically accurate way—what worked for our ancient relatives, living as they did, would not be likely to work for us, living as we do. Anyway, historical accuracy is not the point here. Instead, we strive to re-vision, re-member, and re-create a sacred feeling, a reverence for our planet's pattern, and a joyous way of being. If we consider the idea of the festival—celebrating the sun's rebirth, for instance, or the blessings of the grain—as the seed, then we can invent fresh, relevant, and highly contemporary ways of bringing that seed to glorious fruition in our family celebrations. And if a time-traveling ancestor popped up in the midst of one of them, she or he would still be able to recognize the central image or event that we are celebrating.

MABON

September 20–23

Our book begins with Mabon, the giving-thanks festival that marks the autumnal equinox in September, the moment of equal balance between day and night, light and dark. Traditionally, Mabon is the time of final harvest, a day to celebrate the Mother's gifts with family and community and, as the nights begin to lengthen, to take stock of all we have reaped. The American cultural holiday of Thanksgiving has left many of us with a nasty feeling—it's hard to rejoice when we know how things turned out for the natives who so generously shared with those first settlers. Mabon gives us a chance to celebrate with whole-hearted thankfulness all of the splendid, varied harvests that we have brought in over the past year. Rich with contrasting images of earthy abundance and the dimming of the sun's power, Mabon marks the beginning of the turning-inward time. And we can imagine our ancestors, faces painted white and black, circling together in a sacred dance that honored the interweaving of light and darkness in the spiral pattern of life.

SAMHAIN
October 31

Our cultural Halloween still has the shreds of this ancient festival of the dead clinging to it. A night to honor the Crone who is born anew after midnight, Samhain's mystery reminds us of our roots that reach deep into the dark earth, bringing up memory and power into this witchiest night of the year. Samhain teaches us to make death less terrifying: we prepare special foods and set a place at our table for dead loved ones, remembering them with reverence. Our ancestors knew that on Samhain the veil separating this world and the next is thin, making communication between the worlds a real possibility. The ideal time of all the year for doing divination, Samhain encourages us to listen to the wise voice within, to trust our own ability to see into, and shape, our futures. The Celtic New Year's Eve, Samhain is a time for both reflection and looking ahead; the next day brings winter and the still, dark time of looking inward, attuning ourselves to our inner wisdom. The darkness swirls with dead leaves driven by the chill winter wind as we light our carved pumpkins and sit beside the fire, dreaming of our own dead, and of the many choices, opportunities, and great mysteries that lie before us.

YULE
December 20–23

The winter solstice in December is the time of greatest darkness: the sun is at its lowest point in the sky, and the night is the longest of the year. One of the great turning points of the cycle, after Yule the days begin to lengthen, so this festival (similar in spirit to Hanukkah and Christmas) traditionally celebrates the return of light and hope to the dark and frozen world. Yule is filled with both noisy celebration and quiet reflection; our ancient relations built huge fires on Yule Eve and danced around them all night long to call up the dawn, turning and turning to bring about the change, both inside and out. And the perfect stillness of Yule's images—candles shining bravely in darkness, the sacred green tree that echoes nature's vibrant life in the midst of seeming death, and the Earth Mother who nurtures her miraculous Sun Child—reminds us that, just when things seem most hopeless and bleak, the pattern shifts and light returns.

IMBOLC

February 2

Observed at the beginning of February, Imbolc traditionally honors the seeds beginning to waken and stir beneath the earth. Imbolc celebrates the visibly longer days and encourages us to spring-clean and prepare for the busy season ahead. The ancient Celts called this Brigid's Day, in honor of the inspirational triple Goddess of that name. At Imbolc we ask for inspiration and guidance for new plans and projects, and we give some thought to the unseen mysteries unfolding in the dark. Just as the dark earth gestates life that sprouts and flourishes in the spring, so we honor our own times of dark power, gestating the growth that will sustain us in the warm and sunny months of creativity to come.

OSTARA

March 20–23

The spring equinox in March focuses on the balance of light and dark, but at this point in the wheel, light is triumphant and the days will become longer than the nights. Paying homage to all new life, Ostara, like the cultural Easter holiday, brings grasses and chicks and eggs into our lives to demonstrate the exuberant power of fresh beginnings. With the spring equinox, we find the energy and freshness in ourselves to burst out of the dark egg of winter inactivity, and we celebrate all the abundant evidence of life's continuation with joy.

BELTANE

May 1

This ancient festival of fertility and sexuality celebrates nature's amazing capacity to reproduce itself. Set at the beginning of May when the world is brimming with sensual vitality, Beltane connects us to the flowering that is taking place all around us. A day for appreciation of our bodies and their divine capacity for pleasure, the ancient Beltane honored sex in its creative aspect, as the great joy-giver and bringer-in of new life. As we picture our ancestors weaving their garlands around the maypole, both phallic symbol and representative of the great World Tree, we remember a time when sex was not a sin—when open and guiltless lovemaking in the fields was a sacred act that was believed to promote a greater harvest in the fall. Beltane becomes a reclamation of the body's holiness.

LITHA
June 20–23

The summer solstice in June honors the power of the sun: on this longest day of the year, the sun is at its zenith, or highest point in the sky. Litha festivities encourage us to celebrate the sun's life-giving warmth and our own ability to make things grow. With its radiant solar images and fiery colors everywhere, Litha urges us to abandon ourselves to the joy of this peak moment. Our ancestors built blazing hilltop bonfires on this day or lit great wheels of straw, which they rolled downhill to be quenched in the water of a river or stream. It is good to enjoy the warmth of the sun's gigantic fire that gives light and life to our planet—and to realize its staggering power, as well. Too much of its radiant energy can mean drought, sunburn, or skin cancer; even at this climactic time, we consider the need for respect.

LUGHNASAD
August 1

This festival at the beginning of August marks the first harvest. Traditionally a time to honor the sacrifice of the grain that gives its body so that we may be fed, Lughnasad reminds us to be mindful of the many ways in which the Earth Mother meets her children's needs. When we engage all aspects of ourselves—hands, mind, feelings, will—in a ritual bread-making, we come closer to the ancient reverence for the loaves that stood between our ancestors and starvation and that were the hallowed embodiments of Goddess and God. We end the book with this affirmation of the sacredness of all life, and of our own sacredness as well.

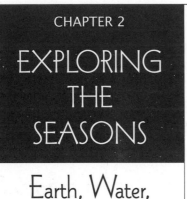

CHAPTER 2

EXPLORING THE SEASONS

Earth, Water, Fire, and Air

THE ELEMENTAL ENERGIES

Four of the eight festivals are peak moments, rich with the energies that each of our four seasons embodies. The other four festivals mark shifts or transitions, ushering in the new after the old season has peaked and declined. Ancient people had a powerful vision of the meaning behind those seasons, of the significance for humanity—and for all of life—in these four movements of the great dance. We can begin the journey toward recovering our oneness with nature by understanding these four vital and distinct seasonal experiences from the traditional point of view.

To our ancestors, the seasons directly corresponded to four magical elements—earth, water, fire, and air—building blocks of life that are also related to human nature, to basic modes of being. The noted psychoanalyst Carl Jung identified four distinct personality types corresponding to the elements, and the four suits of the Tarot, with their ageless wisdom about humanity, echo this idea of four basic ways to order, understand, and interpret our life experience.

From this perspective, every year becomes a journey through each of the four elements, giving us a chance to experience them wholly, to redress any imbalance in our lives. Although we develop this idea of connection and correspondence more fully in each of the seasonal chapters, the following overview will start you thinking about the ways in which nature teaches us about ourselves. There is a beautiful interrelationship implied in this vision that is both delicately balanced and rooted in strength and permanence. Once you have opened to it, the correspondences suggest a mode of living in awareness of the larger picture. And you will find that children are able to grasp this larger picture with relative ease; once you have articulated (or, better yet, actively demonstrated) it to them, the elemental vision of the seasons—and of human nature—makes complete and satisfying sense to them.

These correspondences are the seasonal elements as we have come to know and dance them, both by ourselves and with our children. They are taken from the Western European traditions that make up our own heritage. For those of you who are attracted to other paths—the Native American way, for example—we hope that you will be moved to discover how those other visions of the great pattern differ from the one we offer. Find the pattern that makes the deepest inner sense to you.

AUTUMN—WATER—THE EMOTIONS

Water is autumn's element, related to tears, flow, feelings. It is often a time of letting go, releasing, allowing life to seemingly slip away: many of us find ourselves becoming sad or depressed as the days shorten and the leaves fall. But the watery autumn also encourages us to dream, to look for the patterns around us that illuminate the meanings behind our reality. It teaches us to honor our inner knowledge, to listen to the wise, intuitive inner voice. Dreamy, emotional, and longing to merge or bond with others, autumn's water element has much to teach us about honoring our feelings.

WINTER—EARTH—THE BODY

To enter winter is like going deep into a snow-covered cave: winter teaches us about our physical selves. In winter, we see the shapes of things: without the camouflage of grass and plants, the hills take on a stern beauty underneath their quilt of snow, trees reveal their elegant skeletons, and water turns to stone. Forced to confront our bodies—slipping on the ice, stamping our frozen feet to keep them warm, sniffling with colds, longing for sleep when the long nights urge hibernation and the healing energy of dreams—the earth connection of winter counsels us to take care of our health, to listen to the body's wisdom, and to ground ourselves by honoring the physical. And winter teaches us to respect our own seasons of darkness, which, like the earth now lying fallow, have the power to gestate so that new life can once again be born.

SPRING—AIR—THE MIND

In spring, the silent skies of winter become alive with birds again; to many ancient cultures, birds and their element of air related to the swiftness of thoughts. A time for new beginnings, the sprouting of young things, reviving fresh breezes that sweep away the cobwebs from our minds, making lists and planning the projects we want to achieve during the growing time—and sharing these with others so that they can blossom—spring teaches us about communication and the inspiration of new ideas.

SUMMER—FIRE—THE WILL

Passion and drive, and the spiritual flame that impels us to action, are all related to fire and to the hot and vibrant summer that brings things to fruition. As the world grows and ripens all around us, the summer fire connection teaches us about recovering our own inner zeal as the key to making good things happen in our lives. The fiery radiance of summer gives compelling proof of its power to enhance and enliven—or to wither and parch if not regarded with respect. The impulse of positive energy urges completion of projects and the celebration of abundance everywhere.

ANCIENT TRANSITIONS

Once we become familiar with the order and pattern of the festivals and their seasons, we begin to notice something odd. Have you ever wondered why Litha is often called midsummer when our calendar says it's only the first day of summer? Or why the winter solstice is supposed to be the first day of winter, but it's been cold and bleak outside for weeks, and the old Yuletide carols refer to it unmistakably as midwinter? The answer lies in our ancestors' vision of the transitions that mark the seasons—and those vary from our modern calendar in significant ways.

To the ancient Celts, for instance, Samhain (now our cultural Halloween) was the last day of autumn; by the following day, winter had arrived. If you live in a northern region, as we do, you will probably see the wisdom of this—the bright leaves have usually blown away by early November, with snows and sleet forcing all but the bravest of us indoors. By the time Yule finally rolls around, it's felt like winter for quite a while, and the midwinter term for the solstice makes sense.

Beltane, the festival of sensuality and fertility, could be said to usher in summer's time of fulfillment, so the midsummer description of Litha fits as well. And by Lughnasad, you can feel a palpable change in the earth's energy. Even though the leaves won't begin to change color for a few weeks yet, the green world becomes quieter, more reflective, as all of nature goes to seed. We feel that the growing season is over and nature has begun its descent toward decay. Autumn could be said to start here, with Mabon as the apex, just as Litha is the climax of summer, and Yule of winter. And, to complete the pattern, it's good to know that the mild Irish climate prompted the ancient Celts to consider Imbolc the first day of spring. Ostara, then, is spring's midpoint, the central embodiment of seasonal forces.

What happened, basically, is that our culture turned all the peak moments into transitions, and mostly forgot about the transitional ones—only Groundhog Day and Halloween still evoke a whisper of their ancient origins in Imbolc and Samhain.

Another way to understand the pattern of the ancient seasonal celebrations is to visualize the wheel of the year as a clock face, placing the festivals evenly around it. Yule becomes 12:00 A.M., the darkest middle of the night—but an instant after midnight, morning has begun. Imbolc falls at 3:00 A.M., when the world begins to stir in its sleep, sensing dawn's approach. Ostara at 6:00 A.M. is the clear, inspiring light of sunrise, and Beltane at 9:00 A.M. is the full, sweet morning light. Litha is the noon of the year when the sun blazes at its highest point—and then begins its decline. Lughnasad at 3:00 P.M. is the mellow, golden afternoon as shadows begin to lengthen. Mabon at 6:00 P.M. is dusk, as we say goodbye to the sun and the longer days and begin to welcome in the dark. And Samhain at 9:00 P.M. is the deep night, the blackness of the Crone's cape as it whirls across the moon.

For the purposes of this book, we've chosen to keep the seasonal activities and festivals in the calendar pattern that is most familiar to all of us. But once we perceive the clarity of the old view—once we recognize the peak points in the dance—we find ourselves seeing the yearly cycle in a new way, weaving our knowledge of what is coming soon and what is passing away into a unified fabric.

SEASONAL ACTIVITIES FOR OUR CHILDREN

We have carefully chosen the activities in this book to foster interaction with, respect for, and enjoyment of the energies of each season. There are watery activities for autumn that develop relationship with your child's inner wisdom and offer balance for family relationships. Earthy activities in winter nurture respect for the dark, still time and for the groundedness of stone. Airy spring activities inspire and delight. And the fire activities of summer make all our young ones into sacred embodiments of solar energy.

Children learn by both acting out and taking in. Most of us who have children, or who teach or counsel them, have discovered their amazing capacity for entering into, for becoming part of. With total absorption, a child can watch a snowflake melt, or a bee gathering nectar from a flower, or the patterns of light and shade formed by leaves and sun and wind. Children inhabit their world in a way that most of us have forgotten, incorporating what they see and touch and taste and hear and smell into their own bodies completely and naturally.

Because many children spend more time outdoors than the grownups in their families, they already have a stronger sense of the changing pattern than we do; for us, this book is a means of our rediscovering what they already know. Encouraging our young ones to pay attention to the world of nature becomes an exercise in simply getting out of their way.

When we give our children focused things to do around the seasons and the earth's festivals that engage what they already feel—by involving them in simple, meaningful activities that resonate with their own half-conscious ancient memories—then they can experience the seasonal dance and its sacredness with even greater depth and wholeness, with every aspect of themselves. And we will have helped our young ones to become the conscious and contemporary embodiments of ancient magic.

DISCOVERING THE GODDESS

EXPERIENCING THE EARTH AS SACRED

The full moon shines brightly on the sacred gathering of women. There are five of them, holding hands around a very old oak, its trunk twisted and furrowed with age. One by one, the women approach it. One hugs the tree. Another rubs her cheek against its rough bark. A third kisses it and strokes its trunk. They name it, using a syllable from each of their names. They sing it a song. They dance a dance around it, watching the moon make silver shadows on its leaves and the acorns just beginning to swell beneath its branches. Later, after the Circle, they will return, one at a time or in groups of two or three—to give the tree a little love-gift of tiny silver bells tied to its branches, or to nestle a small statue of the Goddess in its hollow. One woman reads it a poem she just wrote. Another sits with her back touching its trunk and can feel her tension headache ease. To them, this tree is a friend, inspirited and holy. Because this is so, each of them has become more aware of the terrible waste going on all around them. They are committed to using recycled paper products whenever possible; they participate as a group in a tree-planting project in their community; and two of them are active in the struggle for rainforest preservation.

Alone, tired, and drained, another woman sits on a riverbank. She takes off her shoes and allows the cool water to lap gently against her feet. Gradually, the peace of lapping water and warm wind, the quietness—only wind in branches, birds weaving their songs above her head—and the spirit of water and wind begin to fill her with peace. Her feet become thirsty roots, drawing up the nurturing water to her parched inner self. She sighs deeply and feels herself filling with a sense of the Goddess. She notices that her toes are touching something heavy and hard on the river bottom and she leans over and pries up a rock, dripping, from the water. She turns it over and over, marveling at its color, its solid smoothness. As she stills her mind and continues to focus on the stone, she sees that it has a shape like a crow, her power animal, half-hidden in its intricate whorls and patterns. She returns to her work refreshed and renewed.

Three children play at the beach beside their parents. Running backward and forward like small seabirds, they gather bits of garbage—soda cans, bottle tops, and plastic wrappers—washed ashore by the tide. They will take a full bag home to recycle or discard, but for now they beam at the clean beach they have helped to restore. They begin to form a great Earth Goddess out of sand, mounding the massive shape with damp hands, pouring water gathered in a bucket around her so that she rises out of the water like Aphrodite. They garland her head with seaweed and give her shell earrings and a necklace of tiny, water-smoothed pebbles. Then the whole family joins hands and dances in a circle around her, singing and laughing, until the tide comes in. Later, as they drift off to sleep, each child remembers the Goddess they all made together. The youngest thinks about the shells and pebbles washing back out to sea with the tide, and about all of the refuse he helped to pick up. The middle child has kept a tiny canister of sand from the Goddess's body. He holds it in his hand, under the pillow. And the eldest thinks dreamily of the painting she will do the next morning, a painting of Aphrodite made of sand and shells and seaweed.

Many of us were raised in a Judeo-Christian tradition that taught human superiority to the earth, which was reviled as lowly and inferior to Spirit. Women, because of their instinctive connection with the earth and with other living creatures (as well as because of their "messy" monthly bleeding and intuitive power), were considered lowly and inferior, too. But the word is definitely out that the old patriarchal way of relating to our planet won't do much longer; it is bringing us closer and closer to the destruction of our own particular species, closer to making the entire planet uninhabitable for any but the hardiest insects and one-celled creatures. Every day it becomes clearer that female power was—and is—terribly threatening to the patriarchal mind, and with good reason. After centuries of suffering abuse and calumny, women are becoming aware that they were, in fact, the creators of civilization—that the ancient matrifocal societies lived in peace and gracious harmony with the earth for thousands upon thousands of years.

The Goddess-way has special importance as a healing path for women, after centuries of crippling patriarchal oppression. For men, whose roles under the patriarchy have been no less constricting, the Goddess offers the same promise of wholeness; many of us believe that it is the feminine power to relate, to create, to embrace, and to nurture—in men as well as women—that may be the saving of us all. And for children, growing into the women and men who will be the future caretakers of this planet, the Goddess-way offers a blueprint, not only for living well now but for embracing a hope-filled future.

So there has been some much-needed re-visioning going on, and the unifying force behind a great deal of it has to do with the Goddess. Who is the Goddess? What does her way offer our world?

THE ROOTS OF GODDESS WORSHIP

Archaeologists have found countless ancient statues of the Goddess buried in the earth. Some are small enough to hold in the hand. Others have pointed legs to plant in the ground—as the center of a ritual circle, perhaps, or to guard the entrance to a sacred cave. Many are marvelously rounded to emphasize the mysterious powers of the Life-Giver, the Milky One, with her pendulous breasts and her womb ripe with many children. Sometimes she has no head; she is fertility, continuously giving birth, and it is her roomy hips, substantial belly, and nourishing breasts that are her vital characteristics. Sometimes she squats and we see the baby crowning. From her all things come: children, both human and animal; plants for food and healing. Every cave, every dark opening is her vulva. The wings of flying birds flow like hair across her sky-cheeks. Rivers are her flowing breast milk, endlessly rich with life; hills and mountains are the sensual contours of her majestic body.

But the Great Goddess appears in other aspects besides the maternal, the Earth Mother. She is also the Destroyer, who takes back what she has created in order to make room for new life, gathering it up and returning it to her limitless self so that it can be reborn. Or she may be the bird-headed shamanic Goddess who flies on the dark currents of dreams, who rides the smoke from the cave fire up through the top of the sky and crosses over into other worlds. In this guise she gives not food but mystical healing, her wisdom dancing itself snakelike in the patterns of the life-spiral. Her priestesses dance in a line, winding in long serpentines deeper into the sacred groves, the sacred caves, the sacred spaces. Some wear crescent moons on their foreheads. Others twine their arms with living snakes, calling up the earth power at ley lines and energy centers. Others open their arms to heal the inwardly wounded, the spirit-sick, with the soul-saving power of touch, the sexual mystery that both blesses and transforms.

Every woman is touched with her magic. For eons past reckoning, women opened their garments and blessed the grains with their vulvas, to encourage growth and ripeness, ripeness as sweet and powerful as their own. Every birth and every act of creation was a holy miracle, a calling down of the Goddess in her endless cycle of renewal. As Marija Gimbutas writes in *The Language of the Goddess,* "Pre-industrial agricultural rites show a very definite mystical connection between the fertility of the soil and the creative force of woman. In all European languages, the Earth is feminine."

From cave to village to community, she encouraged the human capacity for working peaceably together, not only to survive but to thrive. With her all-encompassing power, nurturance, and compassion, the great female Goddess showed people how to live—creatively, with spiritual richness, cooperatively rather than competitively, and with deep reverence for and interaction with the great cycle of life—for perhaps the first two hundred thousand years of our history.

Riane Eisler is a visionary archaeological scholar and passionate advocate of a partnership society, a healing counterpoint to the prevailing dominator mode. As she says in *The Chalice and the Blade,*

> Our reconnection with the earlier spiritual tradition of Goddess worship linked to the partnership model of society is more than a reaffirmation of the dignity and worth of half of humanity. Nor is it only a far more comforting and reassuring way of imaging the powers that rule the universe. It also offers us a positive replacement for the myths and images that have for so long blatantly falsified the most elementary principles of human relations by valuing killing and exploiting more than giving birth and nurturing.

Historically, the cultures that hold earth as an embodiment of the divine have been the easiest on the planet. This makes perfect sense—if the ground you walk upon is Goddess, you're going to treat it with the utmost respect. If the other creatures are manifestations of Goddess, then you'll avoid wantonly destroying them. Global ecology suffers when people place themselves outside of the wheel; there is a terrible arrogance in seeing humanity as above the rest of life on this planet. But when we affirm our place on it, the benefits are many. First, we will commit ourselves to correcting the ecological mess in which we are presently sitting. Then we will begin to feel a tremendous kinship with the other creatures—they become our allies, our teachers. And finally, we feel ourselves firmly and lovingly held in the web of life, connected to all.

The oldest known artifact of a human figure is the Goddess of Willendorf, chubby and faceless, arms resting on breasts. A dynamic reminder of the earth-centered beliefs of our Paleolithic ancestors, replicas of her thirty-thousand-year-old figure are now worn as pendants by contemporary women everywhere. When we say that the Goddess is rising, we mean this both literally and figuratively. The little statues are being unearthed, brought up out of their ancient burial grounds, to share the remembrance of earth-loving consciousness with our diseased and troubled time. Knowledge of the Goddess, suppressed and denied for so long, is back among us once again. Her spirit—her values, her magic and power—is blossoming everywhere as women and men reclaim her ceremonies and rituals, her earth-honoring way of being in the world.

As Jean Shinoda Bolen writes in *Crossing to Avalon*,

> I have a sense that the Goddess—"the Woman that is in the heart of women"—is revealing herself to humankind again. She is appearing in our dreams as a numinous figure, sometimes as a larger-than-life dark woman, sometimes as a goddess, sometimes as a guide. "The Woman that is in the heart of women" is an inner figure. She is feminine wisdom, knowledge that comes through the heart, a way of knowing that became discounted and devalued with patriarchy, which substituted obedience to outer authority for this inner knowing. In Greek mythology, she was Metis, the Goddess of Wisdom, whom Zeus tricked into becoming small and swallowed when she was pregnant with Athena. She was Sophia, whom the church fathers banished along with the Gnostic heresies, and she was the Shekinah, the forgotten feminine face of God in Judaism.

Astrologer Demetra George has a theory that, like the Greek goddess Persephone after her six months with Hades or the Sumerian goddess Inanna after her descent into the underworld, the Goddess principle is now re-emerging after long centuries of darkness—renewed and ready to act as a force for healing and planetary regeneration. The times of darkness and decay may be an undeniable and necessary part of the great cosmic pattern. But there is great joy in being alive to see this resurgence of the Goddess principle and in knowing that we can take an active role in helping to further it in the world. We can be the dynamic bringers-in, the co-creators of a culture that will nourish and sustain all of life.

But exactly where do we look to find workable models that we can emulate as we re-create our culture? Examination of our ancient roots is inspiring, empowering, and helpful, but we cannot return to the absolute primitive simplicity of a preindustrial world —although we can do our best to live more simply and to halt the cancerous overgrowth of technocracy. Somehow we need to find a workable balance.

Many of us turn to visionary fiction when we seek blueprints for a better future. Starhawk, brilliant ecofeminist and Goddess-centered witch, gives us such a vision in her novel *The Fifth Sacred Thing,* which presents an earth-loving, cooperative community of the future that honors cultural diversity and lives in deep reverence for the planet, creating joyous ritual celebrations in which everyone takes part. And Starhawk is not alone; all over the earth, people are beginning to imagine a different life, a culture based on sacredness, respect, a spirituality grounded in the earth. We can imagine together, and we can share our vision with our children.

CREATING A LIFE-AFFIRMING CULTURE BEGINS AT HOME

People are never slow to tell us, "You can't change the world single-handedly." But we're not single-handed. There are many, many of us. And we're not out waving banners or proselytizing or pounding our fists on manifestos. We work—or, rather, play—from the inside out. We involve our children in a joyful, creative connection with the Goddess. Then those children go off to their schools and to their friends and to their community and share what they have experienced. It becomes obvious to everyone that these young people are on to something great—not because somebody told them, "This is the way to change the world," but because it works, it's real; it's fun in a deeper, more satisfying way than many of us have ever known.

We can envision entire groups of people—young and old—peacefully and joyfully creating celebration rather than watching endless acts of violence on television or engaging in warplay or cutthroat competitive games. And as the earth-loving, earth-honoring Goddess rises more fully into our world, we will all be her celebrants.

CHAPTER 4

NATURE'S SACRED WORLD

Goddess consciousness often starts with the natural world and our attitude toward it. Over the past five thousand years, patriarchal culture has taught people to be separate from nature. Rationalizing all manner of greed and exploitation, the view that the earth was put here to serve humanity—that we are created to be its dominators—is the root of our present ecological nightmare. And by stealing a sense of the sacred from nature—by making it lowly, inferior, dead—the sky-god cultures produced a cruel rift in our inner natures and paved the way for widespread alienation and psychosis.

On a more personal level, many of our parents regarded nature as the enemy; family picnics were punctuated by cries of "A wasp! Quick, get the poison spray!" Squirrels, marauding at the bird feeder, were the targets of BB guns, and garden snakes were beaten to death with shovels. The lawn was sprayed to rid it of "pesky weeds," and only a chosen few of nature's myriad flowers were allowed to bloom. But people were being given hints of the real price of this imbalanced and soul-denying way, even in the controlled Eden of suburbia: there were years when dozens of birds were found lying dead on the chemically treated, perfect emerald lawns. Children developed weird allergies and respiratory ailments from overexposure to chemical cleaners and pesticides. And the world, to those children, seemed a dead and spiritless wasteland.

Now there is a growing impulse for change. As we open to the sacredness of life—to the spirit-teachings that all creatures have to offer, if only we look at them with open, human eyes—we rediscover our own place in the whole picture. Irrevocable ties bind us to all the lives that share this planet with us.

In *The Geography of Childhood: Why Children Need Wild Places,* Gary Paul Nabhan and Stephen Trimble recommend three concrete and specific actions that we can take with our children to counteract the deadening cultural tendency. We can help them to become intimately involved with plants and animals; we can give them direct exposure to wild animals living their routine lives in natural habitats; and we can encourage them to learn from community elders about their local biosphere. Not every community has the wonderful opportunity to learn directly from indigenous native teachers (in which case, you might want to read traditional Native American tales from the tribes in your part of the country), but even local residents in their seventies and eighties remember details of a more nature-focused lifestyle earlier in this century that give a special sense of place to where we live.

One of the most important things we can do for and with our children is to actively reclaim a sense of the sacred in nature, a sacredness of which we are a part. This chapter gives some practical and immensely enjoyable ways to begin re-inspiriting the natural world around us.

ANIMAL TEACHERS

Perhaps nothing deepens our experience of nature and her sacredness more than really noticing and honoring the animals that inhabit her. Recently, Cait's young son watched one special squirrel build her nest in the maple outside the front window, laboriously, a mouthful of leaves at a time. We celebrated when she brought home a mate—wonderful! Now there were two squirrels to watch and love. We saw them grow fat on the Native American corn we put out for them and watched as they winterized their nest in autumn, tucking more leaves here and there to keep out the chill; throughout the long, severe winter, we worried and left them food. And then we rejoiced over the sight of five small offspring scampering up and down the tree in spring. Squirrels will never be the same to us; we have opened our hearts to them. Their incredible agility, their vitality, their alert and furry beauty are sources of wonder and delight. We realized, through watching and caring about them, that they have spirit and tremendous value; they became our teachers, with much to tell us about both preparedness and play. All this is in pointed contrast to the prevailing cultural notion that squirrels are worthless "tree-rats," a notion now completely alien to us.

We had no idea that there would be enough interest or drama in the doings of a squirrel family to keep a child engrossed—but there was. We were amazed at the fascination we felt just watching these little animals.

Another year, it was a wasp's nest in the window that enthralled us: from a single wasp building a papery gray chamber to an entire community of wasp sisters all laboring together to protect and nurture their young, we watched an endlessly fascinating progression. These wasps seemed to know our scent and never bothered us. They became our friends. And they taught us about cooperation and protectiveness—we learned that wasps do not mess with you unless you threaten them or their young. In contrast to his friends and classmates, Cait's son has no fear of wasps now. They are kindred.

If we allow our children to simply hang out and watch the lives around them, we give them the opportunity to connect. Intimacy, respect, and love grow with continued observation. And once we begin to notice, we find that thousands of small lives are intertwined with our own—the trees, the weeds, and even the soil under our feet are all teeming with life. Learning about birds, squirrels, earthworms, spiders, or ants becomes an endlessly fascinating occupation, well within the reach of most of us, no matter where we live. And if our homes encompass any wild land—or if we live near a preserve or park—we can add involvement with many other creatures as well.

In this way, our children learn to be respectful of others' lives; it becomes unthinkable to watch someone thoughtlessly torturing or destroying any creature, and they will speak out. One six-year-old of our acquaintance heroically came to the defense of a daddy longlegs whose legs were being pulled off one by one by a teenaged neighbor. The younger boy, who knows most of the arachnids living in his house by name and has learned a great and abiding respect for them, was so impassioned that the older child backed down, backed off, and allowed the creature to escape. Environmental activism starts in just this way.

We have found that children are often drawn to different creatures at different stages in their lives. Observing our young ones as they observe becomes an additional source of knowledge and richness for the adults who care for them.

Set aside some time with your children to simply look while sitting outdoors, or inside, through a convenient window. Comment quietly on what you see. Put out some food for the creatures and then watch them enjoy it. See if you can recognize individuals; with time and repeated visits, it's often possible. Name them, if you like. Notice how they move, how they eat. Encourage your children to imitate them or draw them or write about them. You may want to learn more about the animals from library books or nature magazines. Your children might want to engage them in a deep inner dialogue, taking them on as power animals and animal allies (see the activities in the Samhain section of Autumn for more on this).

Involvement with creatures deepens with time. Give yourselves the time it takes to really notice and connect.

TALKING WITH FAERIES:
TREE SPIRITS AND OTHER GREEN ALLIES IN YOUR BACKYARD

The idea of talking to plants to help them grow better is not new—many of us made friends of our avocado plants back in the 1970s. But those people who really know about such matters—the members of the Findhorn community, for instance, who created a green oasis from barren land, and Wise Woman herbalists such as Susun Weed and Pam Montgomery—have taught us that the rooted, green growing things have spirits with which we can communicate. Now we can encourage our children not only to talk to the plants, but to listen carefully, too.

Listening to the trees or the weeds becomes an opening to intuition, a dialogue with Source. In much the same way that children build deep relationships with the animals around them, they may be taught to value the individual trees or weeds that share their space.

To small ones, faeries are inarguably real. Now there seems to be adult-based evidence for them—not in the popularized guise of cute and fashionably thin winged nymphs, but as presences that may be sensed and known and honored. Some herbalists call them "devas" and base much of their knowledge (later borne out by study and investigation) on what the devas tell them.

When Cait first moved to her Hudson Valley home, she and her son went on a morning ramble to meet all of the trees and plants growing on their land; they found one corner of the property filled with sturdy milkweed plants that simply hummed with life. There was a palpable high-vibration sweetness, a holiness hovering in the air that blazed out at them. It was their first direct experience with faeries. When they looked at a magical herb book later, they found that milkweed is traditionally believed to attract them.

Invite your little ones to sit near trees and plants, relax, and see what images or words enter their minds. If they know that the green ones have something to say to them, they will try to listen.

For some specific activities designed to build a loving relationship with the trees, see the Lughnasad section of Summer. By opening to the wisdom and sweet energy of trees and plants, we enrich our lives immeasurably. If you have learned to love a particular tree—if it has become a person, a spirit to you—then you will be less likely to wound or scar any tree with a jackknife, or hack one down for no reason, or even thoughtlessly waste paper.

Spirit involvement with the other beings on this planet is one key to true ecological awareness. If all things have spirit, we will be more likely to care for and conserve them.

WEED WALKS:
WILD FOODS FROM NATURE'S PANTRY

But if all life is sacred, how can we bear to eat any of it? Many of us are vegetarians because we can't live peaceably with the thought of eating animals. But if the green things have spirits too, how are we to survive?

As Alexandra Hart, editor of *Earth Circles News,* explains it, "The Native American term *'all my relations'* implies that we make sacrifice of our bodies to one another. The term *'sacrifice'* means *'to make sacred.'* If the grasses and the fruits are my sisters, they are made sacred with the sacrifice of their bodies to mine. It is incumbent on me to be worthy of their life. They *become* me and I become them. We are one."[1]

We need to teach our children that we, too, are sacred. We are as much a part of nature as are the trees and the animals and the plants. True, deep knowledge of this makes the act of feeding our bodies a holy one. And those who regularly speak with the plant spirits report that they actually want us to eat them; the green things seem to rejoice in the give-away.

With just a little study, most of us with access to a yard can experience this spirit-satisfying edible greenness directly and joyously. Prepare to be amazed: even children whose

---
1. *Alexandra Hart,* Earth Circles News 5 *(Summer 1994): 1–2.*

diet is strictly limited to pizza and hot dogs will eat wood sorrel—and enjoy it. Suddenly, the land becomes alive with green treasure. And constant interaction with the different phases or cycles of your weeds is a great side benefit for families rediscovering the sacred rhythm.

We have gone on "weed walks" with children varying in age from the toddler years to the late teens, and all of them, without exception, were completely enchanted. There is a real, wild magic in discovering that many of the common weeds growing under our very noses are both delicious and free for the taking—a satisfying link with our gathering ancestors, perhaps. And adults will be amazed to learn that the plants so many think of as noxious pests and enemies of the manicured lawn possess incalculable health benefits as well as food appeal.

First, you will need to get a field guide (Stefen Bernath's *Common Weeds Coloring Book* is a pleasant alternative, and your children will enjoy coloring their finds) to make absolutely sure that you and your little ones know what you're eating; by identifying plants with a field guide, you may be certain that anything you put in your mouths is perfectly safe. We list only those plants that are both common and distinct. We also made a few considered omissions: nettle, for example, grows freely and has tremendous nutritive value, but it can sting the unwary. And although it's not easy to confuse red sumac with its poisonous white relative, we decided not to take the chance. You just can't go too far wrong with the plants we chose to list.

Next, be certain that the area you are harvesting has not been sprayed with chemicals or toxins. The easiest way to do this is to harvest from your own land only, which of course you keep pesticide- and herbicide-free. (A few years ago, a "lawn-care specialist" came to call and offered a free evaluation of our yard; although we warned him that we had no intention of spraying to kill any of our precious weeds, he was insistent. He actually found one or two wonderful plants that we hadn't known we had; they are now flourishing.)

You will want to avoid picking any plants growing within three feet of roadways to avoid heavy-metal contamination. And be aware of areas patrolled by neighborhood dogs—if it smells weird, don't pick it. We try to harvest only a portion of any one plant in an area, so that it will grow there again. Take only what you need and intend to use; you and your family will feel good about not wasting these embodiments of life's sacredness.

Once you have filled your gathering baskets, you may wash your finds by simply plunging the contents into a bowl of cold water and then shaking them dry or allowing them to dry while spread on a towel. If you are planning to steam or stir-fry your greens, just put them in the skillet with the droplets of water still on them: this is usually sufficient for cooking. For recipe ideas, see Susun Weed's *Healing Wise* (which is a wonderful source of information about the curative properties of weeds, as well) or *Plantworks* by Karen Shanberg and Stan Tekiela, which is aimed at children and is also a field guide (both are listed in Suggested Reading).

CHICKWEED

Delightfully called "Little Star Lady" by Susun Weed, chickweed is often the first edible green to appear in spring; in some regions, it appears before the snow is completely gone. Growing close to the ground, chickweed's tiny leaves and diminutive starlike white flowers are a challenge for children to find, but they are sweet, lettucelike, and delicious.

CURLED DOCK

Another early spring green, the lemony tartness of curled dock's first young leaves is popular with children. Older summer leaves may be added to the family stock pot, and the thickly growing, dark red-brown seeds in late summer or early autumn make a deliciously crunchy addition to salads, soups, and casseroles.

DANDELION

Hard to believe that some people actually spray their yards to kill them! Dandelions are a treasure trove of goodies. One taste of dandelion cordial is enough to convert many adults, and children, besides enjoying the picking process for its own sake (only plantain is more plentiful and easy to find), are usually enthusiastic over dandelion-flower fritters. The young greens are great in adult salads (children dislike the bitterness), and almost everybody likes them steamed or stir-fried. Grownups may want to try roasting the roots and making a delicious coffee-like beverage from them. Children love to blow on the dried seed heads and make wishes. Dandelion has something for everyone.

GARLIC MUSTARD

Not every child likes the spicy garlic taste of this weed when raw, but it usually gets rave reviews in stews and stir-fries. Adults will enjoy it in salads. Hardy (like chickweed, another very early spring green), abundant, and easy to find.

LAMB'S-QUARTERS

A favorite salad green with youngsters because of its tender, sweet blandness, lamb's-quarters have distinctively shaped leaves and are common in most regions.

PLANTAIN

Nicknamed "way bread" because it is edible and grows everywhere, this humble wayside-growing plant has been used for hundreds of years by hungry pilgrims or other travelers on foot. Most people prefer it cooked, if given a choice. Delicious when boiled lightly and covered with cheese sauce or made into quiche—there's a super recipe for this in *Plantworks*—plantain will become a family favorite. But every child should know about plantain because of its medicinal properties. It's also called the "Band-Aid plant": when your little ones get cut or scraped or stung by a bee, they can chew up some plantain and put it on as a poultice and the injury will heal more quickly.

PURSLANE

Considered a nuisance by many gardeners, one taste of purslane's succulent sweetness is usually enough to send children running for the gathering basket.

RED CLOVER

Lovely purplish flower heads make this weed a favorite for children to pick. The flowers are a bit much when eaten raw; make them into fritters with a lightly sweetened batter, or place them in boiling water for tea. We like to dry them in bunches hung upside down in the kitchen—partly because they are so pretty, but also because the dried flowers make a tasty tea.

WILD VIOLET

The vivid purple flowers make a beautiful and unusual addition to salads in early spring, and the leaves are a popular snack with children all summer long, either in salads or munched-as-you-pick. They are also fun to find: heart-shaped, a little slimy on the tongue (like okra, only a little less so), and sweetish.

WOOD SORREL ("SOUR GRASS")

Of all the raw greens tried by children, this one is the hands-down favorite; something about the tangy tartness, like that of curled dock but much more tender, has been making children smile and pucker their lips for years. The tiny okralike seedpods are a special rare treat when they form toward the end of summer.

Children who are encouraged in these simple ways will begin to turn naturally toward the sacred outdoor world for comfort, strength, and inner nourishment. When a child has had a rough day at school, it becomes a healing journey to go for a weed walk-and-nibble, or to watch a butterfly sunning itself on a leaf, or to rest against a giant oak and feel its gentle stability. Just sitting quietly, watching, and listening become paths for stilling inner conflict and opening to life. With this comes a quiet awareness of our own deep connection to every aspect of that life, of our own deserving place in nature's grand design, of our own sacredness. And we feel ourselves dancing with the dear earth around us.

CHAPTER 5

DREAMS

Messages from Underground

Besides a reverence for nature, Goddess consciousness implies honoring our inner worlds, the depth and magic of our secret, nighttime selves. There is a growing awareness that dreams, largely neglected in our culture, are a vitally important key for our lives. Research on the Malayan Senoi and the Naskapi of the Labradoran Peninsula—both peaceful, indigenous societies where dreams are an integral part of life—has done much to alert us to the value of dreams. These people are taught to honor dreams from earliest childhood, and they are healthy, loving, and harmonious, both individually and as a society. If this is due to a constant interaction with dreams—as researchers suggest—then we may have much to learn from them about dreaming's impact on us all.

Working with dreams gives us real information about the self. Dreams are, in fact, messages from the Deep Self, where change, healing, self-confidence, and greater awareness gestate and from which they may emerge to manifest in our waking lives. Even the most seemingly trivial dreams come loaded with information that reveals much about the inner state of the dreamer, if only we take the time to explore them. For an adult attempting to resolve a life issue, for a parent trying to understand a child's problem, or for a child looking for nighttime adventures that satisfy the spirit, dreams offer inspiration, wise guidance, and answers to many of our questions.

It's never too early or too late to begin working (or playing) with dreams; even the youngest children can be taught to approach their dreams meaningfully and to reap the benefits that dreamwork offers all of us. And you will probably find, as we did, that children are naturally curious and eager to explore this mysterious and exciting aspect of themselves.

This chapter offers practical suggestions for dream recall and dream-keeping and gives ideas for activities around dreams that will benefit the entire family. By giving our young ones the keys to their dreaming selves, we give them what is possibly the most significant and far-reaching tool to wholeness of any that we know.

DREAMS AND THE VERY YOUNG

We can encourage our children to begin paying attention to their dreams in several ways. Even the littlest ones often remember their dreams; when we show interest in them by asking, "What did you dream last night?" (and truly listen to their replies) or by writing down the dreams for them in a special notebook, we show respect for their inner selves in a way that is bound to have positive impact on their self-esteem.

We can honor our children's dream images by remembering them and incorporating them into daily life: "That reminds me of that dream you had last week," or "Remember the dream you had last night? Did the boat look like that one?"

We can ask questions that allow the child to become more present with the dream, more aware of it. Questions such as "How did that make you feel?" or "What did the pirate look like?" or "What color was the turtle?" can lead the child back into the dream, with our loving support and companionship.

Very young children need the validation of our listening and respect around their dreams. Then, when they are old enough to begin keeping a dream journal and doing actual dreamwork themselves, they will have a foundation on which to build.

NIGHTMARES

Frightening dreams must be taken as seriously by the adult as by the child who has had one; it doesn't do to say, "Forget it, it was just a dream." Scary dreams (if they aren't simply a sign of blood-sugar imbalance brought on by sweets before bed) are often a signal that something needs attention. Encourage creativity around these: "If you could dream that dream over again, what would you do differently? What would you take with you this time? How would you make the dream end?"

Ask the child to draw a picture or tell a story about the dream; this gives the child a measure of control over the frightening feelings the dream has brought up. Acknowledge these feelings: "That must have been really scary. You were in a pretty tight spot in that dream." It can be very comforting to be heard and understood in this simple way.

You may want to invent a ritual action in which your child participates, as another means of gaining some control over the strong feelings generated by the dream. As an example, when one horrified little girl dreamed of a terrible seed that, when she threw it on the ground, caused the whole world to blow up, her mother encouraged the child to draw a picture of the seed, then wad it up and place it (with supervision) in the family fire, sprinkling salt in afterward, and then burning some smudge herbs to completely purify the space. "Now it's all gone," the child reported with satisfaction and relief.

There are several methods of preventing nightmares that partner our inner wisdom with the Earth Mother's fruits—these are time-honored, traditional folk-ways to soothe our dreaming self and ensure sweet, restful sleep:

- Keep a hyacinth plant near the bed: its scent is a reputed folk cure.
- Burn some cedar or sage before bedtime.
- A piece of jasper, worn or placed under the pillow, is a traditional anti-nightmare stone.
- A dream-catcher hung above the bed is a Native American cure: bad dreams are said to become entangled in its web, while the good dreams, being smarter, can find their way through to descend upon the sleeper.
- Catnip and chamomile, taken as a tea before bed, are time-honored ways to induce sound sleep.
- Marigold flowers or an onion, placed under the bed, are said to prevent nightmares.
- Bay leaves hung above the bed or placed under the pillow protect the sleeper from night terrors.
- Peppermint under the pillow is another nightmare preventative.

Children are often eager to try these magical methods; we have found that the simple act of taking steps—no matter which—to prevent a nightmare from recurring becomes the cure, all by itself.

Adults and older children may want to try some techniques for allying with "bad" dreams: nightmares can become teachers and friends if approached in the proper frame of mind.

You may want to go back into the dream, either in a guided meditation or by using auto-suggestion to re-enter the dream in sleep. This time, take with you what you need, or be prepared to ask any hostile creatures what they want. Knowing that no real harm can come to you in a dream is very empowering. Dreams may make heroes and heras of us all: since actual, physical risk is nonexistent, dreamland becomes the place for drama, heroics, and daredevil feats not allowed to us in waking life.

But for young ones, it may be helpful for you to make waking-life analogies from the events or images in the child's dream that make sense of it for you, to address the issue that is being brought up in symbol-language for the child. For example, children who dream of abandonment may need extra reassurance; those who dream of being injured while doing something they know to be dangerous may need stronger or better-defined limits.

AGAINST INTERPRETATION

Drawing analogies to our children's waking lives, however, is not to say that you need to figure out what the dream "means"—only that you take steps to respond to the feeling it evokes. We actively discourage interpretation and suggest that if you own one of those little "Dictionaries of Dream Symbols and What They Mean," you throw it out immediately. First of all, no one can know what your highly unique and personal dream symbols "mean" (if, indeed, they "mean" anything at all: like a good poem, a dream symbol just *is*). But the symbol or dream image itself is whole, significant, and weighted with spirit-value, and it offers itself to be worked with or simply mulled over. As Carl Jung, the great psychoanalyst, wrote in his book *Memories, Dreams, Reflections,* "I have no theory about dreams. I do not know how dreams arise. . . . I share all my readers' prejudices against dream interpretation being the quintessence of uncertainty and arbitrariness. But, on the other hand, I know that if we meditate on a dream sufficiently long and thoroughly—if we take it about with us and turn it over and over—something almost always comes of it."[2]

Older children and adults are capable of holding their dream images and turning them over as Jung suggests; for younger ones, it becomes our joyous responsibility to do some of this meditative work for them. By simply holding a child's dream image in our conscious-ness for a period of time, we grow into deeper understanding of her or his vibrant dream-ing spirit.

---

2. *Carl G. Jung, quoted in Dick McLeester,* Welcome to the Magic Theater, *p. 34.*

REMEMBERING DREAMS

Older children will be ready to begin actively recording and dialoguing with their dreams. But any dreamwork presupposes that we are able to remember the dream in the first place. So, since everyone has dreams but many of us don't recall them, here are some hints for you and your older offspring to help you seize the dream before it flies away.

1. Before you go to sleep at night, try autosuggestion. When you feel yourself getting sleepy, repeat the following several times in your head: "Tonight I will dream and I will remember my dreams." This takes persistence, but it will work. Don't give up.

2. Drink some Dream Remembrance Tea before bed; not only are the herbs good for dreaming and dream recall, but your full bladder will wake you up later in the night and give you a chance to write down some key points from any dreams you just had. Children who dislike the taste of this tea could try a drop or two of mugwort tincture on their tongues or in a glass of juice before bed. If bedwetting is a problem for your child, forget the tea and use the mugwort tincture instead.

Dream Remembrance Tea

¼ cup dried mugwort
2 tsp. dried rosemary

Add the ingredients to 2 cups boiling water. Steep at least ten minutes, strain, sweeten with honey if desired, and drink.

3. Stress, too little sleep, and alarm clocks all interfere with normal, healthy sleeping and dreaming (as do alcohol and drugs). If you are tense at bedtime, try soaking in a warm, soothing bath with a big mugwort "tea bag" (a handful of dried mugwort tied up in a handkerchief will work fine, or you can use a muslin tea bag purchased from the natural-foods store) or having a massage. Children (and adults, for that matter) love to be stroked and gentled into sleep and you don't have to be a licensed practitioner to learn how. If a full-body massage seems too daunting to you, try just massaging the feet or patting the back or tummy.

   Make sure your bedtime is early enough to permit at least six or seven hours of uninterrupted sleep; we often dream our deepest dreams after our bodies are fully rested. For some adults, that may mean as much as eight hours or more of sleep a night. Children, of course, usually need even more.

Try waking yourself up a little early in the morning so that you can rest in bed and mull over your dreams—and write them down—rather than catapulting yourself into the day. It helps if you are allowed to awaken naturally rather than to the shrill insistence of an alarm; even a clock radio startles the dreaming self and tends to make the dream flee. It's surprisingly easy to kick the alarm habit. Just try autosuggestion before bed. "Tomorrow morning I will wake at 7:30," repeated several times just as you are beginning to get sleepy, will plant the idea in your subconscious. It may take a little practice, but in time you will find that it really works. We haven't used an alarm for years.

4. If you wake up and know that you've had a dream but can't remember it, reposition yourself the way you were lying when you were asleep. By some fluid alchemy, this will often bring back the dream.

5. Once you are able to remember even one dream and write it down, you have given a positive message to your dreaming self, which says, "I'm here. I'm listening." If your Deep Self has shut down from years of neglect, you are now giving it the message that its effort will not be wasted and that you are eager for more. It will respond.

THE DREAM JOURNAL

Once you have started remembering your dreams, you can become the keeper of them. The best way that we have found for you and your children to do this is through the use of a dream journal. Keeping a record of our dreams gives a powerful message of respectful attention to our Deep Self, which invariably results in more and deeper dreams.

The most effective way to record your dreams is in a special journal used only for this purpose. The following hints will allow you to keep a journal for yourself or for your young children. Older children will want to start dream journals of their own.

1. Keep your dream journal beside the bed, so that you can write down your dreams as soon as you wake up; we usually have only eight minutes or so to remember the dream before it begins to fade. If you wake up in the middle of the night with a

dream, write down some of the main actions or images from it to help you remember more fully in the morning.

2. When you write down your dream, try to remember events, characters, colors, sounds, objects, feelings, and words that were either spoken or thought. Don't judge or analyze the dream, just write down everything you can remember.

3. You may want to write your entries in the first person, present tense ("I am standing on a turtle's back" rather than "I was standing on a turtle's back"). This not only makes the dream more present as you write, enabling you to recall more details, but it also brings an immediacy to later rereadings of the entry.

4. You may want to make sketches or drawings of dream objects, to help yourself remember their shapes. This simple act can be extremely helpful, as your sketch often reveals a likeness to other significant things.

5. Include the date and give your dream a title based on the most important action or image in it. Was there an object that seemed significant in the dream? What did you do in the dream?

6. Include notes on important things that are going on in your life at the time. Then see if you can find correlations among these waking-life events and your dreams.

7. The dream journal becomes a wonderful tool for self-understanding. Periodically reread it and see if you notice any patterns or images recurring.

THE DREAM ADVISOR

We confront many situations in life where a little expert advice would be helpful, and the Deep Self is the best advisor we can choose—if we can learn to work with the curious symbol-language that it uses to communicate with us. If you or your child is facing a difficult choice or task, or you would simply like some information, insight, or feedback from your inner Wise One, here is a simple technique for obtaining what you need.

After getting into bed, and just as you are growing drowsy, direct your question, stated simply, to the Dream Advisor. Remember that cut-and-dried questions are alien to the Deep Self and will be resisted. Rather than "Should I take the job?" or "Does Zoe like me?," try "What do I need to know about this job?" and "What would it be helpful for me know about Zoe?" Repeat your question several times. Then write down your dreams the next day. It may take several nights before your Dream Advisor gets around to your question, and the results are likely to show you more about your possible state of mind if you take the job, or about your own deep intuitions about Zoe, than anything else.

Children love to perform conscious physical acts that connect with their own inner wisdom, using the simple gifts that the earth gives. Crystals, herbs, flowers, plants, and other natural ingredients can be used to make talismans around dream questions that will fascinate and deeply satisfy our children. (See chapter 7 for more on making talismans.)

Here are two folk talismans to try when you or your child has a question to ask the Dream Advisor:

1. Write the question on a piece of paper. Add a pinch each of dried sage and thyme and nine apple seeds. Then fold the whole thing up, tie it with a piece of string, and sleep with it under your pillow. As with any talisman of this nature, each ingredient has meaning and significance (much like each element of a dream). Apples have a connection in the universal unconscious with wisdom—they are the fruit of the Goddess and of hidden knowledge. Their seeds contain the idea of regeneration, rebirth out of darkness. Sage also has associations with wisdom, and thyme is a traditional purifier, to help the dreamer feel both empowered and protected.

2. If you grow poppies, save several seedpods for this simpler version of a dream talisman. Write your question on a small piece of paper. Then cut a hole in the dried seedhead, shake out the seeds, and place your folded paper inside. Sleep with the seedpod under your pillow. Poppies have a centuries-old association with sleep as well as with the mysterious and hidden. Even if your conscious mind is unaware of these talismanic associations, your Deep Self knows and remembers.

ENCOURAGING DEEPER AND MORE MEANINGFUL DREAMS

Although any dream, if we pay it enough attention, has much to tell us, there are some dreams that are more deeply significant than others. Such dreams often come to us when we are in crisis or in transition, as guideposts and messages of hope from our inner selves—many of us can recall at least one or two dreams that had a profound effect on our lives. But there are ways to encourage such clear and magical dreams even during ordinary times.

Autosuggestion, once again, becomes the simplest method for inviting deep dreams into your nightly life. Before sleep, repeat: "Tonight I will dream a deep dream and remember." Or you could make up a deep-dream invocation, a poem to your inner self that will encourage it to send you a dream of substance and magic to occupy both your sleeping and waking hours. Don't worry about your invocation's artistic merit (or lack thereof); if you use imagery that is appealing to you, it will be an effective and direct call to your inner self.

> *Great Owl of Dreams*
> *Wings soft and furred with dark*
> *Soar through my sleep*
> *To that tender place between eyes and heart*
> *Bring me the Dream in your mother-beak*
> *The Dream to feed me*
> *to teach and guide me*
> *Great Owl of Dreams.*

Certain incenses have ancient folk associations with deeper dreams, and their use is a charming, sweet-smelling reminder of our ancestors' earthy wisdom. You can burn frankincense, jasmine, or sandalwood in stick or cone form in a burner, or place some dried cinquefoil or mugwort on a piece of self-igniting charcoal. Try grating a piece of High Joan (or John) the Conqueress root (also known as Jalap root) to burn on charcoal, as well; or you may place a whole root under your pillow—its smoky scent makes a delicious dream companion. Benzoin, a powdered resin, burns with a clean, distinctive aroma; wormwood is another traditional dream-calling herb, but don't keep it where young children may ingest it—you only need to burn a pinch.

Adults and older children may want to try the following deep dream tea (see page 39).

Deep Dream Tea

¹/₄ cup dried mugwort
¹/₄ cup dried peppermint
2 Tbs. dried rosebuds
2 Tbs. dried vervain

Add the ingredients to 2 cups boiling water. Steep at least ten minutes, strain and drink. Sweeten if desired.

There is also a lovely dream tea available from Mountain Rose Herbs that is worth trying (see Resources at the end of this book).

Younger children who dislike the taste of herbal teas might want to try placing a drop of sandalwood or jasmine oil on their foreheads before bed; these are traditionally thought to open the "third eye."

You may make a dream pillow (see page 96 in the Mabon section of Autumn for detailed instructions), or sleep with ash tree leaves, heliotrope, mimosa, or mistletoe hung over the bed or placed beneath the pillow.

Certain gems have a folk reputation as deep-dreaming stones; among them are amethyst, bloodstone, Herkimer diamond (a double-terminated quartz crystal), and opal. These may be worn as jewelry (we caution against young children wearing any kind of necklace to sleep, but rings are fine) or placed under the pillow or beside the bed.

Or you could combine any or all of these elements and make yourself a deep-dream talisman. Chapter 7 will help you learn how.

FEEDING YOUR DREAMS

One of the best ways to enrich your dreamlife is to give the Deep Self lots of inspiration. Feed your dreams with poetry, artwork, myths, and fairy tales; all of these will enlarge your vocabulary of images and will often spark a deep dream by virtue of their deeply human appeal.

Bedtime stories are a time-honored method of soothing children and readying them for bed, but the bedtime story may now take on a deeper function—nourishing the dream. We have found that an element of the universal is what the Deep Self enjoys most; folk and fairy tales have been feeding dreamers for centuries and are far more effective than the fluffy Disney versions, which seem largely devoid of real gut-and-bone meaning.

You could also try choosing a Tarot card before bed and allowing its archetypal image to accompany you into sleep. This often yields rich and surprising results.

By sharing the power of dreams with our children, we open a door to a priceless world, one where great change, growth, and deepening become not only possible, but usual. By encouraging our children to become the keepers of their dreams, we give them a gift of magical awareness that will last a lifetime. And if you are exploring this dream landscape for the first time yourselves, you and your children will gain an added sense of partnership as you travel together on the night journey.

CHAPTER 6

YOUR CHILD'S INNER WISDOM

The Wise One within. The still, small voice. Deep power. Inner wisdom. No matter what we decide to call it, this reservoir of ancient knowledge is both universal—rooted in racial memory, stemming from the Larger Forces—and deeply personal. It knows our answers even before we've formed the questions. With its help, we can choose our paths wisely, heal ourselves, change our lives. The inner Wise One can give us the gift of loving and compassionate self-knowledge. And it is a part of every human.

Our culture has suppressed this knowledge and negated the entire concept of inner wisdom. An important part of our work as adults and as parents is to rediscover this well-kept secret, incorporate it into our lives, and then teach our children about it. To begin, we need to recognize the insidious twofold way that our culture continues to deny and devalue our gift of inner knowing.

First, most of us are taught from birth that we must look outside ourselves for the answers to any pressing question, including matters of our own health and well-being. We learn very early in life to give our power over to authority—to the teachers, doctors, political figures, and ministers/rabbis/priests who are the power-holders, the answer-givers. The entire structure of our society rests on the concept of power-over. And in submitting to outward authority, we often lose our sense of inner worth, inner power, spiritual authenticity. In reclaiming for ourselves and our children the concept of power-within, we can be wonderfully and dangerously subversive.

Second, it is the surface, the superficial, that commands attention today. In fact, most of us grew up not knowing that there is a layer of reality—a rich and fertile reality—beneath the surface that we can contact, explore, and learn from. In all this loud and crazy focus on the superficial, the quiet voice of inner wisdom is continually and thoroughly drowned out. Our current Western worldview embraces and values only the rational/intellectual; many of our "leaders"—political, industrial, or religious—have little or no use for anything other than that which is left-brain, linear, logical. The intuitive, the heartfelt, is demeaned and belittled; it doesn't serve the needs of the powerful, with their demands for product, for consumption, and for our meek cooperation in our own oppression.

The good news is that there is a great underground renaissance going on, an awakening of respect for our own intuition and for those powerful psychic gifts that are not supernatural at all, but the natural birthright of every child and adult. These gifts of inner knowing are available to all of us—more highly developed in some individuals, perhaps, but universally human all the same. The secrets of inner wisdom that have been kept from most of us for so many centuries are now being unlocked and shared through many different means.

Many of us have found that learning to listen to our inner guide becomes much easier if we enlist the help of a deck of Tarot cards, a set of runes, an I Ching book, or a pendulum—all ancient and respected systems for contacting the inner self. Many would argue that the Deeper Power—call it Goddess, God, the Higher Force—is contacted and engaged in this way as well.

Our ancestors called the practice of working with a system to contact the deep wisdom, the beneath-the-surface reality, "divination." Through divination, we contact the divine in ourselves, the Goddess or Wise One within. Divination is a tool for self-knowledge, self-change, and coming into greater awareness of and better relationship with the numinous powers.

Adults are currently enjoying the new interest in dialoging with the inner Wise One. But the idea of teaching techniques to our children to contact the inner voice is a relatively new one. We maintain that it's never too early to show our little ones how to listen to their own inner wisdom. Bringing up our children to be in harmony with their inner selves can only result in healthier, more balanced, and more empowered adults—and perhaps a saner, more heart-centered culture: divination helping us to co-create a divine-nation. Fortunately for all of us, there is an ever-increasing variety of tools, keys, and allies available today that can help us to do this.

Choose your tools to suit each individual. For a visually oriented child, the Tarot, with its seventy-eight striking pictorial cards, may provide the key. Highly kinetic children may want to work with a pendulum or will enjoy throwing the three I Ching coins and drawing the resulting six-lined figures. And children with verbal leanings may prefer runes—simple symbols with written meanings for each—or the formal meanings of the I Ching hexagrams. It becomes a source of both fascination and pleasure to experiment with different methods and see which ones evoke the strongest response from your young ones. Your family may end up using several systems, varying them according to mood and need.

And of course, it isn't even necessary to choose a preexisting system to do inner work. Some children may be satisfied to explore their dreams or to simply engage their lives with conscious awareness. When we treat every symbol or event that appears or happens to us in waking life with interest, respect, and eagerness to learn more about it, then life takes on an added fullness and mystery that even the youngest child can begin to appreciate. By dialoguing with waking reality in the same way that we've learned to dialogue with dreams, we begin to see the significance of the tiniest details of our lives, and we gain an appreciation of the many weird and wonderful synchronicities that occur with greater and greater frequency to those who are conscious of them. And as we grow in consciousness, we gradually move from a victimized position ("Why did this have to happen to me?") to an empowered one ("What am I meant to learn from this?"). All you really need is a willingness to go deeper.

Divination systems such as the Tarot, the runes, or the I Ching have been important allies for centuries. Whenever our ancestors went in search of inner vision, they were likely to use something of this nature. These systems are keys to unlock the inner self. They make use of the principle of synchronicity—the idea that there is no coincidence and that every card or rune or hexagram that appears was meant to appear, meant to be learned from. Humans have an innate ability to see the pattern and intuit the personal meaning from apparently random events—this is one of the gifts of the inner Wise One. Reading tea leaves, apple peelings, nutshells, or bird entrails falls into the same category, since this involves interpretation of pattern and an openness to the significance of seemingly random shapes.

We include some techniques and ideas for using these rediscovered ancient methods with your children, encouraging each of you to contact your inner wisdom and make it a conscious part of your lives. You may already be familiar with the Tarot or the I Ching and own and use a set of runes; for you, as well as for those who are just beginning to explore, we offer a few innovative group approaches to these systems that will involve the whole family in an interactive way. You will find that it is possible to have lots of fun and still gain insightful results—the inner Wise One has nothing against a good time. In fact, you may find, as we did, that group divination activities will provide some of the most mutually satisfying playtime you can spend together.

PENDULUMS

Divination doesn't get much simpler than the pendulum, and even though its use is limited by its cut-and-dried, yes-or-no format, it has been known to give valuable information, especially in matters of physical health and bodily preference. Your inner self knows what your body does and doesn't need, and the pendulum will swing to prove it. Ferreting out the answers may be a little time-consuming—if, for example, you feel you need a vitamin supplement and you ask your inner wisdom, via the pendulum, which one it is that you need, you'll have to go through every vitamin one by one in order to figure it out.

Younger children may have difficulty staying sufficiently still for this to really work, but it's usually fascinating to the seven-and-up crowd. You can invest in a fancy store-bought pendulum carved from special wood, complete with a crystal tucked away in a secret small chamber and a pure silk cord, or you can make one that will work just as well from string (embroidery floss is fine) or thread, and something with a little weight to it, from a fishing weight or a bolt to a star anise seed or a small crystal point. Some people swear by a simple needle and thread, but we've found that air currents can be too great a factor for a pendulum as lightweight as a needle.

The traditional length for a pendulum string is the same as the distance between the outstretched thumb and little finger, added to the measure of the widest part of the hand. You can each have a personalized pendulum to call your own. As your children grow, you will occasionally need to lengthen their strings.

When you ask a question, the pendulum will "answer" by swinging and rotating. Most people's pendulums will rotate in a clockwise direction for "yes" and a counterclockwise direction for "no." Others will reverse these directions or will swing in a circle for one answer and back and forth in a straight line for the other. So, to use your pendulum you first need to establish which type of movement means "yes" for you and which means "no."

To find out how your pendulum will respond, sit comfortably at a table and hold the string about eight or nine inches up from the pendulum between the thumb and forefinger of your strong hand (the one with which you write). Now ask a yes-or-no question to which you already know the answer. For example, hold the pendulum a few inches above a piece of red paper and ask, "Is this paper red?" Then look away, or chat with a friend, or hum a little song—and then look back at the pendulum. Note the direction or type of motion: it is your "yes." Now ask "Is this paper blue?" Look away for several moments, hum, think about what you had for lunch, and then look back at the pendulum. Note what it's doing now. It will be different from what it did last time. This is your "no."

Your children will enjoy taking it from there. Try having a family pendulum session, with everyone using his or her own. Compare notes: does everyone's move in the same way? How long does it take for the movement to start? Try asking the same question: Do I need more greens in my diet? Does the color orange make me feel relaxed? Did I get enough sleep last night? See what the answers tell you about each person. Do all your answers agree?

And if your family is as prone to losing things as ours is, you will be glad to know that the pendulum can be used to find them again. It's a roundabout way of doing it, admittedly, but it works—and your children will be enthralled. Ask a question using a location where you might have left the lost object: "Did I leave it in the kitchen? Did I leave it in the bathroom?" Just keep asking until you get a "yes." Then ask for more specific information: "Did I put it under the bed? Is it in my toy chest?" Theory has it that we really remember everything, but newer information is overlaid on top of old information. The pendulum helps us to retrieve what we already know.

TAROT

Even though you could make a life's work of studying the Tarot—and many people have—years of advanced study are not a necessary prerequisite in order to work with it, play with it, and gain insight and incalculable benefits from it. The depth and wisdom of the Tarot's ancient symbolic language is accessible to everyone; all you need to do is look—simply look, and then describe what you see. As happens when you mull over a dream image, the images on the cards, when seen through your individual filter, will yield surprising information. Everyone will see the same card in a different way. In fact, you will see the same card in a different way if you look at it a day later. And it's how you see the card that makes all the difference.

If you want some basic information—how to choose a deck, what the four suits of Tarot mean—or if you find yourselves bewitched by the cards, as we are, then by all means read some of the books in Suggested Reading. Tarot has been our favorite guide and ally for years, and our choices reflect our passion for it.

Tarot cards offer a language of symbols that can help unlock the feelings and needs that children sometimes have difficulty expressing, especially to adults. The images on the cards can give free voice to the inner self, conferring the same license as speaking from behind a sacred ceremonial mask. Working with the cards together can be a wonderful way to encourage youngsters (particularly those who are in the throes of preteen and adolescent self-consciousness) to tell you what's on their minds, through "objective," shared, and always nonjudgmental discussions of the meanings of the cards. Maura's son has an eleven-year-old friend who was getting into trouble in school and had been sent for counseling to a therapist. When he spent the day with us, we took the time to do some Tarot activities together to see what was going on in his life. He was easily able to recognize the difficulties that his sudden outbursts of anger were causing, and the cards showed that it was time for him to let go of that earlier behavior pattern, which no longer worked for his more grown-up self (which was exactly what his therapist was helping him to do). The cards encouraged him instead to embrace the humorous, creative, artistic side of himself and to welcome growth rather than fight it. He was reassured by envisioning a positive, happy outcome as he let his true self become visible.

Our own offering to the vast body of Tarot literature, history, and thought is a quietly revolutionary concept for interactive Tarot-play. Nonthreatening and enjoyable, Tarot-play is a perfect way to introduce children and adults of all ages to the evocative and illuminating power of the cards. Even if you've never opened a book on the Tarot, you can get a deck, try one of these activities, and start reaping the benefits immediately. You'll also have a lot of fun.

THREE-CARD SURPRISE

For two or more players, this activity works best with children eight years old and up.

All participants sit in a circle with the cards facedown in a heap in the center. Everyone reaches in and uses both hands to gently mix them. Then the designated dealer gathers them up into a deck and deals three cards to each player.

If you have any cards that are upside down in your hand, turn them right side up. All the players take turns choosing the cards from their hands that best fit the following categories and placing them faceup in the center of the playing space, sharing their feelings about the pictures on the cards and inviting feedback from the other players.

The picture I like best. Pick the one that appeals most strongly to you and explain why you like it.

This one reminds me of you. Pick the card that reminds you of one of the other players and explain why. It could be that the figure on the card looks like one of you, or the feeling you get from the picture reminds you of that person.

Surprise. The final card that is left in your hand. Describe it aloud. What do you see in it? What message does it have for you? See what everyone else thinks.

TAROT HAT

For two or more players, this activity will work with younger children. It also makes a great party activity for groups.

Everyone mixes the cards in a pile. Take turns standing in the center of the playing space while the player on your right grabs a handful of cards and places them gently on your head. The object of the game is to keep at least one card balanced on your head—if you can do it, this card becomes your Tarot Hat. Look carefully at your Hat card. What's happening in the picture? If there is a person or animal shown on it, try imitating its position or activity. How does that feel to you? Do you like your Hat? You may find that your Hat makes you feel stronger or smarter or more energetic.

If you and your children enjoy the Tarot activities above, we recommend our first book, *Tarot Games: 45 Playful Ways to Explore Tarot Cards Together.* It's filled with games for both children and grown-ups that give you access to the wisdom and power of the cards—and the inner self—in an entirely new and playful way.

RUNES

Although the Tarot's roots are rumored to reach back to ancient Egypt, actual decks only began to surface in the fourteenth century. The runes are far older. Called the I Ching of the Vikings, runes were originally used for divination and also for spell-casting and other kinds of reality-altering magical work.

Ralph Blum's popular *Book of Runes,* often sold as a set with runes, is available at bookstores everywhere, but the definitions are a bit difficult for children to grasp. To make and use your own set of more child-friendly runes, take a look at the bean rune activity on page 115 in the Samhain section of Autumn.

Runes may be consulted whenever you or your children need more information about something; we know families who choose runes whenever they need to make a decision that will affect everyone. If there are pressing issues or concerns, runes can give insight and advice. To learn how bean runes may be planted in a ritual way, see page 154 in the Ostara section of Spring; they may also be sprouted and eaten or allowed to grow.

HOT RUNE

This family rune activity is a variation of the time-honored Hot Potato game that yields significant information while everyone has a great, rowdy time.

Sit in a circle and have everyone choose a rune at random. Then, to the tape-recorded song of your choice, pass the runes to each other—no order required, so it becomes a free-for-all very quickly—until the music stops (take turns being the designated music-stopper). Some of you may be caught with several runes, while others will be empty-handed. If you're caught with a rune, great! Examine it and relate the meaning to your life, sharing ideas and input together. Everyone wins.

I CHING

For basic how-to information—how to throw the coins, how to translate the results into lines—we recommend Diane Stein's *Kwan Yin Book of Changes.* As well as giving clear, concise explanations, the book offers nourishing feminist interpretations of the hexagrams rather than the sometimes punitive meanings found in the patriarchal versions.

The actual method of notating the results of your coin-throws is a little complicated. Older children can learn how to figure it out on their own, but you will probably want to tell younger ones whether their line is broken, unbroken, or moving, and then allow them to draw their own hexagrams.

It is usual for individuals to throw their own hexagrams, but you could try having each family member take turns throwing the coins until six throws have been completed. The resulting hexagram will be a group effort—very helpful if it relates to a group issue or decision—and will reflect the sum of each person's input.

When factors are hidden or unclear, when feelings run too deep for verbal expression, or when an issue seems too big for a child to handle, then it can be an act of loving understanding to reach for the bag of bean runes, or the three special I Ching coins, or the child's favorite Tarot deck. By simply bearing witness to the insights she or he will gain from those helpful allies, we promote the self-reliance and self-empowerment we all need and long for. And by honoring the child's inner wisdom by engaging it in conscious, enjoyable, and meaningful activities, we deepen our connection with each other as we play.

CHAPTER 7

SELF-EMPOWERMENT IN A POUCH

Making and Using Talismans

Talismans offer us a means of applying our inner wisdom in a practical and physical way. The making of talismans is an ancient and respected magical practice that has been known to Wise Ones for centuries. It is an amazingly effective method of working toward desired outcomes from the inside out, because, in order for any good thing to happen to us, we need to make sure that we will allow it to happen. Talismans prepare the ground by shifting our consciousness toward those good things. It is a vital first step.

Our children are in so many ways powerless and vulnerable, at the mercy of larger forces beyond their control. Teaching them the basics of talisman-making can become a key to self-empowerment. Often, it is the simple action of taking steps—any steps—toward rectifying a problem or gaining a desired outcome that produces the hoped-for result. The fact that we do not have to wait helplessly but can concentrate and act in positive ways to effect change gives enormous hope and confidence.

Making a talisman becomes a technique for focusing every aspect of the self—body, mind, feelings, and will—toward the specific purpose or issue at hand. Some of the ingredients are chosen from traditional sources, giving a degree of deep authenticity to the proceedings; others are chosen from the heart, making an important personal connection.

Magic has been defined as the ability to change consciousness at will. Trance and visualization may easily be seen to fulfill this criterion, but the humble folk magic of gathering suitable materials and unifying them toward a single purpose is just as valid and effective a means of achieving this. There is also a healing and empowering wisdom in recognizing the potential for transformative magic inherent in all things, no matter how small or seemingly insignificant.

A talisman is defined as a collection of objects put together with a specific purpose and conscious intention. There are also single-object talismans, but we have found that the act of combining is a powerful one, and it probably works best for young ones just beginning to do this kind of work. Many people use the words "amulet" and "talisman" interchangeably, while others insist that amulets usually are made to keep undesirable things away—such as ill health or danger—while talismans have a more attractive quality, serving to draw good things toward the maker. Either way, talismans not only focus our inner forces toward a specific purpose, but they seem to activate outer universal forces in our favor, as well. Synchronous events and positive "chance" occurrences often increase dramatically after you make one.

To make an effective talisman, it is not necessary to believe that it will work (although children usually have much less difficulty in this regard than adults). What *is* necessary is a strong sense of really needing and wanting the hoped-for outcome. It is this needing/wanting energy that makes a vital connection in one's inner self with the talisman and that fills it with power.

Talismans answer myriad human needs and desires. Your child may make one to find a friend or to do well in school; to make herself feel safe or to protect your home; to help a sick companion animal get well; to feel self-confident—the list of possibilities is infinite. Adults, of course, can make them too, in answer to a different set of needs.

The one thing that you must never do with talismans is use them as attempts to manipulate others. Magical coercion is unethical, dangerous, and apt to produce unforeseen and nasty results. This is why you wouldn't make a talisman to get Nathan to be your friend, but you might want to make one to help yourself become a friendlier and more likable person, knowing that, if Nathan never comes around, someone else who is just as wonderful (or even more so) will certainly come along.

Talismans, like focused prayer or the sending of energy, are often highly effective in healing, but we usually ask the permission of the ill person (or animal) before doing healing work of any kind, including making a healing talisman. Often, people need their times of sickness as respite from the daily grind, or as a time-out so that inner growth or progression is possible. Companion animals will let you know in their wordless way; practice listening to them when they are well, so that you will be able to sense their will when they are not.

Some talismans may be worn or carried—if your child needs relief from painful shyness, or wants to feel strong and powerful, she or he could make a small talisman to wear around the neck or tuck into a backpack, where it will be a constant companion. Other talismans work their magic tucked away out of sight—home-protection ones generally are hidden from view in a closet, cupboard, or drawer. And still others are placed where they will be seen often, as reminders of your intention and the steps you are taking to bring it about.

You can use a wonderful variety of containers to hold your talisman. Some children like to sew their own pouches, or you can buy one of the many silk, brocaded, crocheted, or woven ones available today. If you can find one in a color that fits your purpose (see Correspondences on page 204), then use it, by all means. A self-empowerment pouch in a vibrant shade of dark red or purple will have a different effectiveness than a pale pink one; color is deeply connected to our inner selves and becomes a powerful ally in any kind of inner work.

Bottles are another traditional container, especially for talismans that include fluids; herbal teas, salt and water, and saliva all make good ingredients. Other possibilities to house your talisman include envelopes, boxes, tins, or bowls—let your personal preference and synchronicity lead you to the choice that feels right to you. You will often come across the perfect yard-sale or thrift-shop find just when you need it most.

Sometimes you might be inspired to put a talisman in a hollow tree or stump or bury it in the ground; imagine what a strong feeling, imbued with nature magic, these choices would add.

CREATING A TALISMAN

There are several steps in constructing a talisman, steps that resonate in the inner self, activate it, make it pay attention, and begin sending energy toward the desired outcome. These steps are clearing, constructing, sealing, and acting.

CLEARING

It is often necessary with older children and adults to clear any thoughts holding them back from receiving what they need and want. Many of us have been taught that it's selfish and wrong to want things for ourselves, so talismanic work may activate guilt ("I shouldn't be doing this—this is greedy and selfish of me"). Young ones seem to have no such hampering feelings and are ready to run wholeheartedly toward their desires. But we older ones must remember that we deserve to have all we truly need. We deserve to be happy. When we have contacted our source of inner joy, we become a beacon for everyone around us— in this way, an individual's own personal happiness shines brightly for all. The Goddess way does not teach that there is any particular virtue in suffering. By embodying the fullness of the Goddess—by embracing all the joy of which we are capable—we create more of that wonderful, inspiring, nurturing energy in the world.

After you have established your worthiness of every blessing that life can give, you need to clarify the exact nature of your present need. It's difficult for a talisman to do its work if the purpose behind it is hazy. You can focus your inner self by being specific here.

CONSTRUCTING

Now comes the fun part. Collect as many ingredients as you like, using Correspondences on page 204 for ideas and also trusting your own inner wisdom. Suppose you want to make a talisman for success in your schoolwork, and the "correct" herb for this, according to the tables, is sage, but, for some unfathomable reason, you feel strongly attracted to dill. It is your inner self that you are working to empower here—if it responds to dill, then dill it is.

Your possibilities for talisman ingredients are practically limitless: from the nuts, seeds, flowers, and herbs that are the Great Mother's green gifts, to feathers, shells, crystals and stones, or things crafted by human hands, the talisman becomes the place for wonderful connections to be made between your need and the objects that surround you. A pictorial representation of the desired outcome is a powerful tool, as well. Cut-out magazine pictures, photographs, your own drawings, or Tarot cards all make wonderful affirmations that your desired outcome exists and is attainable. And don't be afraid to involve other senses besides your sight; smell is an ancient road to the Deep Self, and essential oils make fine additions to the talisman.

As you place the ingredients in your container, imagine your desired outcome as an already accomplished fact. Know that everything you put into the talisman is connected deeply to your need. Visualize yourself enjoying the fruits of your magical inner work. See chapter 8 for more information on how to visualize.

SEALING

Once all of your ingredients have been safely placed in their container, you need to seal it: that is, do a small ritual that lets your inner self know that the talisman is finished, magically closed, and ready to start generating power and energy in your life to work the changes you desire.

Many options are available to you here. You can seal the top of the bottle—or box or envelope—with melted beeswax, candle wax, or sealing wax. You can tie a pouch closed with twine or cord, knotted three times. You might want to repeat an ancient rhyme that Wise Ones have used for centuries:

> *By knot of one the spell is done*
> *By knot of two it shall come true*
> *By knot of three, so mote it be.*

"So mote it be" is a traditional phrase, similar to "amen" or the French "ainsi soit'il," meaning "thus it must be," or "may it be so." Little rhymes like this one have been used universally in magical work—what they lack in poetic terms is more than made up by the soothing quality of the rhyme and repetition. A magical rhyme becomes another way to still our head voices and get right to the Deep Self.

You may want to take a breath and then exhale over your talisman, or use saliva (or tears) to seal it. Place your hands over the talisman and send your energy into it. Any method of involving the body—with its breath or its fluids—gives a message that you are sacred, that every part of you has magic and holiness.

Once your talisman is sealed, you will want to make sure that it stays that way until it is no longer needed.

ACTING

Once the talisman is finished, you need to back up your inner work with some pragmatic, concrete, and practical outward action. You can't expect the talisman to work unaided. If you want to pass the math exam, you may make a special talisman to help you calm your mind, rid yourself of worries that keep you from concentrating, and give you some confidence and hope. But you also need to study. Or if you made a friend-attracting talisman, by all means wear it, but also be sure to create situations where you will be with other people. If you stay hidden in your room, your talismanic magic will be greatly hindered.

When the outcome has been attained, you may want to open your talisman and burn, scatter, or bury the ingredients. Gratitude to every aspect of your Self, and to the universal forces that flow through and around you, can be freely expressed at this time. Feel good—no, feel *wonderful*—about the power you have discovered in yourself to effect change.

EXAMPLES OF TALISMANS

Talismans, like dreams, are unique and highly personal to the makers of them. However, because we want to give you some idea of how they operate and are constructed, we offer these examples—not to be imitated, but to be taken as inspiration for your own.

SWIMMER'S TALISMAN

One young friend, terrified of the water but determined to learn to swim, made the following talisman to help him get past his crippling fear.

In a little blue-green glass bottle, he placed the following:

> a piece of sea-colored aquamarine
> a nose plug
> water mixed with sea salt to purify his mind of fear
> a bay leaf for protection
> a picture, cut from a magazine, of an Olympic swimme*r*

As he stuffed each ingredient into the bottle, he visualized himself swimming strongly. When he added the rolled-up magazine photo, he moistened it with his saliva and thought about the many fluids that flow through his body, connecting him with water.

He sealed the bottle with beeswax, wound a silver cord around the top, and poured some tap water over it. He took this talisman with him into the bathtub, where he visualized floating safely in the arms of the warm and nurturing water. He began to visit a local indoor pool, where he held his talisman and dabbled his feet in the water. Eventually his parents signed him up for individual swimming lessons. The talisman, which he now kept in his gym bag, made him feel safe; no harm would come to him, he felt, as long as it was nearby. Eventually, he was able to learn the breathing and the movements that allowed him to swim; as a final test, he brought out the bottle and allowed it to sink to the bottom of the pool. Then, mustering all of his confidence, he went underwater to retrieve it.

Once he had truly learned how to swim and had realized that the water was not his enemy, he opened the bottle and extracted the nose plug, which he buried, and the stone, which he kept. Then he took the bottle to a nearby river and shook the remaining contents into the water, saying a little made-up rhyme of gratitude. Then he took the empty bottle to a recycling center and released it into the bin with a joyful heart.

SELF-AFFIRMING TALISMAN

Some young people are oblivious to issues of appearance (girls who relate strongly to the Goddess Athena, for instance, may be more concerned with the results of their latest research project). But for an individual whose personal attractiveness is an important part of his or her life, it can be terribly painful to feel unattractive or different. One of the nastier results of woman-demeaning, patriarchal thinking is that women who don't fit the conventional notions of beauty are devalued and made to feel worthless. Here is how one teenage girl found the courage to feel beautiful just as she was.

First, she found a small wood-backed mirror at a local gift shop. As she looked at her reflection in it, she repeated three times, "I am myself and I am beautiful in my own way." This was the most difficult (and possibly the most powerful) part of the process. She placed the mirror in a special carved wooden box, which her mother had given her on her thirteenth birthday. Then she added orris root powder, traditional to make one feel irresistible; a small piece of amber, an ancient beauty and self-confidence stone; and several photographs of unconventionally beautiful women that she had found. Many of these had strong and unusual features illuminated by inner strength, serenity, vibrant intelligence, passionate belief, or spirit-fire. Then she added a drawing of her face that she had done while looking in the mirror, to take its place among these.

She chanted, "All of us are sacred, all of us are beautiful," as she wound the box with red cord. Then she knotted it and held her hands over it, visualizing the completed talisman glowing with radiant, affirming energy.

She kept the box in front of her dresser mirror, where she saw it every morning as she brushed her hair before going to school and again at night before going to bed. She slept with it under her pillow whenever she felt the need. She carried the box to school in her backpack once but ended up worrying that it might get broken. So she found another piece of amber, dusted it with orris root, and wore it in a tiny pouch around her neck—a sort of talisman-to-talisman communication and constant reminder.

Whenever she needed a boost, she would hold the box in her hand and repeat, "I am myself and I am beautiful in my own way." She reports that the process, although sometimes slow, was amazingly positive. She could gradually feel herself holding her head higher, walking with more confidence and power. And her friends began saying, "What have you been doing to yourself? You look great!"

When she was finally able to look in the dresser mirror and repeat the affirmation with real conviction, she opened the box, burned the photos and her own drawing in an ashtray after giving thanks, added the orris root and amber to the pouch she wore, and placed the box on her windowsill. She kept the small mirror in her backpack, wrapped in a cotton kerchief, so that she could remind herself of her beauty, value, and power whenever she wanted.

Talismans are not only empowering and hope-giving, but they also encourage us to creatively dialogue with our inner wisdom. In the act of choosing just the right ingredients, we find solace, enjoyment, and a deep satisfaction. The making of a talisman becomes a healthy way to honor all goodness and to celebrate our own ability to change and grow.

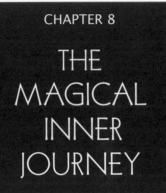

CHAPTER 8

THE MAGICAL INNER JOURNEY

It has become common knowledge that guided meditations (also called "guided imagery" or "creative visualizations") are highly effective tools for personal transformation as well as to greater relaxation, stress reduction, and healing. But, until fairly recently, it was a technique used by and for adults. Diane Mariechild's powerful *Mother Wit: A Guide to Healing and Psychic Development,* a Goddess-oriented selection of guided meditations, includes a wonderful chapter on creative visualization for children, and Maureen Murdock explores the applications for children fully in *Spinning Inward: Using Guided Imagery with Children for Learning, Creativity, and Relaxation.* Now parents, educators, and counselors everywhere are beginning to appreciate the potential for growth and change, centering and relaxing, that guided meditations have to offer young people.

This chapter will give you some helpful ideas on beginning to explore these valuable techniques with your children, beginning with visualization, which is the cornerstone of a guided meditation.

HOW TO VISUALIZE

Visualization is one of the most important and basic elements of any kind of meditation, healing, or ritual work. The first reaction of many people is to say, "I can't do it!" But anyone can. In fact, chances are you're doing it right now. If you can read a printed word on a page and see an image in your mind, you are visualizing automatically. It is a human gift, to be able to see things with the mind's eye. In fact, visualization is rarely just visual; all five senses can become deeply alive, like a dream that feels more real than waking reality. As Starhawk says in *The Spiral Dance,* "When the inner senses are fully awake, we may see visions of extraordinary beauty, smell the blossoms of the Isle of Apples, taste ambrosia, and hear the songs of the Gods."

The marvelous truth about visualization is that it engages the inner space where reality can actually be changed and where deep-self issues can be healed. But there is also a grave responsibility implied here; negative or frightening images, when nurtured and allowed to grow in the vulnerable inner self, can do real damage. Most of us have seen the trance state that prolonged television-watching induces in children. The mindless violence and horror of many films and television shows is doing terrible harm to those children, and to us as well.

Children love to visualize; their elaborate games of pretend and the legions of invisible pals that befriend them show how instinctive the process is, even for the youngest child. By encouraging practice in this invaluable technique from an early age and continuing to journey together as the child grows, we replace the images of brutality with images of healing. Visualizations become gifts we can give our children—and ourselves—again and again.

Here are two simple exercises to help get you and your children started on consciously visualizing. You can either read these aloud, pausing between sentences to give the images time to develop, or make a tape and play it; that way, you can all practice together. Begin by getting comfortable, preferably sitting (if you lie down, you run the risk of having your visualization punctuated by the sound of snores). Once you've mastered the circle visualization, you may want to try a more advanced visualization like the orange visualization, which involves the senses of touch, taste, and smell as well as sight.

Circle Visualization

Close your eyes and take a few deep breaths. Imagine a big white movie screen. Now a huge green circle appears on the screen. It fills the screen. It is perfectly round. You can make the circle change to another color. What color is your circle now? You can make the circle change again. What color is your circle now? Take a few more deep breaths and open your eyes.

Close your eyes and take a few deep breaths. Imagine that you are holding a sweet, juicy orange slice in your hand. It is cut in a perfect circle; enjoy the beauty of its shape. Now hold it up to your nose and enjoy its sweet, citrus scent. Your mouth begins to water for a taste. Carefully tear the peel with your fingers and open the circle, holding the peel in a straight line: the orange forms little triangles pointing up. Nibble one of these orange segments now and enjoy the delicious taste and the sticky, warm juice that drips down your chin and fingers. Now take a few more deep breaths and open your eyes.

PREPARING FOR GUIDED MEDITATION

A guided meditation is a sustained visualization, a magical inward journey. Approach each one you do with delight and anticipation; you never know what you'll experience, but it is certain to be exciting and meaningful. As with any work that involves the inner Deep Self, it is wise to practice three simple but vital preliminary steps before you begin.

1. **Relax.** Get comfortable, and become conscious of your breathing—not forcing or changing your breathing pattern, but simply noticing it. Then, beginning with your feet and working upward, relax each part of your body. Some people imagine each part becoming heavy or soft, while others wriggle or tighten first and then relax. Listening to soothing music and burning incense or a special candle are also effective methods of getting your body into that stressless, receptive, relaxed state that is a prerequisite for a meaningful visualization experience. Children love having their feet massaged or their backs gently rubbed before their inner journeys.

2. **Ground.** This means literally getting in touch with the energy of the earth, allowing it to flow through you. Unless you do this, you run the risk of expending your own vital energy and becoming depleted or burning out. The time-honored method for grounding is a simple meditation (a sort of premeditation meditation) called the Tree of Life. We offer an abbreviated version on page 62; as with any of our meditations for children, we've stripped it down to the bare bones so they don't get antsy. Repetition of this meditation deepens our sense of the earth's power by making a literal connection between earth energy and our own bodies. When you are journeying with others,

you can experiment with imagining the branches touching each other, energies flowing together. (There is a beautiful, more fully articulated version of the Tree of Life in Starhawk's *The Spiral Dance* that you may want to try yourself or with older children.)

3. ***Protect yourself.*** Whenever we engage nonordinary reality, it is vital to make all participants feel protected and safe. By grounding ourselves in our physical bodies and setting a boundary of magical space in which our bodies will remain protected, we can allow our inner selves the freedom to journey.

In order to create a safe space, you will need to affirm these three keys to inner protection (silently if you are meditating alone, or aloud, if you're leading a family journey, so that all the participants will hear):

> *You are safe and protected.*
> *You will be able to come out of the journey any time you wish.*
> *You will remember everything that you experience.*

Sometimes, it is enough just to hear these words. But it can also be helpful to picture your space surrounded by a glowing warm light; or to visualize the room encased in a magical safety bubble; or to imagine yourselves held lovingly in the arms of the Mother. Simple images such as these actually convey a great deal.

You may also smudge the space (and each other) with sage and cedar or sprinkle a little salt and water around the perimeter of the room. Children love to help with this, and both of these age-old rituals are highly effective, as they communicate a sense of safety directly to the inner self.

Some adults worry if they go on a guided meditation or shamanic trance journey they will never come back. Unless your journeys involve the use of heavy psychotropic drugs, this is practically impossible. Even if a journey is interrupted before its conclusion, you can always come back to ordinary reality—feeling a little spacey and incomplete, maybe, but still fully functional. You will want to do all you can to prevent interruptions—take the phones off the hook, use a quiet time and space that would ordinarily be private—but if a neighbor knocks on the door or you hear your cat embroiled in a scrap outside, don't panic; simply do what you have to do, and then resume and finish the journey when you can.

Experiment to find the meditation time that works best for your family. After school or before dinner are often good times to wind down, and one of the added benefits of doing this kind of activity is the deep relaxation it produces. You will find that your evening is much less stressful after a family meditation. And always include time to share what you experienced; revealing our inner selves to one another is a special way to grow closer. You may want to encourage storytelling or artwork around the images that evolve during your inner journeys.

If you want to practice doing some meditations alone or with your children after enjoying the ones in this book, we highly recommend Diane Mariechild's *Mother Wit*, which includes a section for children. And Maureen Murdock's *Spinning Inward* is filled with ideas and exercises that are wonderful for the whole family. Also, Shakti Gawain's *Creative Visualization* is another valuable resource that gives a good, solid grounding in the technique.

Experiencing guided meditations together deepens our connection with one another. When tough times hit—the illness, stress, separations, and disasters that are an inevitable part of life—meditations help us to cope, as individuals and as a family.

◆─────── Tree of Life Meditation ───────◆

Sit comfortably with your eyes closed. Breathe deeply and fully in and out for a few breaths. Now picture tiny white roots sprouting out of the base of your spine and traveling down into the earth, the fertile, nourishing earth. See these roots beginning to draw up the life-giving energy of the earth, drawing it up into your body, filling it with energy and light. Your sense of aliveness grows with every breath, until you imagine branches of energy bursting from the top of your head, bursting out and arching back down to the earth again, returning to the earth, one continuous circle of energy.

At this point, you may either continue with the guided meditation of your choice, or take a few more deep breaths and open your eyes.

ENCOURAGING THE SHAMAN IN YOUR CHILD

Shamanism is becoming widely understood and accepted as a powerful method of accessing wisdom, healing, and personal transformation; it is a basic human ability that can be practiced by people everywhere. Because of its increasing popularization, it is now possible for adults to read any of several excellent books on shamanism or to take workshops to learn actual shamanic techniques. But we believe that children, too, can be shown how to experience the shamanic trance journey, giving them access to greater self-understanding and personal growth. Shamanism becomes a path of healing for our children and for our communities, both immediate and global.

What, exactly, is a shaman, and what does a shaman do? The word comes from Siberia, but shamans are found in virtually every indigenous culture. What a shaman does is to journey in nonordinary reality, often with the help or in the company of a power animal. Journeys take place in a state of altered consciousness or trance, usually brought about by the rhythm of a drum or rattle. Shamans often journey to help other people; as Michael Harner describes in *The Way of the Shaman,* "The shaman may journey for the purpose of diagnosing or treating illnesses; for divination or prophecy; for acquisition of power through interaction with 'spirits,' 'power animals,' 'guardians,' or other spiritual entities; for establishing contact with guides or teachers in nonordinary reality, from whom the shaman may solicit advice on tribal or individual problems."

Like many of those on the Goddess way or the path of earth-connectedness, shamans see the spirit in all things; a tree or an animal can be just as important a teacher to a shaman as a human being. Shamanism opens the door of communication. Shamanic journeying deepens our earth-knowing.

We have chosen to use guided meditation to begin the process of journeying with your children, but this is not a must: you could simply explain the basics, put on a drumming tape, and let each individual find her or his own way.

BASICS OF SHAMANISM

As Vicki Noble points out in *Shakti Woman: Feeling Our Fire, Healing Our World—The New Female Shamanism*, a shamanic trance journey is not really the same as imagination, a guided meditation, or creative visualization. As she says, "While it may include each of these forms, the shamanic trance journey itself is an actual movement out of one body (the physical) and into another vehicle (the energy body, the light body, the spirit body) and another dimension. Where the spirit body travels to is up to the individual shaman, who slips through a crack between the worlds to enter another time zone or another plane." Children are naturally adept at this, being able to achieve the trance journey with little effort and with wonderful results.

It is important to begin any shamanic journey work with the three preliminary steps described under "Preparing for Guided Meditation" (page 60). But also keep in mind that, although this whole idea may sound weird or even a little scary to some of you, journeying to other planes is a safe and natural experience. A shaman, unlike a schizophrenic, knows the difference between the ordinary reality of here and the nonordinary reality of there and has the ability to shuttle back and forth between the two places at will. Shamans know about boundaries and become adept at passing through them.

People trance lightly all the time—we just call it fantasizing, daydreaming, or "spacing out." A shamanic trance is a trance with conscious purpose. You will be able to come back whenever you wish. And the insights you gain through the process will have a significance and a positive impact that can deepen and change your life.

Finding your power animal is a good prelude to shamanic journeying, but it is not an absolute prerequisite. Following the looser, feminist shamanic process described by Vicki Noble, rather than the more rigid and linear techniques set out by Michael Harner and others in the 1980s, we have come to believe that there are no real "rules" that, if strictly adhered to, will guarantee a "successful" journey. All journeys are meaningful and valid. This feminist way feels much more heart-centered and embracing, giving each individual more personal flexibility and respect for whatever she or he experiences. But you may find that children, in particular, feel safer and more secure if their guardian animal accompanies them into other magical realms. The Samhain section of Autumn includes a meditation (page 110) that enables your children to meet their power animals and begin establishing a relationship with them.

Most journeys begin with an opening: a cave mouth, a burrow or hole in the ground, a well, an elaborate carved door—whatever your inner self is drawn to. When this opening is entered, it becomes the gateway to other planes. Many of us have found that our openings become tunnels going down into the earth—which is very helpful in getting us from ordinary to nonordinary consciousness—but your journey may take you up, or over, or through. Maura's shamanic journeys begin when she sees herself walking through a waterfall into the rock passageway behind it, which opens into the world of nonordinary reality. Eventually, you leave the in-between place and find yourself in magical space and time.

Once you are there, be prepared to meet guides and teachers, often in surprising form—remember that not only power animals can give you information here. Trees, plants, rocks, personal ancestors, figures from myth, and infinite other possibilities exist as sources of insight and knowledge.

At the end of the journey, you will return through the in-between place and emerge from the opening through which you first entered. Then you may wriggle your fingers and toes, stretch, and come back to awareness of being in your body.

The final step in becoming comfortable with the shamanic journey is to simply find a rattling or drumming rhythm and allow each individual to journey unscripted; again, the only elements you need to remember are the magical opening, meeting with a teacher—often the power animal—in a magical landscape, and then returning through the opening.

Although many adults find it easier to journey in silence and stillness, your child may want to move around or talk during a journey, and that's fine; guided journeys often incorporate dialogue, as the person in trance describes what she or he is experiencing.

We have found that just before sleep is often perfect for very young children's first experiences with journeys, since they are more relaxed and receptive at that time. (Some of those bedtime journeys will inevitably end up in slumberland. If this happens to your child, don't worry—simply finish the meditation out loud, just as if she or he could hear you. When your little ones drift off to sleep in the company of their power animals, they often have especially meaningful or magical dreams.)

FIRST JOURNEY

This introductory guided version of the shaman's journey for little ones is meant for that half-awake, half-asleep time. After your children have become familiar with the technique, you can journey in broad daylight at whatever time you choose. Or you may be surprised to find that your child won't need any verbal cues at all but will be off and running after the merest suggestion from you.

Once your child is in bed and the lights are dimmed, make sure that she or he is feeling relaxed, grounded, and safe. Try patting their backs rhythmically in lieu of a drum—it works in a beautifully tactile and powerful way. You may want to memorize the following journey map or use it as a guide for your own version (it's difficult to read in near-darkness).

Close your eyes and pay attention to your breathing for a little while—how you breathe in, pause, and breathe out in a very peaceful rhythm, over and over again. Now begin to imagine that you are walking in a field. The moon is shining brightly overhead, and it is early summer. The warm breeze smells sweet and flowers bloom in clusters all around you. Their colors look different in the moonlight. You breathe in their scent with enjoyment, feeling the deep peace and beauty of the night all around you. You look down at your feet and see that you are on a path, a path that stretches smoothly out in front of you, with sweet-smelling flowers and grasses rising up on either side.

You follow this path, all silvery in the moonlight, and you see that it is leading you toward a dark and grass-covered hillside that rises up in front of you. As you approach, you see that there is a door in the hillside, an opening that is just your size. You walk right up to this doorway and enter it.

Now you are standing in a tunnel that is leading down into the earth. It smells warm and rich, like the earth. You begin to walk down this tunnel, and you reach out with your hands to touch the walls on either side of you. They feel dry and smooth. The earth beneath your feet is soft and makes your footsteps very quiet. You go downward and downward, deeper and deeper into the earth. Finally you see a light ahead of you. You see that there is a doorway at the other end of the tunnel, and you run toward it now, eager to find what wonderful place your tunnel has brought you to.

You step out of the tunnel into bright daylight. You look around in amazement. You are in a magical land.

Now you see your power animal, who rushes up to greet you. Together, you explore this special place. (Pause for a while.)

Now your animal tells you that it is time to return. You go back to the tunnel's entrance and, together, you enter it. Together, you walk up the tunnel, upward and upward, up toward the doorway in the hillside. You can see the doorway now. You and your power animal step out of the doorway onto the path and walk together through the field, back through the sweet-smelling flowers, back toward your bedroom, back to your bed, where you are lying.

Now stretch, and wiggle your toes, and open your eyes.

After a few of these bedtime experiences, children may be ready to make more independent journeys—journeys in which their inner selves provide more of the details and the experience follows their own internal guide.

ANOTHER JOURNEY

Read the following journey aloud or make a tape so that the reader can journey as well, leaving pauses of one to three minutes between paragraphs. We strongly advocate using a background drum or rattle to keep up a rapid rhythm—the primary method of trance induction among modern shamans—as the beat takes you out of ordinary reality very quickly and pushes you on. You can all rattle together, or you can find someone willing to drum while everybody else journeys, or you can always make use of one of the many tapes produced specifically for shamanic purposes. The tapes are timed, which is comforting— you know exactly how long each journey will be—and its beat becomes more rapid or uses a distinct rhythmic pattern to let participants know when it is time to return.

◆————————————————————————————◆

Relax, ground, and cast a web of safety around yourself.

Listen to your breathing, becoming aware of the peacefulness of its pattern. Now imagine that you are standing in one of your special power places. It could be a windswept hillside, a sunny beach, a dark and mysterious forest—any place that feels sacred and powerful to you.

Next to you there is an opening of some kind: a well, a rabbit hole, the hollow of a tree, or the mouth of a cave. You enter this opening and find yourself in a tunnel leading down into the earth. You journey down this tunnel now.

Now you see a light ahead of you, a light in the darkness of the tunnel. You approach and find that it is a doorway into a magical land. You step out into this magic landscape and there you see your power animal.

Your power animal has something important to tell you or show you. Take some time now to listen. Your animal may want you to follow it. You may ride on its back, or fly.

Now it is time to return. Together, you and your power animal journey back to the doorway of the tunnel, and you step inside. Quickly, you walk back up the tunnel, back toward the opening, until you are standing in your power place.

Now come back to awareness of being here in this room. Wiggle your fingers and toes, stretch, and open your eyes.

A PROGRESSIVE JOURNEY

With her many years of experience, Vicki Noble has developed a progressive shamanic journey through which she guides participants; we include a summary of it to give you an idea of the possibilities for activity that exist on the other side. You may want to try this, or a similar script, with your children or by yourself, as a next step.

First, as with most journeys, you enter a special opening. Then, on the other side, you will hear or see water; you immerse yourself in it, for cleansing and healing. (The watery sound of rainsticks make a wonderful adjunct to this part of the journey.) You step out of the water and find a garment waiting on the shore for you to put on. Make an altar from things you find, and stay by the altar for a while, praying or clarifying your intentions. Then, when you begin to explore the terrain, you meet with a special plant (sometimes an herbal remedy that you need) and an animal that teaches you about something in the body. The animal leads you to a sacred enclosure, where you will find an ancient guide who has known you for many lifetimes and who loves you very much. When you go, alone, into the enclosure, your guide communicates with you using words or touch or telepathy. Gifts are exchanged. You ask for advice. Then you take leave of each other, and you return with the animal to your altar. You leave the garment there, and ask the animal if it wants to return with you. (At this point, the animal may jump into your body, lodging in a particular place.) If the animal chooses to remain on the other side, it will give you something of itself to bring back with you. Then you re-enter the tunnel, and return to ordinary consciousness.

So many surprising and wonderful things can happen on a shamanic journey. Your animal may take you on its back to other even more incredible places. Together, you may fly or swim or run tirelessly, effortlessly. You may even become your animal. You may also receive information from unusual sources: rocks, trees, and waterfalls may all communicate with you, or you may meet important human or extra-human guides. You may undertake your journeys for fun or for self-knowledge; if there is an issue or concern on your mind, a journey will often give surprising information, wise insights that transcend the knowledge of your conscious mind.

Eventually, you can journey for one another—a powerful method of healing and problem-solving that allows your own power animal, or the guides that you meet, to give you information about the person for whom you are journeying. Simply begin your journey with the other person's need in mind. You will remember the important information to repeat afterward. Often, the words or images you get may seem like utter gibberish to you, but they will make perfect sense to the other person.

Become magical travelers together. By reclaiming these nonordinary methods of healing ourselves and each other, and so becoming wiser and saner human beings, we help the world to grow in wholeness.

CHAPTER 9

THE HEALING CHILD

TEACHING WELLNESS:
ATTENDING TO THE BODY

Very young children are completely present in their bodies, feeling every joy and every pain with total physical intensity. With age and time, however, many of us seem to lose touch, to a greater or lesser degree, with the body and its wise knowing, its miraculous self-healing power, its incredible system of warnings. To that increasing lack of attention, add the cultural distrust of the physical and the allopathic medical practice of treating the body like a machine, and you often end up with the mind dissociated from and entirely overshadowing the body.

Many adults simply are not fully *in* their bodies; they have learned to close off from the body's signals, ignoring and suppressing them—and they become numbed, literally out of touch. For some, abuse was the trauma that triggered this split. For others, the simple workings of a culture centered on the rational mind did the job. In any case, what is often needed for the adult is a reintegration of body and mind. And children need our support and encouragement to keep from succumbing to cultural pressures that teach the supremacy of the mind and see the physical self as "lower," of lesser value.

We believe that the first step in becoming whole—engaged in a body-mind partnership—is listening to and learning from the body. Attending to it, becoming aware of its messages and their significance, is an important first step in the prevention of disease. Maureen Murdock makes this point very clearly in *Spinning Inward*, telling us that "possibly one of the most valuable things we can teach our children is how to attend . . . how to be fully present in mind and body at each moment. . . . The word *attention* comes from the Latin *attendere*, 'to stretch forward.' What do we wish our children to stretch toward? The values they see mirrored around them in our competitive, stressful, consumption-oriented society? Or a clear sense of who they *are*?"

If our bodies are feeling uneasy and out of balance, we need to know. By responding to the cues our physical selves give us, and by encouraging our children to pay attention to the way they feel, we can avert many of the full-blown dis-eases that often result from continued neglect or suppression of body wisdom.

Here is a guided meditation "check-in" that can be done regularly as a family to encourage listening to the body. You may wish to adapt the language of the following meditation if you are doing this with very young children.

✦———————— Body Check-In ————————✦

Relax, ground, and establish a sense of safety. Now close your eyes and listen to your breathing. Notice how long it takes you to breathe in, to hold for a moment, and then to release the breath. We breathe so naturally, without being consciously aware most of the time. Take a few moments now to be aware of the miracle of breath. Breathing in life, the air that sustains us. Breathing out all that is no longer needed. As you continue to breathe, gently and naturally, become aware of your feet. How do they feel? Are they tingly? Cold? Tired? Is there any discomfort there? Or are they warm and soft and relaxed? Now become aware of your legs. How do they feel? Notice any sensations that arise when you send your consciousness there. (Continue moving up the body, focusing on the genital area, lower abdomen, solar plexus, chest, lungs, and throat, as well as hands, arms, shoulders, neck, ears, nose, and head. Use whatever terms your child will understand.)

Now you have listened to every part of your body, and you remember what you felt. Take a moment to thank your body for its wisdom. And now, imagine that the air that you are breathing is glowing with warm, golden light. Picture each breath filling your entire body with this warmth and radiant golden glow. Your body is a wonderful place to be. Now stretch, wiggle your fingers and toes, and open your eyes.

You could do a shortened version of this body check-in at night as you put your children to sleep. Then, if there is a tummyache or a sore throat beginning to make itself felt, you can either do a guided meditation (which often segues into soothing sleep) or give an appropriate remedy.

One great benefit of this type of body attention is that some holistic courses of treatment will become more effective for you: homeopathic remedies, for instance, work best when taken at the very onset of symptoms. If you've been in the habit of not noticing illnesses until they reach such proportions that you can't possibly ignore them any longer, then homeopathy was probably not your treatment of choice. But if you do occasional check-ins with your body, notice any discomfort, and take immediate steps before an illness reaches full-blown status, then homeopathic remedies are highly effective.

Illnesses are often physical pictures of inner states of being: if you are angry but suppressing the anger, you may develop a bladder infection from literally being pissed off. If you feel you carry the burdens for everyone else—do all the work, tote more than your share of the weight—you may be prone to backaches. Even some children's ailments can be seen as a kind of body language that corresponds to psychospiritual feelings. Writing about children's "growing pains," psychologist Richard Bromfield says, "Bodily pains can reflect inner turmoil. Just as some people vent their frustrations through alcohol, violence, or angry outbursts, others take their feelings *into* their bodies. Stress resulting from the experience of overly high demands or expectations may come to expression in a tender and irritable belly. Analogously, intense anger and frustration, if held inside, can lead to torrid headaches."[3]

If you want a clearer picture of the inner state that needs attention or the issue sending out a distress signal, we recommend working with the Tarot. Cait's book *Tarot for Every Day* includes many exercises for loving and honoring our bodies, for clarifying issues that may be manifesting physically, and for healing those issues—all with the help of this ancient symbolic language that bridges the inner self and the conscious mind. Building on the techniques in chapter 6, children can learn to use the cards to put their feelings into words and pictures and to get them out, clearing and cleansing themselves of anything that may be bothering or upsetting them.

Or you may want to try a shamanic approach: when your child is ill, you can journey for her or him, allowing guides or power animals to give you insights or healing advice. The previous chapter will help you to begin working in this way. You can gain amazingly specific and valuable information from the other worlds, if you are willing to open to them. For example, a woman became concerned when her ten-year-old son began to have diffi-

3. *Richard Bromfield, "Growing Pains,"* Mothering *72 (Fall 94): 48.*

culty sleeping and was overly anxious at being left alone, even during the day while she was working in another part of the house. She decided to undertake a shamanic journey for him to find out what could help. On her journey she was approached by a large female deer, who looked at her with gentle and loving eyes. "She looks like Bambi's mother," the woman thought. Then she instinctively knew that her son's anxiety was in response to her own recent hospitalization for a serious illness and her slow recovery. When her son had seen the film *Bambi* at the age of four, he had cried aloud, "I love you, Mommy!" at the wrenching scene during which the mother is killed by hunters. She had hugged him close then and realized that she needed to do the same now, even though he was older, reassuring him that she wouldn't leave him. In time, she felt, he would see that she was in no danger and would be able to resume his growth toward independence; meanwhile, she would quietly let him know that she was always nearby and available if he needed her.

Most parents can sense when their child is developing an illness; as one friend describes it: "When she doesn't shine, I know she's getting sick." The dimming of our children's natural radiance is often a cue that their resistance is lowered. We can become aware of the cues that our children's bodies give us, and respond—as well as encourage them to do the same. By inviting our children to listen to their physical selves, we encourage them to begin taking healthy responsibility for their own well-being.

But it is also important to note here that we don't necessarily see illness as a curse. There are times when allowing ourselves to receive the extra nurturing provided by a day or two in bed is just what the Wise Woman ordered—and the same holds true for our children. Another interesting phenomenon noticed by many parents is what we like to call the Blessed Bug effect: often, after our little ones have been down for a day with a fever or tummyache or other bug, they emerge able to do something they couldn't do before—as if, during the extra hours of sleeping and just lying around, they had time to put the pieces together. Developmental leaps may need just this kind of extra not-doing-anything-else time. If adults could learn to view their minor illnesses in this way, looking forward to the inner developments they might portend, it would be a much needed step in the direction of positivity around sickness.

Even the most conscious people tend to get caught up in what Susun Weed deplores as the "Heroic" stance around illness: as long as we do everything right (which includes everything from jogging to juice fasts to colonics) and don't do anything wrong (no alcohol, no meat, no smoking, no stress, no junk food, not even a smidgen of foods that combine at all improperly), then we will be well forever. And if we're not, then it's because we must have done something wrong. Or because we have an unresolved issue. Or because we didn't love ourselves enough.

The truth is, illness is an unavoidable part of life—and the last thing anyone needs, well or ill, is guilt. Rather than getting caught in blaming ("It's because I ate those greasy French fries yesterday!"), the Wise Woman way encourages us to nourish ourselves, both body and spirit. First, by eating plenty of wholesome wild foods—which are often curative as well as delicious, optimum food and medicine straight from the Mother—and second, by feeding the inner self with images of healing, wholeness, and beauty to stimulate the life force or boost the immune system, depending on your chosen terminology.

The ideas for wild-foods foraging in chapter 4 will help you and your children to explore the possibilities growing in your own yard. And the following guided meditations will provide inner support for the healing child (or adult).

GUIDED MEDITATIONS FOR THE HEALING CHILD

The idea of using guided imagery or creative visualization to promote healing is not a new one. Research is presently being conducted that documents its effectiveness as a healing tool and explores the body-mind connection; even the established allopathic medical community can no longer remain blind to its impact.

A new book on guided meditation entitled *Rituals of Healing,* by Jeanne Achterberg, Barbara Dossey, and Leslie Kolkmeier, gives hundreds of possible imagery scripts for different ailments or desired states of health, albeit for adults. And the excellent chapter for children in Diane Mariechild's *Mother Wit* includes several healing meditations for little ones.

We have used the following guided meditations with our own children with marvelous results. Be sure to pause for a few moments between sentences, and for a minute or more between paragraphs, to give the images time to develop.

HEALING STREAM

This is helpful when your little one has actual physical discomfort—upset tummy, sprained ankle, sore throat. With the child lying down (if possible), relax, ground, and make the child feel safe. This exercise works especially well before bedtime.

Close your eyes and listen to your breathing, the gentle rhythm it has, the way you draw in the nourishing air, hold it for a moment, and then let it go. As you breathe, begin to imagine that you are standing in a shallow stream of water. The water only reaches to your ankles, and it makes a lovely sound as it rushes over the rocks and pebbles in its path. You can feel the water rushing past you, washing over your feet, brushing past your ankles on its way. Imagine that all your pain (or bad feeling) is going down your body, down your legs, down into your feet. And that the rushing water is carrying it all away. All of your pain is flowing out of your body, out through your feet, and the rushing water is carrying it away.

Now you can feel the sun shining warmly on your shoulders and the top of your head. It is filling you with good feeling. You stand bathed by the stream and bathed by the warm golden light of the sun.

Now take a deep breath, wiggle your fingers and toes, and open your eyes.

At the end of this meditation we usually notice that our little ones have gone soundly to sleep. If this happens to yours, whisper an affirmation into their sleeping ears: "Tomorrow when you wake up, you will feel all better." And they frequently wake up well.

Diane Mariechild describes the effectiveness of using a Pain Stone, which was a small black stone that she had found. Whenever one of her children had an ache or discomfort, they would put the Pain Stone over the spot and picture the pain leaving the body and entering the stone. Then the stone would be washed and put away until next time. For children, particularly, having a concrete object to hold is a powerful helper in any kind of inner work.

BODY DEFENDERS

Try this meditation when your child is threatened by a viral or bacterial infection. With the child sitting or lying comfortably, help her or him to relax, ground, and feel safe.

Close your eyes and pay attention to your breathing for a few moments. Your body takes care of you, drawing in the air you need and getting rid of what you don't need any more. Whenever you have a cut or scrape, your body heals it without your even having to think about it. Your body is filled with powerful healing energy. As you breathe gently and naturally, imagine that this healing energy is like millions of tiny golden lights—like fireflies, only they don't blink on and off, they glow all the time. Imagine that anytime you have a scrape or cut, these little golden lights go to work, cleaning it up, repairing it, making it better.

Your golden lights are your body's defenders. Whenever a germ gets into your body and makes you feel bad, the golden lights rush over to it and surround it, taking away its power and making it harmless.

Imagine that, all over your body, inside and out, your golden lights are glowing brightly. Imagine that they are surrounding any germ they see. Imagine all the germs lying powerless, while the body defenders celebrate their victory.

Your body is filled with magical healing energy. Your body defenders are strong and so are you. You can trust the golden lights. You can help them in their work by resting now, and by eating and drinking nourishing foods. The body defenders are your wise inner friends. Any time you feel bad, you can imagine the body defenders helping you, making you feel better. They are working now.

Now take a deep breath, wiggle your fingers and toes, and open your eyes.

HANDS-ON HEALING

One of the simplest and most soothing things you can do for a sick child (or adult, for that matter) is to practice hands-on healing. A body of evidence is beginning to accumulate around this ancient technique, suggesting that it can effect miraculous cures, even of the terrible life-threatening diseases spawned by our technology. But even if your little one just has a bad case of flu, hands-on healing gives relief and a deep feeling of being cared for. Although there are many possible approaches, we have found the method presented here to be the easiest and most effective.

With the child lying down comfortably, sit so that you can touch her without straining or stretching. Explain that you are going to do something that will make her feel better by sending healing energy into her body. Then begin to sing a simple song out loud. There are many tapes of circle songs available that will work beautifully, and many contain messages of healing. You will repeat the same song, over and over, until the healing session is over. The repetition, like that of a mantra in transcendental meditation, helps to still the conscious mind so that the inner self can become more active. As you sing, allow your hands to rest on or above any part of the child's body that you feel needs to be healed. This technique honors a deep body-knowledge: often, your hands will know exactly where to go and how long to stay there. If thoughts arise (Am I doing this right? What about touching over there?), just continue to sing, and let the thoughts go. Allow your hands, as much as possible, to think for you; those of you who practice meditation regularly will find this easier to do.

Some children are docile patients when they are sick, willingly staying in bed. Our sons tend to be the opposite; often it is only when we are actually practicing this hands-on technique that they are able to sleep and get the healing rest they need.

Although we cannot detail the full scope of healing techniques possible here, it is good to be reminded that we can take our health, and that of our families, in large measure into our own hands. We choose how we undergo illness; our attitudes about it and about ourselves when we are ill are strictly up to us. We can teach our children healthy attitudes about issues of wellness by refusing to treat the body as the enemy. Instead of blaming it and ourselves when we are sick, we can ask ourselves healing questions: What does this have to teach me? In what way is this illness my ally? And we can choose to treat our ailments in natural ways that honor the body-mind partnership and provide optimum nourishment in the Wise Woman tradition, honoring and trusting the body's wisdom and healing power.

Children are often marvelous healers themselves. If you are going to perform a healing ritual for a friend or family member who has requested one, you may wish to involve your youngsters, if they want to take part. If the ill person is present, try the hands-on healing described above: children often have a great instinctive knowing about how this is done, as well as a wonderful, pure energy that they send wholeheartedly and without any blockages or reservations right to where it's needed. If the healing is for someone who is physically absent, children can be taught to direct their healing energy by singing, rocking in a rocking chair, or using a drum or rattle, and strongly visualizing the person well and whole.

Our culture is only just beginning to become aware of the power of focused energy (some call it prayer), of the healing that can be accessed through inner work—such as guided meditations or exploration with Tarot—and the undeniable connection between body and mind. Now we can raise a generation of children who know these things and have practiced techniques around them from earliest childhood. The impact on generations to come can only be one of healing, wholeness, and well-being.

CHAPTER 10

THE FAMILY ALTAR

By taking the time, effort, and space to set up a special, sacred spot in our home, we tell our children in a direct and tangible way that our spirituality is a vital part of our lives and that we are willing to honor it. And we plant the idea that our homes are sacred places—that they are part of something bigger, something magical, just as we all are. By refusing to relegate spirituality to big churches, mosques, synagogues, or other institutions, we affirm our power to make something special and holy, ourselves, that celebrates the divine. The small becomes infinitely precious, just as our children are.

Setting up a family altar is a satisfying activity for children. It becomes a place for them to celebrate their achievements and to display personal mementos or objects of special significance for everyone to see and appreciate.

Family altars become symbols of unity in diversity. Different people create it, contributing their own unique offerings. It provides a visual link with other family members. And it teaches children to respect the symbols and objects that are important to others, honoring their individual spirituality.

Because it is a place for the family to bring nature indoors, it has a special breath of the Mother's wildness about it and becomes a satisfying link with the earth. Christmas, with its age-old pagan custom of the decorated evergreen tree, is usually the only time that most Americans bring the natural world into their homes in any conscious way. Family altars encourage us to do this all year long, giving us beautiful reminders of the seasons and our own participation in the great cycles.

A family altar may become the heart of the home, a place to go to when you need nurturing or a sense of inner peace. Sharing quiet time beside it, caring for it, decorating and embellishing it, become heartfelt and deeply meaningful activities that deepen our connection with one another and with the Deeper Power.

Over time, the family altar builds an association with our sense of the numinous. Approaching the altar, with its incense and candles, will instantly invoke feelings of serenity, self-empowerment, and Spirit. Many families have found that the room that contains the altar becomes everyone's favorite refuge.

There are no rules to setting up a sacred space at home, but we hope that the following suggestions will be helpful.

- Remember that this altar only needs to be pleasing to you and the other members of your family. There aren't any "Thou Shalt Nots" when it comes to altar-making, and nobody will be giving out prizes, either. It can be as unique and highly individual as you are. Be as creative as you like—have fun with it. Decorate it with things that are significant to you, that appeal to and please you.

- Location is a vital consideration. Will it be in a spot where it is likely to be questioned by guests or visitors who may not understand its intent? Will you be able to have privacy and quiet time beside it, or is it going to be in the middle of the busiest room in the house? Many of us have found that altars work well in low-traffic areas, where you can shut a door and isolate yourself from the hubbub of family life when needed. But if space is limited, you can place yours in a corner, screening it with plants or furniture so that it has a feeling of privacy.

- Just about anything will do as an altar surface: bookshelves, chests, tables, a mantel, the floor—you don't need to rush out and buy the perfect antique whatnot to house it. Use what comes easily to hand. You may want to create an outdoor altar with rocks or a tree stump if your climate is consistent and extremely temperate; weather considerations keep most of us from making the outdoor altar our primary one. But you can have more than one; envision a home and land dotted with sacred places.

- Make sure that there is a contribution of some sort from everyone in the family, including companion animals (cats shed their claws or whiskers occasionally, and these usually find their way onto Cait's altar; the ashes of Maura's beloved dog are in a round tin box under her altar/desk). Children may want to give artwork or other creations to the family shrine. Other possibilities include locks of hair, or small figures of each child's power animal, or a symbol that is meaningful to her or him.

◆ You will want to include something from nature that changes with the changing seasons. Taking the time to really notice what's going on in the outdoor world so that you can make a small reflection of it in your home is a good way to connect with the Great Mother. She changes every day. In a week, many things have come and gone. Your altar becomes as fluid as the seasons. For example, July gives us the first Queen Anne's lace and the orange trumpets of daylilies. Brambles are heavy with the last wild raspberries, but soon these wither and the pokeweed berries begin to purple. Curly dock goes gloriously to green seed, and mullein begins to form its tall spikes. Garlic mustard grows all gangly and its leaves begin to yellow. By August many weeds have dried and seeded, turning a pale brown, and the flowers in the fields or along the roadsides are golden. And as August ebbs away, late summer gives us sunlike Jerusalem artichoke flowers and sheaves of goldenrod, which gradually give way to airy fronds of dry grasses and blood-red clusters of staghorn sumac. Then the dock seeds turn rusty brown and cornstalks begin to dry and rustle in the fields. Soon the leaves will begin to flush and color.

We can only grasp a handful of each perfect gift while it is here and celebrate it on the altar for a time, until each is replaced in turn. After a year of paying attention, we begin to recognize the season by its blooms—in our region, we often have lilacs flowering for Beltane. Purple spires of loosestrife mean that Lughnasad is near, and ripening apples signal the approach of Mabon.

◆ You might want to include a representation of each of the four elements. A crystal or special rock, an earthenware dish of salt, or a green growing plant for North; an incense burner or a feather for East; a candle or a small oil lamp for South; and a cup of water or a seashell for West are some possibilities. Choose what feels right to your family.

◆ The Goddess has many, many faces. Find the ones that speak most deeply to your hearts and include a statue or painting of each (see Suggested Reading for some books that will familiarize you with her myriad guises). Or place an image of whatever deity you choose to honor in the central position of your sacred space. Your altar will become a special home for the Greater Power when you include such reminders of it.

By honoring the changing gifts of nature and the uniqueness of our own gift, we find a place for our homes—and ourselves—on the ever-turning wheel of life. By honoring deity as a part of our everyday lives, we encourage a sense of sacredness in the ordinary. And by creating a spirit refuge with our children that honors the physical body of earth, we give them a positive and life-affirming message for life's continuation on this planet.

CHAPTER 11

USING THIS BOOK

We live in the northeastern region of the United States, and this book was clearly written from the perspective of mild springs that come after cold winters with plenty of real snow, and chilly autumns that follow blisteringly hot summers; our imagery for the seasonal celebrations grew out of this dramatic seasonal variation. But the activities we offer can certainly be adapted for families who live in year-round warmth. For those of you in Florida or southern California, for instance, there may be fewer striking contrasts in the turning of the wheel, but it turns all the same, with subtle differences that you can appreciate and celebrate. This chapter will give you some ideas on adapting the book to meet your special needs.

And although we live, like many of our readers, in a semirural area with access to wild lands, we have included some tips for those who live in large cities—where the natural world is a little harder to come by—or in suburban settings, with neighbors a stone's throw away, where obvious outdoor rituals may raise eyebrows or cause misunderstandings.

This book is meant for everyone. Love and respect for the Great Mother can blossom in all our hearts, regardless of the climate or type of area we live in.

FOR THOSE WHO LIVE IN
YEAR-ROUND WARMTH

Even the warmest and most constant climates have a rhythm to them—there are plants that will only bloom at certain times of year, or climate changes, like prevailing fogs or rains, that mark a specific season. By paying close attention to the subtle changes that are taking place around you, you will find your own personal ways to note and celebrate the passage of the sun through your part of the planet.

Most of the activities in this book will be manageable for everyone, regardless of the weather. And the few that won't can be changed to suit your own area. For example, tropical dwellers who can't bring a bowl of snow indoors for Imbolc could go for a family dip in a nearby ocean, lake, or river as an early-spring purification (something we northerners could never even consider without risk of hypothermia). And you have the luxury of holding all of your ritual bonfires—even the Yule one—out-of-doors. Read Starhawk's *The Spiral Dance* for some Californian versions of the great festivals, or Ashleen O'Gaea's *The Family Wicca Book* to see how one family celebrates in southern Arizona—complete with numerous family camping trips. Even though spring won't have quite the same impact for you as it does for those whose winters are immobilizing and seemingly endless, one of the important messages here is making an internal connection with the heart of the season: all of us have had times of stasis and inaction that felt as if they would never end. Then, when they do, we have real cause to celebrate. By taking note, not only of the gradual shifts in the natural world around you but of your own times of dormancy, inspiration, flowering, and fruition, you and your family will have found your own way around the wheel.

FOR THE CITY DWELLER

Many of the activities in this book require some actual contact with the out-of-doors, which can be difficult for city dwellers. Having both lived in big cities for a number of years, we are certainly aware of the challenge this poses for those of you whose actual experience of nature is limited to watching for glimpses of the moon between tall buildings or touching a few blades of grass that have poked up between the sidewalk cracks.

Some city people have access to back gardens or balconies, decks, or roofs where plants, trees, and weeds can grow. But for others, local parks offer the only direct contact with the natural world—and these are often violent and drug-ridden places. So we include these few, brief encouragements, helpful hints for bringing nature back into your life when you're surrounded by slabs of steel and concrete.

1. Connect with a specific tree, plant, or weed in your neighborhood. If you can see it from your window, great. If not, make a point of visiting it as often as possible. It will become your direct link with nature. Name it. Hang out with it. Bring it little gifts of fertilizer or crystals.

2. Honor the weather. Collect a cup of rainwater. Bring a snowball indoors. When a hurricane or an ice storm hits, even the biggest cities can feel the power of the Mother. Allow yourself to be awed.

3. Notice the insects and other animals that live in your immediate environment. You may not see hawks or coyotes where you live, but pigeons, squirrels, and even spiders, flies, and cockroaches have every bit as much to teach us. Encourage your children to pay attention.

4. Grow something on a sunny windowsill. It is a miracle that never fails to satisfy, and you can have beautiful free plants all year by using carrot tops, avocado pits, or potatoes. Or you can go whole-hog and buy seeds for a windowsill herb, flower, or vegetable garden.

5. Take conscious day-trips to the country and simply be, quietly, outdoors together. Listen. Look. Smell. Bring back mementos: fallen leaves in autumn, seashells in summer, branches broken by the ice in winter. Dig a hole and put your hands in the earth.

6. Pay attention to the sun and the moon. Days lengthen and shorten. Nights may be bright or dim. Notice the color of the sky at sunset or dawn.

Remember that, although it may take a little extra effort on your part, the glimpses of nature that you're able to share with your children become all the more precious because they are rare, special, and not as likely to be taken for granted.

FOR SUBURBAN FAMILIES

What if you live in a neighborhood where people can watch your every move, and dancing in a circle is likely to be taken for devil-worship? This is something with which we have both had some personal experience; several years ago, for instance, someone actually spray-painted a cross on Cait's garage after a particularly exuberant women's Full Moon Circle. But we have also had some pleasant surprises in this regard; our habitual wearing of Goddess necklaces has prompted several wonderful encounters with the like-minded, people who might otherwise never have known that we had a love of the Mother in common.

When Maura went to a workshop on singing chants and rounds with Libana, a wonderful women's music group from the Boston area, she didn't know a soul among the sixty or so women (and a handful of men). But as the singing went on and the group moved into a spiral dance, the woman next to her said, "Wouldn't this be a perfect chant for Beltane?" Realizing that she was among others like herself, Maura began to notice a number of women wearing jewelry with a goddess image, a labrys, or a spiral. A grandmotherly woman sported a bright T-shirt with the words "Goddess Tours 1991," which Maura thought was inspiring and affirming. What had been a company of strangers quickly turned into a celebration of Goddess energy, and the workshop participants and members of Libana all promised to sing the May song aloud on Beltane, no matter where they were. "It's a *movement*," said a Libana drummer, paraphrasing Arlo Guthrie's "Alice's Restaurant." And we believe it is.

As we see it, you can either celebrate discreetly indoors with the curtains drawn, making sure that anything you do outdoors is completely innocuous, or you can invite the neighbors over for a holiday party and explain that you celebrate the seasons, much as Native Americans do, in an effort to appreciate and understand the earth. For some reason, the mention of Native Americans never fails to neutralize fear and distrust, whereas a mere mention of the Goddess (let alone a buzzword like "witch") often seems to produce anxiety among those whose path is more conservative.

Selena Fox and Dennis Carpenter of Circle Network, a Wiccan organization located in rural Wisconsin, have certainly faced their share of prejudice based on misunderstanding, but through their tireless efforts to educate and inform, both in person and in the local media, they have emerged as respected community leaders despite their alternative beliefs, which include open use of the term "witch." Many Wiccans make a point of explaining to others that they practice magic only for good; they differentiate clearly between their earth-honoring beliefs and the destructive and terrifying popular images of Satanic cultists. "What you send out comes back to you threefold, so why would you send out something harmful?" asked a Wiccan high priestess who was being interviewed by a curious reporter on national television. She went on to reassure the reporter that people who practice the ancient earth-religion do so by their own free will, and she pointed out that Wiccans do not send "recruiters" out into neighborhoods, as some well-known Christian sects have done for decades.

Know your neighborhood. If you are likely to face firebombings or other violence if you are candid about your earth-based activities, then be discreet. But if you think that your earth-loving example is likely to generate interest, not hostility, then by all means go public. In just such small and individual ways we are gradually able to effect large-scale change.

CHAPTER 12

FINAL WORD

The Wild Child

The activities in this book have been field-tested with children and adults of all ages. They work. They can bring you and the children you love, teach, and care for into better relationship with one another, with your inner selves, and with the Goddess, that numinous and healing power. By sharing earth-based spirituality with our children, we give them the gift of empowerment and balance. And by living our commitment to the earth, we give our children a way of being in the world that supports growth, healing, and respect for all life.

Many of the activities you will find here encourage children to trust their own deep knowing and actively teach techniques for growing in inner wisdom. They offer a joyful and enjoyable way for children and adults to explore their spirituality, growing and deepening together.

Our work is based on the premise that play can be sacred—and that the sacred can be playful. Children have a low tolerance for pomposity and pretension. For them, freshness, fun, and spontaneity and a sense of the magical are not mutually exclusive, as they have become in so many conventional, established religions. So the activities outlined in this book allow for individuality and a spur-of-the-moment, impromptu spirit. By taking our cues from our children, we open ourselves to our own inner Wild Child and its sense of magical fun. Many times we end up learning more from our children than they do from us; rediscovering how joyful and silly we can be, while affirming deep mysteries, can be a learning experience for all of us. And children have a natural affinity for this kind of experience. Most children unconsciously invent all kinds of elaborate rituals, with little chanted songs, Circle dances, even special shrines made of sticks and leaves and feathers; earth-based spirituality seems to be the natural birthright of every child. In a sense, this book is a way for adults to recover that earlier simplicity—and to help their children become fully conscious of their place on, and their natural delight in, the wheel of the year.

This book is child-centered: its activities were designed to appeal to children in many different moods, with different types of learning skills, leaving plenty of room for their personal tastes and interests. The activities come from several cultures, and they honor the diversity that is such a wonderful part of the human picture. They lead us, in a natural and gradual way, through interaction with living symbols and sensual delights, into a deeper appreciation and celebration of the seasons and of the festivals that are placed like exclamation marks at important conjunctions of the year. However, the ideas you will encounter here are certainly not meant to be the last word, but rather a springboard for your own imaginations. By tuning into your children's needs and feeling free to improvise, you can create your own personalized celebrations, unique and individual. We encourage you to have lots of magical fun.

But suppose you picked up this book and you don't have any children of your own, or any contact with anyone else's? Don't worry; these activities translate beautifully into adult experience, because underneath the serious, staid exterior of even the most civilized adult there lives a wise Wild Child. Our Wild Child is itching to have fun—meaningful fun—longing to dance and howl and revel freely in magical experience and to be honored for the wise and indomitable spirit that it is. And so we have remembered, rediscovered, revised, and devised these simple, enjoyable ways for *everyone* to come home to the wild, to magic, to the Great Mother.

As we deepen our bond with the Mother, and strengthen the relationships within our own families, we form a circle that will extend outward, embracing and nourishing all.

May the planet be well and our hearts whole.

Blessed Be.

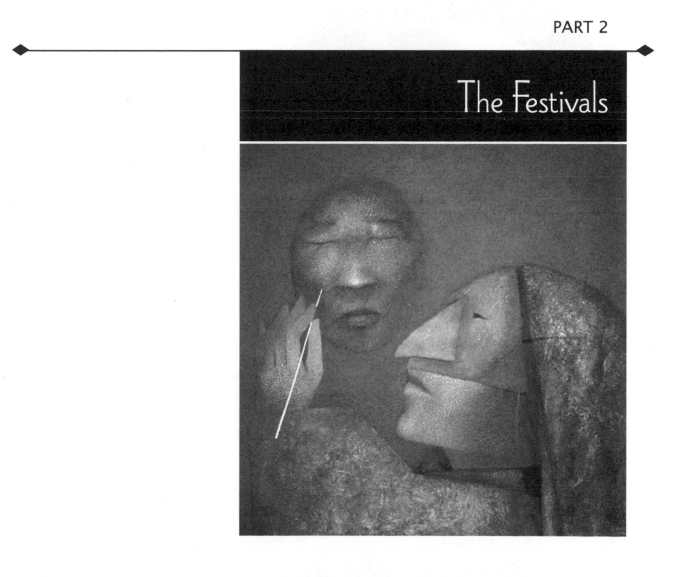

PART 2

The Festivals

AUTUMN

Autumn's dance is one of change and letting go. At first, everything whirls with activity. Furry creatures scurry through piles of leaves, readying for winter, calling "Hurry! Hurry! Hurry!" A hectic carnival of color swoops down with the chill air and swirls through the trees, whipping them into mad glory. We race to gather our children's supplies and warmer clothes before school begins.

But even in the midst of all the swirling colors and motion, we marvel at the sudden silences: the incredible delicacy of the first frost that takes the last insect-songs away; quiet smoke rising from a hearth finally rekindled after long weeks of dark; the stillness of our homes after the children have been whisked off to school.

As the season progresses, we sense more and more strongly that everything is moving away, like the geese that cry from the dark above our children's heads as they lie curled under blankets. The flocks are heading south, and we can feel it all slipping through our fingers. The constant motion and the shifting colors echo our feelings as we begin to turn inward.

This is a time for journeys; the migration of the creatures reminds us every day. But ours becomes a journey within, a season to take stock of our feelings. As nature amazes us with her shifting landscapes and the falling away of all that is outgrown, no longer needed, we take time to appreciate the things that last, that remain deep within us—family, loving relationships, inner wisdom. Sharing this journey with our children, even the youngest ones, and teaching them to listen to the wisdom within is a way to bring them into closer harmony with the earth and with one another.

The autumn begins with glorious richness, golden with the assurance of the harvest finally accomplished. With gratitude and pride we decorate our homes with symbols of the season, symbols of plenty: Native American corn, with its kernels of amber, garnet, and carnelian, and golden corn sheaves standing like Amazon guardians by our doors. And then the wind of Samhain blows all the bright colors away, revealing the stark bones of earth.

The stillness that follows early autumn's intensity encourages us to find our dreaming place. As Samhain ushers in the winter time of outer bleakness, death, and transformation, we discover our own inner richness.

MABON

Autumn Equinox
September 20-23

Like the vernal equinox in March, Mabon celebrates a moment of perfect balance, when light and dark, day and night, are equal. But after Mabon, the nights will be longer than the days. While the earth celebrates the abundance of final harvest, the sun is waning. Finding a way to understand the paradox underlying this complex festival gives it a special poignancy, like Persephone's pomegranate seeds, at once sweet and bitter.

This is the time when, in the most famous version of the Greek myth, Persephone must return to Hades, the God of the underworld, for six months because of the six fateful pomegranate seeds that he persuaded her to eat. Her mother, Demeter, and all of nature mourns her leaving; the gradual decline and death of the fields echo the mother's terrible grief. But Persephone discovers her own power in the underworld, becoming Queen in her own right. And activities that explore our own underground selves, our dreams and our intuitive powers, are exactly what we need to nurture in our lives at Mabon, the falling time of year.

Mabon, like Lughnasad, is named for a Celtic death-and-regeneration god, perhaps the same one who gave his name to the ancient Welsh mythic cycle, the Mabinogion. From Lughnasad until Yule, there is an underlying awareness in these festivals of death as a necessary part of the natural cycle. By incorporating the knowledge of death as part of life into our family celebrations, we do much to dispel the frightened silence, and the resulting inability to cope, that surrounds death in our culture.

Our first activity is offered in the spirit of family harmony. Making and using a talking stick is one way to rectify and heal any family tensions or issues before the long winter months that we will spend cooped up indoors together.

Stringing a dried corn necklace, the second activity, is like wearing a little piece of autumn around your neck; children and adults of all ages will enjoy making and wearing these embodiments of September's bounty.

And to usher in this inward-looking time of dreams, we give you ideas and recipes for concocting your own soothing dream pillows, which will ensure pleasant sleep and deep dreams for the entire family.

Finally, we encourage you to make your door blessing a focus for all of the changes that point to growth, all the important projects brought to fruition, all the accomplishments of the past months; for us as individuals, and for our children, Mabon is a time to reflect on our personal harvests. In so doing, we make our own inner connection with the season.

MABON ACTIVITIES

MAKE AND USE A TALKING STICK

As autumn progresses, colder weather reminds us that soon we will all be indoors together for long periods—chill rain and sleet will draw the curtain on outdoor play. One way to get this time of enforced togetherness off to a positive start is to clear the air and set a ground of mutual respect for all to stand on.

The Native American talking stick is a way of honoring every voice in the group and can be a great blessing for families. Even the youngest children will feel a great deal of pride and importance when it is their turn to hold the stick, knowing that everyone is waiting to hear what they have to say. The talking stick gives real weight and value to our children's ideas, to their thoughts and feelings about our lives as families. By giving our little ones this kind of respect, we encourage them to be respectful in turn.

And it's fun to make one.

This is a community effort: you will make one talking stick for the entire family, not one for each member, so you will need to be sure that everyone has a hand in forming and decorating it.

First, allow the youngest family member to choose a stick from the yard or during a family walk. It will become a sacred object for all of you, but there are no rules here—the stick can be any kind you like, from any type of tree, as long as it is sturdy enough to withstand handling and use. We recommend a diameter of at least an inch. One family we know used a piece of driftwood gathered during a family outing at the beach. Another chose a length of mulberry branch, twisted from the grapevine that twined around it as it grew. Still another found a stubby, knobby bit of oak. What matters is for the stick to be appealing. It will acquire magic with decoration and use.

Making sure that every family member takes a turn, remove the bark by peeling or carefully paring it off with a knife (adult supervision is definitely required). Notice the texture of the newly uncovered wood: look for the runelike tracks of insects burrowing beneath the bark. Now examine your stick from all angles, turning it slowly. Does it remind you of anything? Can you see animals or faces in its whorls and hollows? Your children may like to think of helpful spirits living in the stick that will help them to speak from the heart.

Now smooth the wood as much as possible by sanding with fine sandpaper—unlike many adults, children find this a highly enjoyable process: you may have to stop them before the stick is sanded completely away. Deeply textured sticks, such as driftwood, can be left as is.

When your stick feels silky to the touch, you are ready to decorate it. Allow each family member to add something that feels special and deeply right to her or him. One may wind a leather thong around it. Another may add a crystal or a feather. Still another may paint a design along the side. Any small object or symbol that holds special significance can be used.

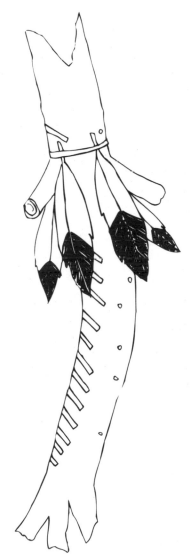

When the decorating is finished, you may want to coat your stick with a beeswax-based polish or rub melted beeswax into it, to protect it from moisture, buffing until it has a mellow glow.

The finished talking stick will feel delicious in your hands—it will invite you to stroke and touch it—and will be magical to look at.

When you are ready to use it for the first time, gather everyone together and explain that the talking stick is passed from person to person. When you hold the stick, it is your turn to speak, and no one may interrupt you. Speak until you have said what is on your mind and in your heart—or you may choose to remain silent—and then pass the stick to the person on your left. If people still have something to add or to say after the stick has come full circle, it may be handed around again. If your meeting is focused on coming to a decision of some sort, the talking stick is passed until a decision has been made that everyone can live with.

We have found that the talking stick truly facilitates family meetings, adding a special depth and significance to discussions of concerns or issues, and ensuring that every voice is heard and given equal respect and attention. To give this kind of sacredness and solemnity to your family councils is teaching a powerful lesson about the process of decision-making and empowerment.

STRING A NATIVE AMERICAN CORN NECKLACE

This is one of the greatest activities around; even young children, with a little adult help, can make a beautiful necklace to wear that is a satisfying symbol of this earth-centered Thanksgiving time. After seeing Cait's necklace, the teachers at her son's school were moved to make this a September project for the entire kindergarten and nursery group, and the results were splendid.

Many adults find this to be their autumn necklace of choice; there is something very right about making this link with the season. The uninitiated are often struck by their beauty, thinking that the simple, humble kernels are actually tumbled rare gemstones. To us, they are—the Mother's favorite jewels.

There is a visual lesson here, as well. Like the world, the necklace is a circle made of different colored kernels—white, yellow, red, and brown. All are a beautiful and necessary part of the whole.

To make your own rare and beautiful necklaces, take a few ears of different-colored Native American corn (last year's corn door blessing, for instance, may be recycled this way) and remove the kernels from the cob. For small, tender hands, this can be a little difficult: try a twisting motion. Once you've got it started, it gets easier, so if your young ones are having trouble with this part, you can start the process for them. Rub the kernels off the cob into a bowl (there will be lots of escapees; if you do this outdoors, leave these, and any leftovers, for the squirrels). Be sure to include all the colors that each child wants in the necklace.

Next, boil some water and cover the kernels with it. Allow them to soak for *at least* fifteen minutes—longer, if your children can bear to wait. The more they soak, the easier the next step will be.

When the kernels have become sufficiently soft, drain them on a towel, spreading them out so you can see the amazing and delicious variety of colors you have. Then thread some needles, making sure the thread, doubled, is long enough to make a circle that will fit easily over your child's head plus about six inches. Plain sewing thread will work fine, or you can use quilting or upholstery thread, if you like. Knot the thread about three inches from the end, pierce the kernels toward the base, where they are softest, and string them together.

Young ones can make random necklaces with whatever comes to hand, and older children can experiment with making patterns from the different colors—three yellow, two burnt orange, two deep red, three dark blue, or any other combination—repeated until the necklace is the desired length.

When your necklaces are completed, tie the ends of the strings together and admire the results. Allow the kernels to dry and harden before wearing; you may want to take them outside and lay them on the earth in the sun.

When they are not being worn, these necklaces may be artfully draped over the tops of picture frames or lampshades or looped between two nails on a wall. Doubled or tripled, they make great coronets for harvest figures, goddesses, and dolls. And the entire family can take turns stringing one to use in the door blessing on page 98.

You may make several in slightly varying lengths and wear them all together—earthy and beautiful. They make wonderful gifts: the garnet-red ones are our favorites to give newly bleeding young women or sisters in a Full Moon Circle. Children love to make them for friends and teachers. You, your family, and the squirrels will all be happy.

MAKE A DREAM PILLOW

Many of us find ourselves wanting to sleep more as autumn unfolds; we love those first really chilly nights that send us running for the blanket chest. Then, there is nothing as cozy as cuddling up under a quilt with only our noses showing, sniffing the sweet scent from our dream pillows that we made together by the fire, and warmly drifting off for a sweet night of deep, meaningful dreams. The longer nights seem to be made for dreaming.

To encourage us in our work with dreams, we stuff our special pillows with magical, traditional herbs that help us and our children to relax, dream deep dreams, and remember them to share or write down the next day (for more on the importance of dreamwork with children, see chapter 5). Younger children especially enjoy stuffing the pillows, while older ones will want to take charge of the entire process, cutting the fabric squares, sewing, filling, and decorating them.

First of all, dream pillows don't need to be the size of regular pillows (it would take pounds of herbs to stuff one!). There are two basic methods. We prefer to make small, plump ones to tuck underneath our regular night pillows during the day. Then, at bedtime, we turn the night pillow over and spend the night breathing the soothing, magical herbal scent left by the dream pillow. Or you can make larger, flattish dream pillows and sleep directly on them—experiment and see which method your children prefer.

To make a small dream pillow, we use two pieces of fabric approximately seven inches square. Larger pillows will be twelve (or lucky thirteen) inches square or so.

Choose a natural fabric such as 100 percent cotton, silk, or linen. Children love to pick patterns and colors that are pleasing to them; ransack the scrap box and see what you can find to recycle. Velvet is especially traditional for dream pillows and many little ones adore it—if you have any remnants sitting around, now is the time to use them. Small pillows can easily be made from old clothing, and the resulting dream creations will have the added attraction of memories associated with them. Although blues and violets are generally considered the most restful colors, we know children who have bright orange dream pillows that work just fine for them, so anything goes as long as the child is pleased.

Once everyone has chosen a fabric, cut out matching squares and pin together with right sides facing. Sew with a simple running stitch one-half inch from the raw edge, leaving a good three inch gap in the middle of one side (younger children will need help with this step). Then turn the pillows right side out, poking out the corners nicely with a pencil eraser.

Stuff both small and larger pillows with about two cups of dried herbs. We have included two recipes below to get you going, but feel free to invent your own personalized dream blends. We always include a generous proportion of mugwort, but some friends don't use it at all, substituting hops or lavender instead—it's really a matter of personal taste and preference.

After stuffing, sew the gap shut. When your pillow loses its scent, simply squeeze it hard a few times to release more fragrance. You can also periodically open your pillows and renew the herbs, burning the old ones in your Samhain fire.

Dream-Pillow Herbs—Flowery Variation

This pillow is especially wonderful if you have grown and harvested your own mugwort at Litha. If not homegrown, mugwort and all of the other ingredients listed here can be purchased from your local natural-foods store.

1 cup dried mugwort
³/₄ cup dried lavender blossoms (very soothing)
¹/₄ cup dried, crushed rose petals

Dream-Pillow Herbs—Woodsy Variation

1 cup dried mugwort
¹/₂ cup dried hops (traditional for restful sleep)
¹/₂ cup dried crushed rosemary (good for helping dream recall)

Other possibilities for dreaming herbs include agrimony (traditional to help bring restful sleep to those with emotional troubles), anise (prevents nightmares), bay leaves (for pleasant dreams), chamomile, clove, lemon balm, peppermint (for inducing fresh, restful sleep), purslane, thyme (eases depression), and yarrow.

Tiny gemstones may also be added to your pillows (not too large or the resulting lumps will defeat the purpose of the pillow!). Both amethyst and azurite have traditional associations with pleasant, healing, or even prophetic dreams. Moonstones make a connection with your lunar, dreaming self, and topaz is said to bring sweet, refreshing sleep.

Your children may want to embroider or appliqué their pillows with special decorations; if they do, this is more easily accomplished when the pillow is still in the flat-squares-

AUTUMN

97

of-fabric stage. We don't recommend fabric paints. Other decorative options include stringing beads and hanging them from the corners or simply sewing around the finished pillow with contrasting thread.

To consecrate your pillows, you can smudge them, put a little salt water on them, breathe on them, place them in the moonlight for a night, or anoint them with a little saliva. Hold them to your heart for a few moments before placing them in your bed for the first time.

You will be amazed at the effect of your dream pillows: most parents find that their children sleep more soundly, have fewer nightmares, and wake up with more interesting stories to tell.

Pleasant dreams!

DECORATE A DOOR BLESSING

Traditionally a way to invite blessings and abundance into the home, the door blessing is a visual statement about our connection with the spirit of autumn and with the Earth Mother. At this season of thanksgiving, a door blessing becomes the conscious focus for our joyous gratitude and appreciation for the bounty the earth provides—and it quietly celebrates our own personal contributions to the great harvest dance.

There are countless ways to make a door blessing. The suggestions we offer below are meant to inspire you to do things in your own unique way; children can always be counted on to come up with innovative and fresh approaches to any project. All family members will work together to make the decoration for the front door of your home, but individuals may want to make similar ones for the doors of their bedrooms.

Roadside stands and supermarkets alike are piled high with colorful dried corn at this time of year. Since most of us don't grow our own, the standard three-ears-wired-together sold everywhere makes a good base for a door blessing, with any of the suggested additions offered below. We have found that the cornstalks sold in huge bunches by our local farm market often have several ears still attached: we remove them and tie three together for a slightly more personal approach to the base. Young ones may enjoy the garnet-colored miniature corn, with ears only about two inches long. Tied together in groups of three, they make a pretty and unusual child-size door blessing.

If Native American corn doesn't feel quite right to you, you could start with a grapevine wreath. If you have wild grapevine growing near you, it is easy to harvest at just this time of year, looping and twisting it together to form a wild, beautiful circle. Or you can purchase one from your local craft shop, which should also offer other attractive possibilities, including wreaths made of willow branches, corn shucks, straw, and wicker. Shop as a family and see what appeals to you.

Tree-lovers may want to use a simple tree branch as a woodsy door blessing, twined and hung with your chosen decorations.

Whatever base you choose becomes your foundation. Now all of you will work both individually and together to decorate and consecrate a door blessing of which everyone will be proud, one that is beautiful and significant to you all.

A hot-melt glue gun will make attaching your additions a snap, but younger children will need careful supervision to avoid nasty burns.

Here are some suggestions for possible additions to your base:

- Cut an apple crosswise to reveal the five-pointed star of seeds in the center. Cut a slice approximately one-half inch thick. Hang this, using a needle and thread to run a string near the top of the slice. The sun and air should dry it beautifully. If you have access to an apple tree, find very small apples and make several slices, stringing them in a necklace to dry. These can then be looped around your base.

- Make a dried corn necklace as described earlier and loop or twist it decoratively. If you decided on a wreath for your base, you could add an ear or two of miniature corn, with its distinctly American quality, to your blessing. For some ideas on how to honor the indigenous people who taught the European settlers how to grow it, see "The Family Mabon" (page 102).

- Make a tiny Earth Goddess from clay, carved apple (it will shrink and brown as it dries, but these make wonderful Goddess figures), corn shucks, or weeds (as in the harvest figures for Lughnasad on page 191), and glue or hang it on your base.

- Feathers, crystals, other gemstones, nuts, large or unusual seedpods, and some of the flower heads and weeds harvested and dried at Litha make lovely additions. The more items you can include from the land you live on, the stronger the visual connection with it will be.

Perhaps most important, be sure to include symbols of what you have harvested this year. For instance, if you have just bought your first home, a tiny house carved out of wood or shaped from clay would make a perfect addition to your door blessing. A woodworker could add a few long curls of wood shaving to symbolize the table or chest just completed. We might include small books made of handmade paper. If your child just learned to ride a two-wheeler, he or she could draw a small bike on a piece of cardboard to glue on. Those just beginning to read could write a word or two on paper and roll it up like a scroll to hang. Or you may cut discs of wood from a tree branch and paint them with your personal harvest symbols. Take some time as a family to think and talk about your achievements over the past months. It gives everyone a happy glow to see their contributions celebrated and honored in this way.

When your door blessing is completed, place it on your Mabon altar, where it will be the loving centerpiece. After your Mabon ceremony, hang it on the door with pride.

CREATING THE MABON ALTAR
DOOR BLESSING, CORN,
APPLES, POMEGRANATE, DRIED WEEDS

For some of us, this is a favorite time of year, when the beauty of fall colors and the energy that cooler air brings after the lassitude of August both enliven and inspire us. Hunting for just the right harvest symbols among the many that abound at this time of year is rewarding and satisfying; your altar is the perfect place for that bunch of Native American corn you just couldn't resist, or for a rough wooden bowl heaped with winter squash and apples. When you stand or sit around the Mabon altar, you will find that its delicious colors, scents, and textures speak directly to our ancient memories of home, harvest, and security.

Because of Mabon's associations with Persephone, you will want to include a pomegranate, usually available in your local grocery store this time of year. And an earthenware vase filled with dried weeds from the land you share is a way to connect with the cycles of the earth: now that the seeds have formed, the plants are dying.

Autumn is associated with water, emotion, and relationship, so you may choose to include a bowl of water; at Samhain, this bowl will take on an added dimension when it is used as a scrying bowl.

The door blessing serves as a focus for your family celebration, so you will want to give it a central place on the altar. And your talking stick, dream pillows, and corn necklaces may also grace the altar and soak up some strong energy there.

SPECIAL MABON FOOD

CORN, BEANS, LENTILS, APPLES

Mabon is the earth-centered Thanksgiving. Delicious and satisfying, Mabon food nourishes us—body and spirit—with its earthy energy. This is the perfect time to start a family tradition: after decorating your table with symbols of the season, and appreciating the beauty of your harvest foods waiting to be eaten and enjoyed, you may want to hold hands and take turns saying what you are personally grateful for at this time of harvest and giving thanks.

Hearty soups, stews, and casseroles made with beans and lentils are traditional for the Mabon meal, and American families will want to make something with corn as a connection with this continent and the indigenous people who were caretakers of this land. Below is a traditional Seneca recipe from the *American Indian Society Cookbook;* it uses both corn and beans and is cooked in water, autumn's element. Your children will enjoy shaping the patties.

Seneca Bean Bread   Makes one dozen

3 cups cornmeal
¾ cup cooked pinto beans
Salt to taste
Mix ingredients with enough water to form a stiff mush. Dampen hands and shape mixture into patties approximately three inches in diameter. Drop patties into a kettle of boiling water or broth and cook gently until they rise to the top of the water. Serve hot.

Butternut or acorn squash stuffed with lentils and nuts also makes a beautiful and tasty main course, with warm corn bread as an accompaniment.

Adults may enjoy a full-bodied red wine with the meal, and apple juice or cider, or pomegranate juice from your local natural-foods store, will be a perfect Mabon beverage for the children.

Any dessert made with apples is a seasonal treat, apple pie being the first that springs to mind; your children may enjoy making little individual apple tarts in a muffin tin. The following recipe has a hearty traditional flavor and appeal.

Spicy Mabon Apple Bread Makes two loaves

2¹/₂ cups grated (peeled and cored) apple
2 cups raisins
1¹/₂ cups boiling water
3 Tbs. oil
1 cup plus 2 Tbs. honey
1¹/₂ tsp. cinnamon
1¹/₂ tsp. allspice
1¹/₂ tsp. salt
¹/₂ tsp. cloves
3 cups whole-wheat flour
1¹/₂ tsp. baking soda
³/₄ cup chopped walnuts

Place apples and raisins in a bowl and cover with boiling water. Pour oil on top and allow to soak for 10 minutes. Add honey, cinnamon, allspice, salt, and cloves and allow to cool. In another bowl, sift or mix together the flour and baking soda. Combine with fruit mixture and add in walnuts. Pour into two greased loaf pans. Bake in a preheated 350°F oven for approximately one hour.

THE FAMILY MABON

This is our time to take stock of all we have gathered, of all that will stay with us during the cold winter ahead. The door blessing was a way to begin thinking about our personal accomplishments and triumphs, our own inner harvests. Taking a few minutes now to honor the resulting creation is good way to begin the family celebration.

Your family may want to wear clothes in autumn colors of olive green, earthy browns, and fall-leaf scarlet, burnt orange, or russet—you could even find clothing decorated with autumn leaf patterns that would be appropriate for the day. Little girls may enjoy wearing wooden pins carved and painted like apples, and your Native American corn necklaces are the perfect addition to any outfit. After hearing the Persephone story, older girls may want to devise a Queen of the underworld costume in her honor.

After the Mabon feast, it feels very right to gather together for the following story and ritual. Because this is a festival honoring both light and dark, both the harvest and the dying of the fields, this activity makes the central dichotomy of Mabon both real and visual.

First, tell the story of Persephone and the pomegranate seeds, either reading the simplified version below or retelling it in your own words; children love storytelling, and this one has been weaving its magic spell on listeners for centuries. The standard version of this story revolves around the forced abduction and rape of Persephone, which is, sadly, probably an apt representation of life for Goddess cultures under the patriarchal conquerors; we have chosen to downplay this aspect. Then there is a much older, alternative version, retold by Clarissa Pinkola Estés in her audiotape *The Creative Fire*, which presents Persephone as being more empowered—but there aren't any pomegranate seeds in it. You may also want to read the version in Carolyn McVickar Edwards's *The Storyteller's Goddess* and discuss how it differs from the more patriarchal one with the seeds. Older children may be ready for the inclusion of Demeter's journey and the Baubo material, with its emphasis on the healing power of female sexual laughter. See Clarissa Pinkola Estés's retelling of this in her marvelous *Women Who Run with the Wolves*.

Persephone and the Pomegranate Seeds

Once upon a time there was a lovely young girl named Persephone, whose mother was Demeter, the Goddess of the growing things. Demeter and her daughter loved each other very much, and they lived in a world where it was always summer— always, green things were blooming and the sun was warm and sweet. But one day, while Persephone was out with her friends gathering flowers, she heard a rumbling and felt a trembling beneath her feet. The ground split open and out came Hades, God of the underworld, driving a dark chariot. He snatched up Persephone and drove back into the earth—the ground closed up again with a huge roar—and all that was left of Persephone was a little bunch of wilting flowers lying on the ground.

Although she looked everywhere, Demeter could not find her daughter. For days and days she searched, too crazed with grief to bathe or eat. So great was the mother's sorrow that the earth began to grow cold and the green things died in the fields. There was no food, and terrible hunger came to the people.

Meanwhile, in the underworld, Persephone soon realized that Hades wasn't really as scary as he had seemed at first; in fact, she had him wrapped around her little finger. He had been so lonely in the underworld, and he told her of his great longing to keep her with him.

Persephone didn't know what to do. She missed her mother and the bright world aboveground. But the dark and magical power of her new status as Queen of the underworld—and her love for Hades—gave her reasons to stay. She felt that she had important work to do in this deep place.

Now, Persephone knew that if she ate or drank anything in the underworld, she would have to remain there forever. So she didn't, though Hades begged and pleaded with her to accept just one morsel of food, just one sip of drink.

Aboveground, Demeter had finally learned where her daughter was. She was furiously demanding justice, insisting that Persephone be returned to her. Hearing this, Hades sadly hitched his dark horses to his chariot and prepared to take Persephone back. But before they left, he offered her one last thing: a pomegranate, ripe and blood-red. Looking him straight in the eye, Persephone took just six seeds— and ate them, smiling a little at the sweet taste of the ruby pulp, then frowning at the bitterness of the inner seeds.

Back they went aboveground, up through a great crack in the earth. In joyous reunion, Persephone threw herself into her mother's arms—and the earth grew rich with flowers once again, and the sun shone warmly, and all things rejoiced and grew. But because of the six pomegranate seeds that Persephone had eaten, it was decreed that, for six months of every year, she must return to the underworld with Hades on Mabon, the autumn equinox, and winter would come upon the land. And every spring she would return to her mother, wearing a crown of apple blossom, and the earth would bloom again.

When the story is done, take the pomegranate you have placed on the altar and gently peel open a section of the skin, showing the blood-red seeds inside. Each family member may take a seed and eat it. Small children will want to spit out the bitter inner pip, but older ones may want to try it. Then take one of the apples from the altar and cut in half, cross-wise, to show the pentacle of seeds inside. Pass the apple halves around so that everyone can take a bite. Explain that this five-pointed star is an ancient symbol of life, health, and wisdom. By participating physically in this paradox of death and life, darkness and light, we have made an inner connection with Mystery in our lives.

To reflect on the watery nature of this season, you may want to invite everyone to place their fingers in the bowl of water on your altar. Feel how the water binds you all together. Then shake a few drops over one another with a sense of fun and celebration.

And you can try this telling little family game. Give each family member a pouch with ten kernels of dried corn in it. Throughout the day, if you are negative to someone—if you say a demeaning word or show a disrespectful attitude—then that person has the right to demand a kernel of corn from the offender's pouch. Saying hurtful things is a giving away of one's inner power and integrity. At the end of the day, count what remains of your ten kernels privately and think about what you have learned.

We find it impossible to celebrate Mabon without an appreciation of the Native Americans who shared their knowledge of corn with the early European settlers. Many Anglo-Americans now cheerfully take on the spiritual teachings of these ancient cultures, just as our ancestors took their lands, without truly thinking about the realities of life for the Native Americans still left alive. It would be good medicine to take a few minutes on Mabon to write to your congresspeople and senators on behalf of the Native American nations. Most live in unspeakable poverty, and, worse yet, are even now in danger of having what is left of their remaining lands taken away. Because uranium has been discovered on the Big Mountain reservation, for example, the people may lose it forever; the Cree Indians in Quebec are fighting to save their homeland from being flooded for construction of another hydroelectric power plant on James Bay. See Suggested Reading and find a few good books on the subject; we cannot help but be enraged by our government's treatment of this ancient culture. Speak out.

It is traditional in our family to light the first fire of the season in our fireplace on Mabon, rather than having an outdoor bonfire; because it is a time to move inward, to celebrate family, this makes the most sense to us. We usually throw in a handful of sea salt and a couple of bay leaves, traditional for protection, and gather around the cheery blaze as the sun sets. You may want to invest in an old-fashioned popcorn popper and conclude your festivities with popcorn made over the fire in the traditional way. If you don't have a fireplace, light several candles (carefully and with constant supervision around very little ones) and bask in their golden glow.

As you watch the light gleaming on the faces around you, know that, even more than the myriad projects in which we involve ourselves, our children are our harvest, ever-growing culminations of care and energy and love. And also know that, like Persephone, our children will one day leave us to find their own power. Hold them close now.

SAMHAIN

Day of the Dead
October 31

This is the only earth-centered festival that falls on the same day as a major cultural holiday; much of our work around Samhain, then, involves undoing the negative cultural messages that have been superimposed on its ancient sacredness. Much of Halloween's imagery comes straight from Samhain's pagan roots, but with a negative twist. Spirits, rather than being the loving reminders of our beloved dead, are frightening and malicious apparitions, against which we must be on our guard. The day abounds with witches, of course, but in a type of Crone aspect that our culture, with its ageism and fear of female power, rejects absolutely. By replacing the stereotypes and unconscious activities associated with Halloween with Samhain's positive knowledge—reverence for death, for our ancestors, and for our own inner wisdom—we give true meaning and depth to one of our children's favorite holidays.

Our ancestors believed that Samhain, out of all of the days of the year, was the one when the veil between the worlds was thinnest—permitting the comings and goings of loving ancestor spirits, who spent the dark hours dropping by for visits and helping out with the myriad kinds of divination activities that were so prevalent at that time. Samhain is the Celtic New Year, and at least part of the reason for doing divination on this night is to receive guidance and information for the coming year. But instead of imagining our ancestors' ghosts leaning over a Ouija board or causing a pendulum to sway, we like to think of Samhain as the perfect night to connect with the spirit of mystery and magic so profoundly felt at this time, when we may open ourselves to our own intuitive power and hear our wise inner voice. Many of our Samhain activities are gentle ways to begin doing this with our children.

The experts disagree on the derivation of this festival's name. Some contend that it refers to an Aryan god of death, Samana, while others point to a medieval Irish word meaning "summer's end." It is usually pronounced "*Sah*-wen." In pagan mythology, this is the night of the god's death, and his simultaneous conception in the dark womb of the Mother: the central message is that death is followed by rebirth.

As part of our effort to reclaim some of the sacredness of this festival for our children, we offer methods for approaching the whole issue of the Halloween costume with greater depth and significance. Rather than choosing sleazy store-bought outfits depicting the latest cartoon character, we encourage our children to create meaningful costumes that give a sense of their own unique power.

The first activity helps your child discover her or his power animal, also called an animal totem or animal ally. Familiar to shamans for centuries, the technique that will allow your little ones to do this is actually very simple, and the resulting information gives a lifetime of empowerment and self-knowledge. The power animal becomes a part of your child's life, lending its reassuring presence to any challenging situation, as well as to the trick-or-treat journey.

Our second activity encourages gentle exploration to discover the costume that is heart-right for your child and gives some pointers for translating ideas into reality. Is your little one drawn to the ancient myths or folktales? Are there any goddesses or gods that have special significance for your child? Do you know much about your early ancestors? Perhaps a particular period in history speaks to something deep within the child. Or children may be inspired to become their power animals. With the tools of guided meditation and storytelling, we can help our sons and daughters to find ways of embodying their deep wisdom.

Nothing can take away our wise inner voice, but our culture has denied all knowledge of its existence and suppressed the means of establishing and sustaining contact with it. One of the most important gifts we can give our children is this simple know-how. At Samhain, a traditional time for all kinds of divination, you can encourage your children to make and use bean runes (a simplified version of the rune system made popular by Ralph Blum); they make sense to even the youngest child. We have also included a fun and enlightening activity using Tarot cards—one of the best tools we know for accessing inner wisdom—that older children may enjoy.

And, finally, to restore spirit-magic to the ubiquitous jack-o'-lantern, we include instructions for carving a spirit guide, with the knowledge of its true use and importance. Beacons that remind us of our dead friends and relatives, these faery lights give a special glow to our Samhain celebrations.

SAMHAIN ACTIVITIES

DISCOVER YOUR POWER ANIMAL

The concept of power animals—magical animal helpers that are deeply connected to specific individuals—is rooted in the bones of our most ancient ancestors. The early shamans knew how to contact power animals and work with them to effect healings, gain wisdom, and receive information not available through ordinary means. Today a new generation of shamans, among them Tom Cowan and Michael Harner, has rediscovered this powerful concept and is teaching it to ordinary people, enabling them to live their lives in a more positive and magical way. The technique for identifying power animals is actually very simple; with a little practice in guided meditation, as discussed in chapter 8, we can share this vital information with our families for the good of all.

Most of us have one power animal that remains constant throughout life—one whose basic attributes are deeply related to our own—and others that change according to the situations in which we find ourselves, perhaps embodying the facets of the inner self that are needed at the time. But suppose you discover that your animal ally is a bear. What does that mean? What does Bear have to teach you? How exactly do Bear's attributes relate to your personality and your life?

A first step in understanding the significance of your power animal is observation of the real animal itself. Watch films or nature programs or read about the animal in books and wildlife magazines. What are your animal's habits? What is its personality? Next, discover how ancient cultures perceived your animal. The owl, for instance, has a centuries-old reputation for wisdom and was depicted as the companion animal of Athena, the goddess of wisdom, by the ancient Greeks. Because of its nocturnal habits, the Celts associated the owl with dreams, and Native Americans believed that Owl was clairvoyant and magical.

Find a deck of the beautiful and informative Medicine Cards, by Jamie Sams and David Carson, which features forty-four different power animals with valuable interpretations of each. In fact, if the guided meditation route to discovering a power animal seems too daunting to you, working with this deck could be an alternative—by allowing each child to pick one special card at random, you can invite the spirit of synchronicity to take a hand in identifying his or her animal totem.

There are great benefits to be gained here, both for us and for our children: power animals give all of us a way to understand our own complex psyches. As Waldorf-inspired educator Claudia McLaren, who uses the concept of animal totems with young children, says, "Every animal is an outward expression of what's in our soul." And in family life, power animals can be helpful in modifying behavior for the good of the group—by referring to a child's behavior in terms of the power animal, the child is more likely to accept necessary correction: "If a mountain lion is pushy and violent and aggressive, then . . . the group looks to see how we can help mountain lion learn a more gentle way. . . . And the child can see, yes, my mountain lion needs help. . . . The totem keeps everyone open."[4]

Power animals can inspire storytelling, role-playing, and other forms of nourishing creativity that provide continual insight and inner enrichment. And the power animal is always there for your child, flying, running, or swimming beside her through every challenge, every situation—comforting, teaching, and empowering.

There may already be one particular animal that attracts your child—one that seems to crop up for her or him constantly, in the form of a favorite stuffed animal or picture book—and for which she or he feels a deep affinity. If so, that may be the animal totem for this particular time in the child's life. If not, try the following guided meditation as a way for both you and your children to make contact with the animal that has something to share with you.

First, explain what it is you are about to do. You may tell your children that they are about to go on a magical journey in their minds, where they will meet a special animal who is their friend and helper. Then make sure everyone is feeling relaxed, safe, and grounded, as outlined in "Preparing for Guided Meditation" (page 60). You may want to play soft, soothing music as an accompaniment to the meditation, or use one of the shamanic drumming tapes available through catalogs or alternative stores. The constant, rapid repetition of the drumbeat helps everyone to journey easily.

--------•

4. *Claudia McLaren, quoted in Jonathan Adolph, "Everyday Magic," New Age Journal, March/April 1993, p. 81.*

Power Animal Meditation

Imagine that you are walking up a soft, leaf-covered woodland path between tall trees. It is autumn and the leaves are all the colors of the fall around you, orange and red and gold. You can smell wood smoke in the cool, crisp air, but the sun feels warm on your face. As you continue walking up the path, you see that it is beginning to lead uphill, getting steeper now, and the trees are being left behind. You are climbing up a steep hillside now, and the path is getting bare and rocky. You see that the path is curving around a bend now, and you can't see what's on the other side. But suddenly you know that there is an animal—a good and loving animal—waiting around the corner to meet you and show itself to you. It could be an animal with fur, or feathers, or scales, or hide. You walk around the corner now, and there you see it—there is your special animal. (Pause for about a minute.) You greet your animal and thank it for showing itself to you. You tell it that you will do everything you can to bring it into your life so that it will always be with you. Then you turn and begin to walk back down the path, waving to your animal until you walk around the corner and cannot see it any more.

Walk down the path toward the bright autumn trees now, walking back down the leafy path, back to this room, back to your ordinary way of being. Stretch, wiggle your toes, take a deep breath, and open your eyes.

Share your results, describing your animals in as much detail as possible. If you like, read the interpretations of any that coincide with the Medicine Cards, simplifying the language if necessary for younger children. Then encourage creative play around each animal; your children may want to unearth forgotten animal toys, or draw pictures, or look for photographs of their animal in magazines. Have them act out the animal, imagining how each one moves, eats, and sleeps.

Bring your knowledge of the children's animals into everyday life. How would Mouse eat that ear of corn? Your Deer seems a little shy today. What do you think Frog would do in your situation? You will find that your children's power animals will tell you quite a bit about each child's needs, personality, and special gifts.

Use your imagination to correlate the animal with the child: a Penguin child (not written up in the Medicine Cards!) may be afraid to try their wings and fly, preferring to stay earthbound. Or maybe Penguin tells you about a love of living in close groups—a Penguin child is not solitary by nature. Or perhaps the Penguin child is able to adapt to harsh and unusual circumstances—the subarctic cold is habitable by only a very select group of creatures. With this kind of objective, imaginative thinking, you can often glean real insights, and you will soon find that your children's power animals have become a constant source of inspiration.

For more information on shamanism, you and your older children may want to see Suggested Reading.

MAKE MAGICAL COSTUMES AND MASKS

Our culture has forgotten that there is a deep magic in costume: by choosing to embody certain qualities, we call them forth from the inner self and invite them into our lives in a very real way. A costume can become a gateway to greater self-understanding and empowerment for our children. And everybody loves to dress up. Our ancestors did it: mummers, costumed dancers, masques and masks, and German fasching rites were all manifestations of the human love of disguise, of taking on the appearance of something other than the self, expanding the limits of the personality.

Like the power animal activity, costume-making gains great depth from guided meditation; it is not surprising that this valuable technique for contacting the inner self is such a help to us at this inward-turning time of year.

For the Samhain costume to take on any real significance, the children need to feel an inward connection with the character or quality they decide to portray—the costume needs to have "soul" or spirit. By giving our children a rich vocabulary of characters and images to draw upon, by encouraging self-exploration in the form of inner journeys, and by giving loving assistance when needed in creating their costumes, we ensure their greater self-esteem and deep satisfaction.

Start a few weeks (or months, if your family is as Halloween-crazy as ours) before Samhain, reading from storybooks filled with characters that will fire the imagination. Carolyn McVickar Edwards's *The Storyteller's Goddess* is wonderful for girls in need of empowering Goddess images to choose from. Grimm's fairy tales, in their original, non-bowdlerized versions, are pretty strong, but they speak to children's spirits in far deeper ways than saccharine Disney stuff—for more on this, see Bruno Bettelheim's influential book, *The Uses of Enchantment: The Meaning and Importance of Fairy Tales.* Jungians have been extolling the virtues of these original folktales for decades now, with good reason. If you can, find a book of myths or folktales that reflect your particular heritage and read these aloud; to identify with a hero or hera from your own ethnic background is a powerful thing all by itself. Mother Goose rhymes are fertile sources of inspiration for young ones. And older children may be ready to listen to any of the tapes from Clarissa Pinkola Estés, or to read *Women Who Run with the Wolves*, or Patricia Monaghan's *The Book of Goddesses and Heroines*.

An element of the archetypal is the key ingredient for children here: aligning themselves with these embodiments of larger forces becomes both empowering and ennobling. A little girl who dresses as Gaia, the Earth Mother, is less likely to litter and will want to deepen her appreciation of the plants and animals around her. A little boy who creates a wizard costume will feel that he has special and unique powers and will want to explore them. And if we, as adults, choose to get in on the act, we can make some powerful visual statements that will go a long way to counteract some of the messages that our culture dishes out. One friend recently made herself a Medusa costume from a bathing cap and a dozen rubber snakes, saying it was a physicalization of the culture's fear of intelligent women.

Your children may be so moved and enspirited by a particular story or character that their search will be over. But if nothing they have read or heard really speaks to them, try the following guided meditation, which calls on their inner wisdom and the help of their power animals, to suggest the right costumes for them at this time.

First, prepare for guided meditation, being sure all the participants are relaxed, safe, and grounded. If you want, you may play soothing music as a background to your journey.

◆———— Magical Character Meditation ————◆

Imagine that you are standing in front of a very large old oak tree. The tree has a hollow in its trunk so big that you can walk right into it, and you do, pausing to enjoy the lovely feeling of being safe inside this beautiful, wise oak. But now you suddenly realize that there is a tunnel leading into the earth at your feet. You decide to enter it, and you begin to walk down the tunnel, touching the walls with your hands as you do, feeling their roughness, smelling the deep, rich scent of the earth, and hearing your footsteps as they crunch against small stones and dirt. The tunnel leads on and on, down and down—and now you see a light ahead of you, a light that means the tunnel is ending and you are about to arrive somewhere, somewhere special. The first thing you see, as you step out into the light, is your power animal, who hurries over to greet you. (Pause for a few seconds.) Now, with your animal beside you, you explore this magical place in which you find yourself. (Pause for about a minute.) Now your power animal lets you know that there is someone you should meet, a person who has a special connection, a special link with you. You follow your animal now as It leads you to a hidden place. You know as you step into this hidden place that the person you will meet there is very important to you. She or he could be straight from a story, or a myth, or a legend. As you step inside, you look up and see this person face to face. (Pause for about a minute.) As you look at this special person, it seems to you that the face you see is changing, becoming more like yours. Now it seems that you are looking in a magical mirror: your clothes are different but your face is the same. (Pause a few seconds.) Taking the memory of this special person with you, you leave the hidden place and, together with your power animal, you journey back to the place of the tunnel. You re-enter the tunnel, and begin to walk up, back to the hollow tree, back to this room, back to your ordinary way of being. Now stretch, wiggle your toes, take a deep breath, and open your eyes.

Once everyone has decided on a character, there are a few helpful hints to keep in mind while translating the idea into a workable costume. First of all, rightness, not perfection, is the key to a magical costume. Even professional costume designers will do well to allow the children to make their own crude approximations, rather than stepping in and concocting flawless adult renditions. If you enjoy sewing, great—but the more hands-on work your children do on their costumes, the better. One little girl we know was happier and more justifiably proud of the Persephone outfit she whipped up all by herself from an old piece of chiffon and some fake flowers than her neighbor was of her fancy Bo-Peep shepherdess dress, complete with hoop skirt and ruffles, that her devoted mother had slaved over for days.

Samhain outfits don't need to be elaborate, fancy, or expensive. We have found that scrap boxes, attics, and thrift shops yield wonderful and unexpected treasures. All we have to do is add an appropriate prop or detail, or a mask, or the right face paint and—voila!—instant costume.

Here are some suggestions. Really, there is a wisdom to limiting the materials for costumes to things that are found lying around the house—as with many Samhain activities, synchronicity steps in. Not so oddly, "making do" out of necessity is often the way to find just the right ingredients for the perfect costumes.

Leotards, tights, and turtlenecks will make a great basis for the costume to start. If you live in a chilly climate, it becomes especially important for your little Aphrodite or Pan to have on something warmer than a toga or a loincloth. Long underwear can also be dyed to look flesh-colored, or, in the case of the goat-legged Pan, painted to look like fur.

Another dashing idea that doubles as a warm overlayer is the magic cape: scads of characters won't leave home without one, and they are ridiculously easy to make out of an old shirt, or a tablecloth, or a sheet, or a scrap.

Adult cast-off clothing is a great boon to the costume maker. Old worn knit tops can be cut and slashed in a variety of creative ways and the edges left raw. In fact, our children have made most of their costumes, including a Saint George (with hand-held dragon puppet made from an old mitten), a wizard, a rock 'n' roll witch (dispelling a cultural stereotype), and a Godfather Death, after the Grimm's tale of that name, entirely from old adult clothing, cut down to size and worn over long underwear or a turtleneck and tights.

If your child has decided on a Greco-Roman character, plain old sheets or large tablecloths make terrific chitons or togas, which were really just big rectangles of fabric, draped, pinned, and belted in a variety of ways. Books on costume history from your local library will show you how it was done.

In fact, most characters from ancient myth, legend, and history wore very simple clothes; the Celts had tunics (an adult top, sleeves cut off, belted, reaching to the knees), capes, and leggings or tights. Again, a book of costume history will show you the basic shape and look to go for, and you can improvise from there.

The most important thing is detail: with just the right magical touch, the sheet or top or cape becomes something extraordinary. Buttons, trim, belts, and costume jewelry are a terrific help. A young friend's Irish hero Cuchullain costume took on an authentic look and feel when he borrowed a beautiful Celtic interlock brooch to fasten his cloak that charmed him completely.

What symbols or props are associated with your child's chosen character? A little Athena might place a toy stuffed owl on her shoulder (especially if this is her power animal), and Persephone needs her crown of flowers, and maybe a pomegranate. Pan should have a reed flute, and Thor needs a hammer.

If your child has decided to become her or his power animal, a simple leotard-and-tights outfit with face paint may be the easiest solution. There are several good books available on face-painting for children (notably one with a set of face paints included, from Klutz Press). Or your child may want to make a mask.

Masks, like costumes, are transformative and bewitching. With the help of some interesting trim and a lot of glue, you and your children can make amazing creations that will change their appearance radically and add some deep magic to it. A word of caution here, though: a mask will severely limit your child's ability to see clearly. Unless you plan to be right there holding a hand, you may want to reserve mask-wearing for inside the home, not for the long trick-or-treat journey.

Start with a cheap black half-mask sold in every dime store at this time of year. Then collect sequins, feathers, costume jewelry, glittery trim, seeds, fake flowers and leaves, small plastic berries or fruits, ribbons, small gemstones, fabric paint—anything you can think of that will lend itself to the effect. Older children may want to work with papier-mâché and build their own creations.

When the costumes and masks are completed, try this special way of wearing them for the first time (not counting necessary fittings). Wait until dark and then turn off all the lights. Help the children dress in their special outfits in the dark and then lead them by the hand to a room with a full-length mirror, if possible, and light a candle. Allow the children to take turns looking in the mirror: the effect is often a revelation and truly magical.

BEAN RUNES—A DIVINATION SYSTEM FOR CHILDREN

Adults everywhere are beginning to enjoy the benefits of working with Tarot cards, runes, the I Ching, and other divination systems that use apparently random chance in combination with our own inner wisdom to give guidance and insight, allowing us to live with greater consciousness and clarity. These symbolic systems, with their roots in antiquity, are a way to order our perception of reality, and they help us to become aware of hidden motivations and impulses that affect our reality.

Children seem instinctively drawn to the magic of the Tarot cards, and there are a few decks available now (notably the Inner Child with its images from fairy tales) that can be used by the young (see below for a Samhain Tarot activity for older children). The strange and mysterious shapes of the runes—that ancient Anglo/Norse language of symbol magic—are equally fascinating to young ones, but if you've ever tried to read the meaning of a

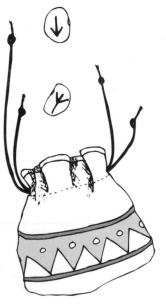

particular rune to a child from the books currently available, you'll know how frustrating it can be.

Because we believe passionately that even the youngest children should have access to keys that unlock their own deep wisdom, we came up with this simplified version of the runes, inspired by Ralph Blum's masterful interpretations but written in language little ones can understand. And when children make their own special sets of runes, their connection with them deepens.

At this time of year, especially, making bean runes becomes a meaningful way to embody the energies of the season—and it's an enjoyable activity. Here's how to make them:

1. Buy a bag of dried, large lima beans and pick out twenty-five beans for each set you are going to make, trying to find ones that are similar in size and shape. Children enjoy counting them out, and they feel very satisfying, smooth, and good to small fingers. This activity, however, is only for children over three years of age; we don't want any toddlers choking on their bean runes!

2. Now, using a Sharpie or other indelible marker, carefully copy the shapes of the runes (see page 117) on one of the flat sides of each bean, leaving one bean blank. Young ones who have difficulty forming the shapes will need help with this.

3. When they are finished, place the bean runes in a pouch or special small bag. The opening of the bag should be large enough for the child to fit her or his hand inside. Older children may want to make and decorate a special pouch for the runes themselves, but there are a wide variety of beautiful drawstring pouches and amulet bags currently available that will do nicely, or you could make one for a younger child yourself. As with the dream pillows, the bean rune pouches may be decorated and consecrated as each child sees fit.

Although it is not really necessary, your child may want to ask a specific question before choosing a rune. As with any kind of divination, there is a preferable way to go about this. Rather than asking cut-and-dried questions—Will I pass the exam? Does Justin like me?—ask for information: What do I need to know right now? What information will help me?

Younger children may only need to choose one rune, while older ones can benefit from a three-rune spread: the first becomes past influences, the second the present situation, and the third a possible outcome, if things continue on their present course. If they don't like the look of the third rune, they can choose a Right Action Rune, one that will give them information on the action or attitude that would be most helpful to them now. You and your older children will want to see Suggested Reading for more information on runes.

When the children are ready to choose a rune, they place a hand inside the pouch and mix the beans with their fingers. Then, without looking, they pick one or more runes to bring out for examination. There are no reversed or upside-down meanings here; simply turn any upside-down runes around so that they're right side up.

After the children have read the meaning of their chosen rune, or you have read it to them, they may want to think about the following questions: What did this say to me? How does it relate to my life? What do I think of what the rune said? Often, the runes will bring out the child's hidden feelings, thoughts, and fears about a matter, enabling her or him to deal with them in a constructive way.

BEAN RUNES

ᛘ	YOU	Learn more about who you are. Don't be afraid to grow up and change. Meanwhile, be careful: don't do things that could be dangerous.
X	FRIENDS	Finding a close friend. Working and playing together. Learning new things from each other.
ᚠ	MESSAGE	Presents or gifts, messages—a letter, a report card, or an idea that pops into your head. Meeting someone who has something important to teach you. Feeling close to your family.
ᛉ	SEPARATION	Let go of something that you have outgrown.
ᚢ	STRENGTH	Inner changes. Hard work ahead, but it will help you grow.
ᛦ	SECRETS	Nice surprises, good luck.
ᛉ	TROUBLES	Tough times, having to wait. Learning. If you have done or said anything that you are ashamed of, do what you can to make things right.

ᛟ	FRESH START	Prepare to come out of your cocoon, just like a butterfly; new ways, new ideas, new friends may be in store. A feeling of freedom.
ᛋ	PATIENCE	Make good decisions and wait patiently.
ᛉ	PROTECTION	Challenges, new opportunities. Try not to let your emotions get too wild. Take good care of yourself.
ᚠ	GOOD LUCK	Things are going really well for you. Be sure to share your good luck with others.
ᚹ	JOY	Energy, happiness. Seeing things clearly, and possibly changing your mind about something.
ᛇ	GROWING TIME	You can't grow up overnight; it takes time. If you have started a project that is important to you, don't rush it. Enjoy doing it.
ᚲ	LIGHT	Something that you were puzzled about is now made clear to you. Honesty.
ᛏ	SPIRIT WARRIOR	Be brave. Don't give up.
ᛒ	SPRING	Growing. Do a little spring cleaning so you have room to blossom.
ᛗ	MOVEMENT	Going someplace new, moving, making things better.
ᛁ	HEART	Listen to your feelings, what you know deep inside yourself to be true.
ᚻ	CHANGE	Even though some of the changes may not feel terrific, know that your inner self needs them to happen.
ᚱ	JOURNEY	Becoming a better person. Do the right thing, feel good about yourself, and spend some time alone.
ᚦ	DOORWAY	Wait—don't make decisions now. Think about your past, all the things that have brought you to this present moment. Then let it go. The future is right in front of you.
ᛞ	DAWN	The darkness is behind you. Good work. Success.

	ICE	Get rid of old habits that are keeping you stuck. Be patient and spring will come.
	SUN POWER	Energy, healing, expressing who you are.
[blank]	MYSTERY	Good and mysterious forces at work in your life.

SAMHAIN CAULDRON—
A TAROT ACTIVITY FOR OLDER CHILDREN

This activity combines the startling visual imagery of the Tarot cards with one of the central symbols for Samhain—the immense black cauldron of death and rebirth. The cauldron has been associated for centuries with the Celtic goddess Cerridwen, who places in it everything that has died. Then, using her transformative magic, she brings the dead to life again—but in a new and different form. You may want to reread the section on Tarot in chapter 6 before you begin.

On Samhain, the old year dies; the Tarot cards put into pictures for us all of the old things we wish to shed or transform. Then we choose new cards in honor of the new year that begins as the old one ends. These give us valuable information, messages from our wise inner selves that will help us to walk the new year's path in a positive and self-affirming way.

Place a large cooking pot (a soup pot is fine) or a cauldron, if you have one, on the floor, near the fireplace if possible. Then, using a deck that feels right to the participants, everyone mixes the cards facedown in a big circular pile around the cauldron. As you mix, think of the events and feelings of the past year. What do you remember? What did you learn? What would you like to put behind you? You may want to sing a song in unison as you mix; when the song is finished, stop mixing. Then, all together, each person reaches into the pile and chooses a card at random. Keep this card and toss the remaining cards into the cauldron.

Examine the card you chose: it is an image of the dying year. It may show something that you have outgrown, an attitude or state of mind that is no longer needed, or a lesson that you have incorporated into your life. Feel free to show your cards to one another, sharing insights and feedback.

When all have carefully considered their old-year cards, add them to the cauldron: the old year has died and is awaiting rebirth. Each person takes a turn stirring the cards in the cauldron, either with their hands or with a wooden spoon (being careful not to bend the cards), thinking about the hidden magic of the year to come. Then, when each participant is ready, she or he chooses a card from the pot. This is the card of new birth, the vital form that follows transformation of the old and outworn. Look at your chosen card for insights about the coming year. What form will it take? What do you need to keep in mind? If you chose the same card as the first, remember that some things take a while to work themselves out—you may need another span of time before this particular issue is resolved.

Tarot cards often act as keys that unlock our children's ability to speak freely about their deepest needs, fears, and concerns. Sharing the inspirations and insights that are awakened by the images on the cards becomes a deeply moving act—trust and caring and inner wisdom make a nourishing partnership. Engaging in this kind of meaningful exploration and dialogue with our children is a wonderful way to ring in the new year.

CARVE A SPIRIT GUIDE

Carved pumpkin jack-o'-lanterns are a fairly recent American variation of Western European carved turnips. These were hollowed out and lit with candles to show the way back to loved ones who had died, inviting them to visit; they also frightened away any less friendly spirits that might do harm. Your children will be fascinated by the charming effect of candlelight shining through the etched designs on the surface of the turnip—unlike our American jack-o'-lanterns, the decorations are not cut through all the way. Younger children will need help in cutting and hollowing out their creations, but safe, dull instruments will work beautifully to etch the designs, so they can do that step on their own.

To carve one of these more traditional spirit guides, find a large turnip or rutabaga at your grocery store and cut off the top. Also cut a small slice from the bottom, if necessary, so that it will sit flat. Using a spoon, a small knife, and a lot of patience, hollow out the inside so that you can place a small candle inside. If you run out of patience, make the space only large enough to fit a tea-light (a small votive candle in an aluminum cup about $^1/_2$ inch deep.)

Now, using the tip of a dull knife, a pointed chopstick, a toothpick, or some other not-too-lethal object, begin to carve designs on the surface of the skin. Be careful not to break all the way through to the inside, but make sure you scrape away the dark outer skin to expose the yellow flesh beneath.

Unlike the conventional faces that usually define the limits of pumpkin jack-o'-lanterns, we have found that designs such as spirals, circles, or pentacles; Goddess figures; and animals such as snakes, owls, or bats make wonderful additions to the spirit guide. And, most important, if you associate a particular symbol with a special departed loved one—a grandmother who was partial to birds, for example, or a friend who adored roses—you will want to include these as well. Etch designs on the entire surface and turn it throughout the evening to show your work from different angles and be reminded of the loved ones who are gone.

When darkness falls, set a votive, tea-light, or other small candle inside and light it—with constant supervision if there are very young children in the family. The designs will take on a magical glow.

We usually carve one rutabaga spirit guide together as a family activity, and then several pumpkin ones (pumpkin is, frankly, much easier to deal with and its sweet, earthy scent is an instant reminder to us of childhood Halloweens)—one for every member of the family, including companion animals. They give us serenity, connection, and a sense of magic with their elfin light.

CREATING THE SAMHAIN ALTAR
PUMPKINS, SPIRIT GUIDES, SCRYING BOWL OF WATER, BONES, MEMENTOS OF THE DEAD, AUTUMN LEAVES

The entire house takes on a wonderful wildness at Samhain, with candles shaped like pumpkins and black cats, heaps of autumn leaves, and glowing spirit guides everywhere. Your altar will become the heart of all of this.

Samhain honors the Crone, the aged, wise aspect of the Triple Earth Goddess whose maiden aspect is celebrated at Ostara. The Crone is the Goddess of winter, of death, the dark womb from which new life will spring. In the Crone's honor, you will want to drape your altar with black fabric.

The Samhain altar becomes a shrine to our beloved dead: to honor those whom we have lost, we may place photographs and mementos—an aunt's brooch, a grandfather's watch—on the altar, with small votive candles and offerings.

Symbols of the season such as autumn leaves, pumpkins, apples, nuts (especially hazelnuts, traditional on this day), and pomegranates are also fine additions to the altar. If your little ones have found any bones on their rambles during the year, today is the perfect day to display them, along with plaster or other imitation skulls or small skeletons.

You may want to include a bowl of water on your altar, as you did at Mabon, to use for scrying later (see "The Family Samhain" for more about this). And each child may want to choose something special to put on the altar that evokes Samhain for them—a small witch doll, a scarecrow, ghosts made of handkerchiefs or tissues.

SPECIAL SAMHAIN FOOD
ROOT VEGETABLES, APPLES, NUTS, DARK BREAD, PUMPKIN

At Samhain we set a place at our table for the people we love who have died, and we cook a dish or two that were their special favorites. When we eat these, we remember our loved ones in a direct and physical way. We usually put a small portion of every food and drink that we serve for Samhain on a special plate and in a special cup, which are set on the table at the empty place—the Ancestor Seat (or whatever your family wants to call it). Mealtime is often filled with personal reminiscences of these loved ones. At the conclusion of the meal, following an ancient Celtic custom, the plate and cup are placed outside for the spirits who are said to wander abroad on this night.

Samhain is also our night to cook foods that reflect our ancestral heritage: as well as Grannie's favorite cornsticks, we often make—in honor of our Irish forebears—"Bubble and Squeak," a skillet of cabbage and mashed potato that squeaks as it cooks. Pick a dish that reflects who you are, the culmination of countless generations, and give some thought to the amazing chain, reaching back beyond memory, of life continuing itself.

Hearty and flavorful stews, with plenty of carrot, turnip, potato, and parsnip, are perfect for a Samhain main dish, served with a warm, dark bread such as pumpernickel or Boston brown bread. Or you can make patties of nuts and lentils and serve them with a dark vegetable chutney.

This rich and savory soup is another Samhain favorite, and we like to serve it in small, hollowed-out pumpkins instead of bowls.

Samhain Sweet Potato Pumpkin Soup

2 sweet potatoes or yams, peeled or scrubbed, and diced

1 medium onion, chopped

1–2 cloves garlic, minced

2 Tbs. butter or olive oil

4–6 cups vegetable broth or stock

$1/3$ cup canned or fresh cooked pumpkin

Freshly grated nutmeg and ginger to taste

Salt to taste

$1/2$ cup light cream

Cook the potatoes, onion, and garlic in the butter or olive oil for several minutes until slightly golden. Add broth or vegetable stock to cover vegetables and bring to a boil. Simmer until potatoes are soft, about 25 minutes.

Add the pumpkin, nutmeg, ginger, and salt and puree this mixture in batches in a blender or food processor. Add in the cream and return the mixture to the saucepan. Heat, thinning with more broth if necessary, to make a creamy soup. Serve in small pumpkins, with a dollop of sour cream, if desired.

Rich black stout is a fine adult beverage for Samhain, or warm mulled red wine with cinnamon sticks and crosswise-sliced apple floating in it. For the young ones, cider is traditional.

Pumpkin desserts are seasonal and fun: we like to bake pumpkin muffins with raisins and nuts or make pumpkin drop cookies. One year, we sliced Boston brown bread in rounds and spread the slices with a mixture of cream cheese, cooked pumpkin, honey, and spices. Then we placed raisins on top to form skull-like eyes, nose, and skeleton teeth. Another year, we strung candy corn on thread to make edible necklaces to nibble while trick-or-treating, echoing the ones we made at Mabon.

THE FAMILY SAMHAIN

On Samhain morning, your children will want to put any finishing touches on their costumes. This is also the traditional day to pull up the withered remnants of your garden and compost them. You may want to include a visit to a cemetery, especially if it houses the remains of someone dear to you. You could bring special offerings—a letter written to the deceased, a nosegay of dried flowers—and leave them at the gravesite. Even if your loved ones rest elsewhere, explore an old graveyard nearby. Read the inscriptions and imagine what life was like in the 1700s or 1800s. You may find one particular grave that means something to you—someone your age, or someone whose name is appealing. If you do, it can be a gesture of respect and caring to tidy up the grave a little, if it needs it, and leave some dried flowers or other small offering.

When you get back home, decorating the house and front door for the night is a favorite activity; then you may all sit down together to decide which foods should be included in the Samhain feast. Setting the table, with its special Ancestor Seat, is an important part of the day—we like to decorate it with leaves, glowing spirit guides, and other atmospheric goodies so that it echoes the altar.

Everyone will take a hand in cooking the meal. Then, toward dusk, it is time to light spirit guides in our windows—we put one in each of the four directions. You may want to mix some salt and water and sprinkle it all around the house, inside and out, to purify and protect it. Younger children, especially, feel safer and more secure on this night, which the culture has made so potentially frightening, if they know that only the loving and familiar spirits that we have invited will be able to visit.

Then it is time for the Samhain Feast, for sharing the special food, telling our loving stories of the relatives and friends who have left us, and then placing the plate and cup outdoors.

Before trick-or-treating, you will want to spend some time by the altar, holding the mementos of your dead ones and remembering them together, telling funny stories or anecdotes that make them come alive in your children's imaginations. Nothing eases the heartache of loss for a young child like this kind of sharing.

Trick-or-treating takes on a more magical dimension when the costumes have personal meaning and significance. And aside from the excitement of amassing a glut of junk candy, children often respond to the wonder of the night. Our small ones aren't usually out on the streets after nightfall, and there is an eerie magic about walking hand-in-hand down dark roads that look a little weird and unfamiliar by the flickering light of countless jack-o'-lanterns.

When we all return home again, it is time to light the Samhain fire and bring out the Tarot cards, bean runes, and other goodies for receiving the guidance and information we need for the coming year. Now is the perfect opportunity to burn old dream-pillow herbs in your fire: the scent will help to get everyone into a receptive state.

Take down the bowl of water from your altar and sit around it—young ones are usually getting pretty sleepy by this point, so scrying will be easier for them. To scry simply means to concentrate on an object—if not a bowl of water, then a mirror, or a crystal ball, the archetypal scrying object—while in a trance state, so that we see with the inner eye. Sometimes, actual images will seem to appear in the bowl, or in the mind. Or words may suddenly pop into our heads. Whatever happens is interesting and valuable.

To scry, first bring your family into a state of deep, protected relaxation (see "Preparing for Guided Meditation" on page 60). Explain that, for generation after generation, people have scryed on this night. Invite everyone to look into the bowl, allow their minds to wander, and see what they see. Continue to look quietly into the bowl for as long as everyone feels comfortable. Then share what you all saw, felt, or thought.

Before bedtime, you may want to play with the bean runes, or with Tarot cards or some other form of divination, so that everyone will have a little information to sleep on for the coming year.

And finally, as winter makes its presence felt in the chill, smoke-scented wind outside our windows, we tuck our children into bed with their favorite stuffed power animals and weave a wish for protection and well-being around them in the dark. Blessed by the presence of our ancestors, and by the depth and mystery of our own inner wisdom, we greet the New Year with joy.

WINTER

Earth is winter's element. Everywhere we are confronted with its motionless grace: water turns to stone and the world is bleached white as bone by snow and ice. Bare branches remind us of the underlying shapes of things, finally revealed in stark beauty. There is a special silence in winter. The few birds left to us are too busy trying to stay alive to grace the air much with song, and a muffler of snow hushes everything. It can be good to feel nature's power now; despite all of our technology, when a big snowstorm hits, we are immobilized, forced to stop and wait. Winter makes a stillness in us that echoes the season.

Winter has an unqualified way of confronting our physical selves, making us pay attention to our bodies. The simple act of walking takes on an edge of challenge and danger when the streets are slippery with ice. And the prevalence of colds and flus reminds us to take care of ourselves, to nurture ourselves, to allow ourselves plenty of time to sit by the fire and dream, or gaze out at the falling snow and dream, or curl up under a warm quilt and dream.

Children usually adore winter, when snowfalls and bitter cold mean hours of sledding and skating, or coveted days off from school. Only adults, trapped by the demands of unceasing work schedules that know no snow days, often have a hard time with the harsh beauty of this season. By stopping long enough to make snow angels with our little ones— or to follow an animal's tracks, or build a regal snow goddess or fort where the snow is piled high at the edge of the driveway—and then to share stories over a steaming mug of tea, we slow ourselves down to match winter's pace.

After so many months of endless work and striving, we can give ourselves and our children the gift of winter, that time of rest, and peace, and inner nourishment, so that we can reemerge in spring revitalized by its quiet, healing magic.

YULE

Winter Solstice
December 20-23

Perhaps no other festival comes weighted with as much baggage as Yule, the winter solstice. It is both a radiant and a harrowingly dark time. For many of us, the daylight hours may only be glimpsed through office windows: we go to work and come home again in the dark. Added to the stress of attempting to function "normally" when our inner selves crave more rest, more sleep, and more silence is the stress of the cultural Christmas holiday that, not coincidentally, falls just around this time. The shopping lists and shopping lines both seem endless, and somewhere underneath the frantic activity lurks a desperate feeling that there must be more to it than this, more than the mountain of presents under the tree. We can dimly remember a magical feeling that we had when we were small and that may only sadden us now; it seems so far away. How to recapture it? How to give this magical feeling to our children?

As the advertisements on television, radio, and even street corners blare the message to buy, buy, buy—and as we attempt to either confront or completely avoid the pain brought up in so many of us at this emotionally exhausting time—some of us find ourselves attempting to remake this holiday in a different image, and we look to our ancient roots as a way to rebuild what our culture has lost and forgotten.

Many of us attempt to create a few moments of beauty and stillness for our families at Yuletide, as well as some healthy, noisy fun. But it is often the silent image that remains in memory lifelong. Most of us have one or two of these winter holiday memories: the night we rose up from a warm bed in the middle of the night to see the unearthly pearl-gray light after a Christmas Eve snowfall; the candlelight on a statue's face, lighting up the tenderness with which the Mother held the Child.

The imagery of our cultural winter holiday is straight from the pagan past; there was no snow in Bethlehem, and certainly no Christmas tree. But our very bones remember the celebration of the living green when all else is bare and bleak. And there is a wonderful stillness about the Christian tradition of Madonna and child images that so clearly echo the ancient Goddess-worshiping celebration of Yule as the birth of the Sun Child out of the womb of the longest night. Although it was often a noisy miracle, with all-night dancing and singing and noise-making and revelry, somewhere at the heart of the mystery was stillness. Quiet unfolding, as quiet as the dawn rising. The stillness of earth, of winter, balm for all our wounded spirits, our wounded hearts.

Despite the commercial mess our culture has constructed around it, there is a fragile and luminous beauty at this time of year like no other. It is a bone-deep beauty, the beauty of bare rock glowing with light. We find that, as the pretty decorations fall away, what we are left with is beautiful indeed: the shapes of trees, each perfect and distinct, the undulation of the hills beneath a covering of snow. And there is a wonderful bravery in each of us that rises again and again to live, despite our death-dealing culture. We struggle every day, each in our own way, to proclaim the coming of the light out of the darkest time imaginable. We are all Yule lights shining in darkness.

We offer these Yule activities as gentle ways to rediscover depth and meaning at this special time. They will encourage our children to take time out from the composition of endless Santa wish-lists and from the poisonous seduction of the advertising that creates such insatiable greed. They will teach our little ones about the things that last, the same ones that our ancestors discovered year after year with such joy: the stones, the evergreen, the light shining in darkness.

Our first activity reminds us that there are more ways than one to bring the living green indoors. If you can find a cedar tree that has lost a branch or two to ice or wind, you and your children can make your own smudge sticks to burn all year. Use this sweet smoke to herald the sun's rebirth.

Opening to the magic of the rocks and stones that are our wise and grounded companions will help to ground our little ones during this time of frenzy; our second activity encourages us to spend some time with these guardians of winter.

Consciously honoring and celebrating a Yule tree, with special handmade ornaments that call forth each child's unique creativity, is another gift we can give the entire family; there is no more potent magic than bringing nature's wildness indoors.

Finally, we offer a way for you to bring the central image of this festival to life for your children. By making a sacred cave, with its valiant lights flickering outdoors, surrounded by the cold and the dark, we create a visual image of great power, and a lasting memory for all of us.

YULE ACTIVITIES

GATHER AND USE YOUR OWN SMUDGE STICK

Winter is often a cruel time for the trees; harsh weather causes many of them to fall or to snap their limbs and send them crashing to the earth. If your yard, a neighbor's yard, or a nearby natural area has any fallen cedar branches, you may want to try this special way to bring the magic of the living green home with you and keep these valuables from going to waste. Smudge sticks are easy to make and satisfying to look at, and the purifying smoke will make a meaningful addition to your Yule celebrations.

Native Americans have known for centuries that cedar, as well as sage, has special purifying properties, especially psychospiritually; if the atmosphere in your home is tense or unhappy, a quick go-round with a burning smudge is one way to clean things out and restore a feeling of harmony. Native people harvest the herbs and branches ceremonially and prepare the smudge bundles with ritual. Cedar and sage are also burned in bulk in large abalone shells, with feathers used to direct the smoke.

If you want to make smudges but your cedar trees are all intact, you could see if any judicious pruning is needed; it doesn't take much to make a smudge stick. If you do this, your children may want to leave a special gift to thank the tree. (Check a field guide to be sure it's cedar you're taking.)

To make your own homemade smudges, each family member will need to find several pieces of cedar branch that are green, full, and well-leafed, about a foot long. Cut longer ones to this measure. Arrange the branches in a bundle with the tips all facing the same way; these bundles should be about two or three inches thick at their widest point. Then wind the cedar bundles firmly with thin cotton string (embroidery floss works well, and each person can choose the color she or he prefers), starting at the bottom and working up to the tips, then winding back down again so that the thread crisscrosses. Look at the smudges commercially available to see how much string to use. You can sing a special song while you do this, if you like:

All around, all around
Peaceful, peaceful
All around, all around
Peaceful, peaceful
Spirit of the cedar
Calling me, calling me
Spirit of the cedar
Blessing me, blessing me
All around, all around
Peaceful, peaceful

When you have wound the string up and back down, knot it at the bottom and cut off the uneven ends of the branches an inch or so below the knot to make a uniform length. Allow these smudges to dry before lighting. Later in the year, you may want to make a few more with the addition of sage and lavender sprigs from your garden, as well as strands of sweetgrass.

To use your smudge, light the tip with a match and let it flame for a moment, then blow out the flame and allow it to continue smoking for as long as you like. When the air begins to get thick or you're ready to stop, extinguish the smudge by placing it, tip down, in sand, ash, or earth, making sure that no embers are still glowing. Always be very careful when using combustible materials with young ones: homemade smudge sticks are often unpredictable and may drop burning embers on the floor or on your children. Please supervise their use with extreme caution.

If it's difficult to find large, full cedar branches in your area, you may want to try gathering small bits of cedar and allowing them to dry on a tray. Then mix them with dried sage and lavender, making a smudge incense to burn on charcoal or in heaps in a special shell. A Yule incense recipe could also include dried pine needles and small pieces of cinnamon stick (see page 155 in the Ostara section of Spring for more on making incense).

DISCOVER THE POWER OF STONES

All matter whirls at incredible speed, atoms in constant, breathtaking motion. But the rock people are seemingly still. We are all of us surrounded by the stillness of stone; if you dig in any patch of earth, you are likely to find bits and pieces that are unimaginably old and likely to outlast us by countless lifetimes.

Just as trees may be intuited to have individual spirits and personalities, so the humble rocks beneath our feet may be known and their energies felt in ways that have much to teach us.

Children are inveterate rock collectors, often seeing unique power and beauty in a rock that looks plain and nondescript to us. By seeing with the open inner eyes of our children, we can share their fascination for the magic of stone. And when we surround ourselves with rocks that are special to us, when we take time to hold one in our hands or stroke its weighty smoothness or striation, we make a bodily connection with the oldest matter on this planet and with the element of winter.

Particularly at this often harried time, building a relationship with rocks—allowing them to permeate our consciousness in quiet and stillness—is a great gift of peace for the entire family.

First, find some. This shouldn't be hard to do, but you may be surprised at the variety of rocks your children can come up with, and you may notice that particular varieties attract some children more than others. Take small trowels or large spoons outdoors with you to help pry things loose. After all of you have brought your finds inside and thawed your numbed fingers, you may want to wash the rocks in warm water to remove loose dirt and bring them to room temperature.

Now spread them out so everyone can look at them. Pick them up one at a time and really examine them, turning them slowly to savor the complexity or simplicity of their shape and color. Do any rocks remind you of something else? Are there shapes hidden in the stone?

Try this simple exercise: Ask your children to close their eyes and choose a rock at random, and then hold it in their hands without looking. Allow them to sense the rock—does it feel light? dark? heavy? Does it make you feel anything in your body? tingly or slow? energetic or relaxed? Then put the rock aside; choose another and repeat the process, making sure to notice any similarities or differences. Then ask the children to open their eyes. Look at the two rocks and compare them.

Rocks that make your children feel a particular way may be utilized to help relax and ground them, or to energize them when needed. A rock that your child experiences as slow and soothing may be placed near her or his bed to be held before sleep. A small bright-energy stone may be worn in a pouch or carried in a pocket to school.

We have found that keeping special rocks all around the home is a wonderful way to stay balanced and grounded: simply seeing the stones becomes an inner reminder of stillness and serenity. And if you or your child is having a particularly trying day, holding one of the rocks and breathing fully and with attention is a wonderful calming and centering exercise. If you really need a release, try sending your tension or anger into a small stone; then go outdoors and throw it as hard as you can, being sure to avoid breakable objects and living things.

Your children may want to make patterns with their smaller stones or build with them. We have friends with small rock cairns in their living rooms and elaborate stone spirals adorning their children's desks and tables. Some rocks become our companions, sitting serenely nearby as we live out our lives; these become friends that will remember us long after we have changed form.

HANDMADE ORNAMENTS FOR A YULE TREE

The Yule tree is a vital representation of one of the central mysteries of this festival: amid the seeming death all around us, we are given this bright green assurance of life's continuation. Resonating with layers of meaning—the Tree of Life, the World Tree—a Yule tree becomes a sweet-smelling, joyous focus for our festival, and a wild reminder of nature's power.

Many of us are pained at the thought of buying a cut tree. For us, topping a large evergreen becomes a way of bringing the living green indoors without killing the entire tree. Or you may choose to buy a tree with the root ball still attached, to plant outdoors in the spring. If you do buy a cut tree, you can fully recycle it by using its dried needles in pot-pourris, incenses, or pillows and by sawing the trunk into logs to be used for outdoor bonfires. Or you can place it outdoors, still festooned with popcorn and cranberry strings for the wild creatures to eat at this time of famine.

We like to bring our tree indoors during the day on Yule Eve, the day before the solstice. We find ourselves passing it often, simply to inhale its fresh, wild fragrance or to stroke its prickly needles. Some children may want to lie down underneath it, like our cats, to feel themselves embowered by its branches. Once the tree is firmly in place, with plenty of water in its holder and a clean white sheet, snowlike, underneath it, you may want to do a ritual blessing, sprinkling it with salt water, smoking it with homemade smudge, and welcoming it into your home; children love to be an active part of this.

Then you will want to decorate. We like to keep our tree as handmade as possible, using as many natural materials as we can. The final result glows with the energy and time we all spent making our own ornaments.

You will probably want to include some sort of small electric lights—a room lit by their faerylike glow is certainly filled with seasonal magic. Even though candles are more traditional, they are just too dangerous to consider using. And many of us enjoy stringing old-fashioned popcorn and cranberry garlands, lovely to look at now and a thoughtful gift for your local wildlife later.

Here are a few ideas for simple and satisfying handmade decorations you can all work on together. Their imagery is straight from our deep past and will give your Yule tree a visual connection to this sacred festival's ancient roots.

Gingerbread ornaments are everybody's favorites. You can buy several boxes of gingerbread mix and add just enough water to form a stiff dough, reserving some dry mix to spread on your counter when you're ready to roll out the dough. Roll the dough to about one-quarter inch in thickness, then cut shapes with cutters or freehand with a knife. Bake and decorate with icing, if you want them to remain edible, or paints and trim if you don't.

Here are some ideas for cookie shapes that may appeal to your children and will echo the song of the season: suns, moons, stars, Yule trees, goddesses, candles, handprints (trace around each family member's hand), earth globes, circles, pentacles, pomegranates, apples, holly, acorns, snowflakes, reindeer, and spirals.

Other magical possibilities include wizards, witches, mermaids and mermen, yoni and phallic shapes, owls, cats, pigs, and bees (sacred to the Goddess), and any other image that has special meaning to your family.

These same shapes may also be made out of simple flour/water/salt dough and allowed to dry, then painted and given a protective coat of polymer or other varnish. Or you can make a yeast dough and bake your shapes, then paint and varnish. You can also use Sculpey or a self-hardening clay. All of these options are lovely, but they can also be a little heavy, so you may want to keep your ornaments on the small side to avoid bending a branch and having your creation smash on the floor.

And before baking or drying any of these dough-type ornaments, be sure to use a drinking straw to punch out a hole at the top for hanging.

If you made handmade paper suns from molds at Litha, you can gild these and hang them, or use any of the smaller solar images from that festival (see page 181 in the Litha section of Summer). Your older children may want to experiment with making other shapes out of handmade paper.

Tiny grapevine wreaths can be decorated with small red berries or holly, ivy, nuts, and seeds and placed in the branches. Acorns and nuts may also be painted gold, tied with red ribbon and hung. Or you and your children may want to make pomander balls, a sweet-smelling addition to the tree and to your home.

Pomander balls

Use small lemons or apples if you want to hang your pomanders on the tree—larger fruits will probably be too heavy. For pomanders to place in bowls throughout the house, larger apples or oranges may be used. Using a darning needle or other big needle, make holes all over the skin of your chosen fruit about one-quarter inch apart. Place a whole clove in each of these, then roll the pomanders in a mixture of ground cinnamon, allspice, cloves, and orris root. Place the pomanders in a bowl with the spices, turning them daily to continue coating the surface. When dry, place the pomander in a circle of lace, gathered with ribbon at the top, or make a ribbon loop directly on the pomander. Hang them or place them in containers at pulse points in the home.

Small paintings look beautiful framed by the tree's branches: many children enjoy making pictures of suns, mothers holding infants, or other seasonal themes. Punch a hole at the top of the completed painting and hang with a red ribbon loop.

A crystal point hanging from the tip of a branch is enchanting and iciclelike, and small bells add a faery jingle whenever anyone passes by.

It's easy to dry real pomegranates to use as ornaments. Buy a few extra ones at Mabon and put them on top of a warm place, such as the refrigerator or radiator. When dry, they look mysterious and special nestled in the branches.

You may want to make winter figures out of dead, dry weeds, tied together with string or embroidery floss to perch inside the tree (see page 191 in the Lughnasad section of Summer for instructions on how to make a harvest figure).

If you don't have the time or patience to make popcorn and cranberry garlands, you could loop ribbon, braid, or trim decoratively around the tree. Red and gold are the traditional colors for this festival, coupled with the green of the tree.

And you may want to wrap tiny presents, such as small fossils or crystals or seeds for an indoor winter garden, and hide them among the branches for your children to find.

When you have finished decorating the tree, you may feel moved to join hands around it, if possible, and sing it a song or simply enjoy the sight of this beautiful and satisfying link with the Yule season. Then, when the season is past, you may want to save a few special ornaments, dated on the back, to bring out again and again as your children grow.

BUILD A SACRED CAVE

This last activity, more than any other, has a drama and intensity that speaks to the deepest part of all of us. With its own quiet power, it creates a strikingly beautiful image of courage and light that your family will remember all their lives.

The sacred cave is a family project: everyone will help to build the cave itself and make the figures that will people it. Like the Christian crèche or manger scenes so popular in Europe at this season, the sacred cave features a central mother and child, but in this case it is the Earth Mother and the Sun Child who are depicted.

The cave has stone's stability and earth energy. It becomes a representation of the earth, of winter stillness, and the nurturing womb of the dark. It is constructed in one of two ways. If you have a stone wall on your property, you may remove a few of the rocks to make a cavelike opening. Or you can build a cave using rocks and stones found nearby. The mouth of the cave must be large enough to accommodate whatever figures you want to include, as well as a few tea-lights or votive candles.

Pick a sunny day when the windchill is tolerable and you can enjoy working together to haul the rocks to your chosen outdoor location (the cave should be outdoors if at all possible). Then stack them carefully—and with supervision to avoid bruised fingers or toes if your children are very small. We prefer to make ours in a place that is visible from a central room indoors. You can make your cave in any shape you like; we like ours to have a roof as well as three walls.

Then comes the indoor part of the project: making the figures to place in the cave can take hours or days to accomplish and creates a lot of fun in the process. We like to use modeling beeswax, available from art supply stores, to shape ours, with the addition of small beads or pieces of jewelry pressed into the wax, but other options include clay or papier-mâché. Older children may want to try carving the figures from wood or making them from bits of recycled tin, glass, or what-have-you; the figures may become true works of art. To ensure that they can withstand the elements, you may need to varnish some of your creations.

The central Earth Mother and Sun Child are the only must-haves. Other possibilities include crones, horned or vegetation gods, winter figures, wizards, witches, and magical creatures such as mermaids, mermen, or angels.

We always include small representations of each family member's animal totem, plus any others to which we feel an attraction. Our sacred cave becomes a sort of magical zoo, with owls, crows, squirrels, and snakes perched on jutting rocks or nestled in hollows formed by the stones.

You may build your sacred cave any time in December, but keep the figures indoors until Yule Eve. Then, at sunset, bundle up and make a grand procession outside, carrying a basket filled with the figures, some evergreen sprigs, special stick incense, and tea-lights or votive candles. As the sun sets, light a stick of incense and place it in the ground nearby, and then set your figures in, on, and around the cave: the Mother and Child are always in the center, with a candle placed directly behind them. Decorate the cave with the evergreen sprigs and place other candles all around, being careful to prevent any potential fire hazard.

Then, as the dark grows darker and the cold grows deeper on this longest night of the year, say a few words about the courage it takes to shine brightly in the dark, about the turning of the wheel toward light, about the magic of the Great Mother bringing forth the sun once more. Then take turns lighting the candles.

The first time we did this, the effect was immediate and electric: something about the sight of warm golden light shining on stone, surrounded by the cold and the dark, went right to our hearts, touching our deepest ancestral memories.

You may want to sing a carol or two. "The Holly and the Ivy" has strong pagan roots, and "Deck the Halls" has survived untouched by later Christian associations.

Then everyone goes back inside, leaving the candles shining in the dark. Once you've removed boots and coats and mufflers, stand beside the window, looking out at the glowing cave. Its brave presence reminds us all through the dark night that the light will return, that the darkest moments cannot last forever.

On Yule itself, renew the candles and light them again at the onset of darkness. This time the mood is more boisterous: the longest night is past. Next morning, retrieve the figures to pack away carefully until next year. You may leave the cave intact or dismantle it to build again the following Yule.

CREATING THE YULE ALTAR
CANDLES, EVERGREENS, SUN IMAGES, APPLES, POMEGRANATES, NUTS

In a sense, the sacred cave and the Yule Tree become your altars, reminders of the central images and mysteries of this festival, but you may also want to decorate your dining table to harmonize with the great magic afoot at this time.

Candles are a must; living light is crucial to this holiday, but be sure to use extra caution around little ones. If open flames are out of the question, try twining small strings of holiday lights around your dining area and share your Yule meal by their glow only.

Evergreens of all kinds—spruce, juniper, cedar, pine—are also a fragrant and beautiful imperative; your children may literally want to fill the entire house with green. Place an armful in a stoneware pot, make garlands for mantels or stairways, wreaths for walls and doors, and drape festoons over any available table or other flat surface. Just be sure to keep the needles well away from open flames once they have dried.

An old English custom involves twining mirrors and paintings with sprays of ivy, and, of course, holly with its beautiful red berries makes a splendid addition to your decorations as well. Mistletoe, whose white berries were revered by the Druids as the semen of the God, may be hung in doorways for the traditional custom of kissing beneath it—chances are, our ancestors did more than kiss under this sacred fertility symbol! Keep the highly poisonous berries out of reach, however, to make sure your children or companion animals can't ingest them. And as a special token of love, you may want to string a garland of small dried rosebuds, available at florist or craft shops, to twine around a small live tree for a child's bedroom.

We like to put a leafless branch, or a twig tree, available at craft and nursery shops, in the center of our table—its bare wintry beauty is a constant reminder of winter's power. Then, on Yule Eve, we wind it with ribbons and gold trim and tuck small sprigs of evergreen and bright holly berries among its bony branches, laying more evergreen at its foot.

Apples and pomegranates are still appropriate to include on your Yule table. You may also want to gild a few acorns and nuts and tuck them here and there among the greens. If you made more ornaments than your tree could hold, the extras may be nestled in as well.

You may want to hang a golden representation of the sun nearby, as a reminder of the sun's return (see the ideas on making solar images on page 181 in the Litha section of Summer). And many of us choose to include a small statue of a hoofed and horned animal—usually a stag or a reindeer, easy to find at this time of year—on the table to honor these animals of the North and the element of earth.

Cinnamon sticks and pomander balls may also be tucked into the evergreens adorning your table, as well as little sweet treats (special cookies or small balls shaped from chopped dried fruits and nuts) for the family to nibble throughout the season. We try to keep these as healthful as possible, so as not to add the extra stress of too much sugar to the usual seasonal hysteria.

SPECIAL YULE FOOD
APPLES, NUTS, ROOT VEGETABLES, GINGERBREAD, SHAPED CAKES AND COOKIES

Sadly, most holiday feasts in our culture have some dead animal as their centerpiece: the Thanksgiving turkey, the Dickensian Christmas roast goose, the Easter lamb or ham. Certainly, our ancestors looked forward to the festival meal as a chance to indulge in the rare treat of meat-eating; for them, too much meat consumption was not generally a problem as it is for most of our culture. But a new sensitivity to the rights and feelings of animals, as well as to the ill effects of eating toxin- and chemical-laden dead flesh, has inspired many of us to rethink our vision of the festive meal.

Instead of a piece of meat, we like to think of a sun-shaped nut roast or savory pie as the center of the feast, surrounded by simple and delicious side dishes that echo the season: sweet potatoes with spices, honey, and nuts; baked potatoes heaped with sautéed leeks or spinach in a cheese sauce; salads sweet with apples and nuts and raisins; and the crisp-cooked fresh green vegetables (perhaps decorated with strips of red bell pepper) that would have been an undreamed-of luxury for our ancestors at this barren time of year.

Hot ciders and mulled wines, with the addition of brandy or some other strong liquor—variations of the Yuletide wassail still celebrated in carols today—are festive and fun for the adults, as is eggnog, that creamy and delicious reminder of the Great Mother's intoxicating milk. Children will enjoy nonalcoholic versions of the hot spiced cider, with the addition of a cinnamon stick in each steaming mug.

The possibilities for desserts are endless, but we try to include a special shaped gingerbread cake of some kind, generally in the form of a sun or a Yule log, and little cut-out cookies that everyone has helped to make.

THE FAMILY YULE

Our Yule celebration lasts from sunset on Yule Eve through sunset of Yule Day; this seems to be the time that evokes the strongest response in us and in our children. On Yule Eve, after lighting the candles around the sacred cave at sunset, you may want to try another dark/light activity that is one of our favorites.

Turn off every light in the house. Sit together and really feel the dark for a while; this is something we rarely do, and it has a powerful simplicity. Then, walking clockwise or deosil (in the direction of the sun) around the house, begin lighting candles that you have placed in every room. Older children are welcome to participate in this, and little ones like to hold the matchboxes for us. When all the candles are blazing, hold hands and feel the radiant energy of their vibrant lights. Then, if the weather isn't too nasty, you may want to take a quick stroll outdoors, walking out of sight of the house and then returning to see the golden glow in every window. (Please be very careful to avoid fire hazards—you don't want to come home to a smoldering ruin. Try using votives in glass holders, or the large glass novena candles sold in the Hispanic section of most grocery stores.) This Yule vision of home as a warm and radiant beacon is very special.

Lighting the Yule fire, if you have a fireplace, is a traditional way to honor the sun. Our ancestors used huge logs to keep the dark at bay and danced and made lots of noise around the fire all night to call up the sun the next morning. Although you probably won't want to keep your children up for an all-night celebration of this type, it can be great fun to provide noise-makers (pots and pans, bells, rattles, whistles—anything goes) and let everybody go a little crazy; stomping and dancing and creating ear-splitting havoc is a great release for seasonal overexcitement. If you saved any logs from your Yule tree last year, you can use one of these as part of your fire this year—although the pitch in pine trees can clog a chimney, one log once a year shouldn't do too much harm, and it's a lovely way to make a connection from Yule to Yule. And if you don't have a fireplace, arrange a grouping of candles on a raised surface, such as a bookshelf, to keep them out of the way of little dancing feet, and proceed with your noise-making.

If you can, bring your table into the room with the fireplace so that you can share your evening meal by its cheery blaze. If this isn't possible, or you don't have a fire, eating by candlelight or the faery glow of small electric holiday lights is a magical departure from routine that is sure to enchant everyone.

Then, to help excited little ones get to sleep, you can serve a warm carob drink before bed and sit near the fire and the tree, telling stories of the light rising out of darkness. Virtually every culture worldwide has a celebration of this kind; find folktales from your own ethnic background to share.

On Yule morning, we like to rise before dawn and watch the sun come up together, with the scent of our homemade smudges sweetening the air. If you include a few gifts for your family as part of your festival celebration, this would be the perfect moment to open them under the tree, as the room begins to warm and glow with dawn light. We try to keep our gifts as simple, personal, and handmade as we can, saving neon plastic toys, computer games, and the occasional action figure for Christmas morning a few days later. Then, after a special breakfast of sun-colored foods (fresh-squeezed juice and golden pancakes or muffins), you may want to make gifts of food for your local wildlife. We like to fill the empty orange halves left over from juicing with peanut butter and birdseed, and stick fresh cranberries decoratively around the rim. Or you could cut festive shapes from cardboard and spread them with peanut butter, then sprinkle with seeds, punch a hole in the top, and hang them in a bare tree. After placing our gifts outside, we can enjoy watching the birds and squirrels at their Yule feast as we all work together to cook our own.

You may want to eat your main meal early, while the sun is still shining, as a way of marking and celebrating its return, being sure to drink special toasts to it and to each other. Then, as the dusk approaches, light your sacred cave candles and know that the wheel has turned again, the darkness is past, and longer days will return once more.

IMBOLC

Stirring of the Seeds
February 2

Our culture only dimly remembers the festival of Imbolc, once a celebration of the visibly longer days and of the sacredness of fire, particularly the hearth fire. We know it now only as Groundhog Day. But if we, like the groundhog, step outside for a few moments today, we can feel a difference in the winter stillness. Though the ground may be covered in a pall of snow, there is a new freshness in the air, and a sense of possibility, a softly humming energy in the earth. Suddenly, we realize that our winter time of rest and retreat is nearly over and that soon all of nature will be dancing and singing again.

Imbolc celebrates the first stirring of the seeds, deep within the womb of earth. Just as nature is beginning to waken under its covering of snow, the birds to sing again, the seeds to put forth the first tiny shoots, so we can feel ourselves beginning to look ahead, after long months of forced inactivity, to the plans and projects we will work on bringing to fruition in the greening season that is nearly here. Besides creating an Imbolc image of great beauty, our first activity, the light garden, is a way for us and for our children to begin our looking ahead.

Traditionally, Imbolc is the day to make the candles your family will burn for seasonal celebrations all year long, since at Imbolc it can be clearly seen that the light is growing. Making this connection between our own tiny lights and the larger picture is one of Imbolc's gifts to us, and our second activity will give you some ideas for creating magical, scented candles to give a special glow to your family's festivals.

Constructing simple musical instruments with our children and playing them all together becomes an endearing and special activity that is designed to stir and inspire us, awakening our inner energies to meet the demands of the coming spring.

And finally, making a rainstick is easy and great fun, and the enchantment of its soothing sounds remind us of the spring rains that will finally wash the last traces of winter away. This last activity will please children of all ages.

IMBOLC ACTIVITIES

PLANT A LIGHT GARDEN

Like the sacred cave, the light garden creates a visual image of real power and beauty for the participants, one that grows directly out of the symbolism and central meaning of the time. It is a favorite with everybody, old and young.

At Imbolc, energy begins to return to the earth after long months of resting and waiting. The light garden celebrates this feeling of potential in the air and starts all of us thinking about our own potential to create and make necessary changes. It reminds children of their own awe-inspiring ability, like the earth's, to gestate new growth, abilities, and projects.

First, go outdoors and dig up some good rich dirt to fill a lasagna pan or sheet-cake baking pan. (If you don't have access to a yard, buy some potting soil.) Then come back inside and sit in a circle with the dirt-filled pan in the center. Take a few moments to think about what particular ideas, projects, creative ventures, or changes you would like to manifest in the coming months. Would you like to learn how to play a flute? Be able to paint with oils? Is there a book inside you waiting to be written? Or would you like to start your own neighborhood newspaper? Make your own clothes? Run a mile? Learn how to drive? Ride a bike? Paddle a canoe? Both adults and children will come up with lots of wonderful ideas. Then have each person write a few words about each idea—or draw a picture of it—on a small slip of paper. Do as many as you like.

Crumple the papers up into tiny pellets or seeds. Then, taking turns, plant the seeds in the pan of earth. When all the seeds have been planted, each person takes a small birthday candle and sets it into the dirt over the spots where their seeds are buried. Place the pan on the altar where the seeds (and candles) will lie waiting. After dark on Imbolc, light the candles and feel their energy blessing your plans and hopes. You may save the dirt and seeds to plant in your outdoor garden in spring.

MAKE SPECIAL CANDLES

Imbolc is the perfect day for this candle-making activity. Then, throughout the year, whenever you burn one of your special Imbolc candles you will remember the day with affection, and the candles themselves will be imbued with the magical significance of the sun's bright new energy.

Even very young children, with some adult supervision and assistance, can make beautiful hand-dipped candles that will make them proud. We like to use beeswax, purchased in blocks from herbal suppliers, but plain old paraffin will do, with the addition of candle hardener (sold in craft shops), since pure paraffin is generally too soft. Or you can melt down all those little candle ends left over from the year before.

Melt your wax in a double-boiler or over a *very* low flame; wax is highly flammable and you could have a nasty problem if it gets too hot. If it starts to smoke, remove the pan from the heat. And please be sure to supervise little ones carefully around the stove.

When your wax is melted, pour it into a tall coffee can or an institutional-size soup or vegetable can for longer candles. Cover your entire work area with newspapers—this will get pretty messy. Give each participant a length of candle-wick (check your local craft shop) a few inches longer than the can is deep and take turns dipping. Allow the wax to harden for a minute or two between dips. Continue dipping until your candles have reached the desired thickness. You will probably need to add more melted wax to your can as you go along, and if the whole thing gets hard, you can pop it in the double boiler until it liquefies again.

Two thin candles may be twisted together, or three may be gently braided, while they are still warm and flexible.

You may also want to experiment with candles made in molds. The 1960s sand candle is back in vogue and is still just as much fun to make. Fill a bucket with clean damp sand and use spoons or fingers to scoop it out, forming your desired candle shape. You can make a tripod base by poking your finger deeper into the sand to make three little legs, like a cauldron. You may also press an object, such as an aspic mold, into the sand for even fancier effects. Have your child poke a piece of wicking through the bottom of the sand mold and hold it steady while you carefully pour melted wax into it (older children will want to do this step themselves). When the first pouring hardens, add a little more wax to fill the hollow that forms at the top of your candle. When the whole thing has hardened, remove it from the sand, brushing off any excess.

Paper milk cartons also make fine molds; when your candle has hardened, simply tear off the surrounding paper. Smooth metal cans may be used as molds, but you will need to grease them first. Make sure that the top and bottom are the same width, or you won't be able to remove your candle once it has hardened. Use a can opener to remove the bottom of the can so you can push the candle out.

Pillar candles made in cartons or cans look beautiful with dried leaves or flowers pressed into them. Hold the leaf in place on the candle and use the curved back of a spoon (heated over the stove or in hot water) to press the entire surface of the leaf against the candle. It's also great fun to embed little surprises in a pillar candle as you pour. Small nonflammable toys, crystals, charms, or coins that magically appear as the candle burns are sure to delight everyone.

Many of us enjoy anointing our finished candles with essential oils: when burned, their scent is released, adding a special sweetness to our festival celebrations or other important occasions. There are theories about the "correct" way to anoint a candle for magical purposes, but we have found that children enjoy simply smearing their candle with oils—the result is fine. If you want to do things in a more traditional way, you can place a couple of drops of oil in the middle of the candle and stroke and spread them upward toward the tip, then add a few more in the middle and stroke them downward toward the base. It is helpful to visualize the purpose behind your scent choice as you do this. Here are two recipes for scented candles to get you started; then look at Correspondences on page 204 for ideas and invent some of your own.

We generally use tapers (the long, thin, hand-dipped ones) for these anointed candles because they burn down in a reasonable amount of time, but feel free to use a larger candle if you wish.

Imbolc Energy Candle

This will help you feel renewed and ready for spring.

> *basil oil*
> *peppermint oil*
> *rosemary oil*

Anoint a taper with a few drops of each of the essential oils. If you used paraffin-based wax, rather than beeswax, you may either leave it white or make it pale yellow (mix in some yellow crayons with your melting wax, or use a cake of store-bought candle colorant) for this candle. You can press some dried basil, peppermint, and rosemary into the wax before it has completely hardened; we like to add the herbs near the candle's base to avoid fire hazards while burning. Small crystals or gemstones may also be pressed into a still warm candle. Aventurine, beryl, rhodochrosite, and tigereye are all traditionally held to be energizing stones.

As you add your oils, stones, or herbs, imagine your candle beginning to take on the fresh, sweet energies of Imbolc, like an inspiring breeze that will strengthen and revitalize you.

New Beginnings Candle

Burn this in honor of new life. Whenever we start something, a new beginnings candle adds an element of celebration and sacredness to the event.

> frankincense oil
> lavender oil

Anoint your candle with a few drops of the essential oils. (The candles may be beeswax-gold, white, or pale green.) As you spread the oils around, imagine the candle glowing with positive energy; visualize the power of a fresh start, a new chance to make good things grow. You may add a small peridot or piece of jade to the candle; their green color, which reminds us of the greenness of the earth after the snow has melted, will enhance the growth-promoting energies of the candle.

Your children may enjoy making simple, beautiful candleholders for their candles out of Sculpey or self-hardening clay, painted with symbols, patterns, and colors that are meaningful to them.

The first time you light one of these homemade candles, make a special ceremony of it. Turn out all other lights and appreciate with reverence the brightness of its flame. Imagine a time when flames like these were all that stood between you and the dark—when any nighttime activity was lit by nothing greater than their glow. Enjoy its warmth, the way it makes the room and your faces look softer. And really notice the dancing of its flame, vulva-shaped and rainbowlike, its colors varying from blue to purple to red to gold. When you and your family become conscious of a candle's energy, through shaping and scenting and decorating it, and when you take the time to enter into its shining spirit, it becomes the perfect way to honor the Mother. Once you have really seen one, you will never look at candles in a casual way again.

MUSIC WITH HEART

Music is a great awakener; as the seeds begin to stir, you can inspire and enliven yourselves with your own special family sounds. You don't have to be a professional to keep a beat or sing from the heart—children are naturally rhythmic and respond fully and with great delight to all kinds of music. And they're usually fascinated by the making of simple rhythm instruments. With a few tin cans, cardboard tubes, or dried gourds, you and your young ones can have hours of creative and musical fun together.

Here are a few ideas to get you started on your very own magical band. Although more elaborate instruments can be made with woodworking tools and a little skill, these sound-producing activities are simple, satisfying, and easily accomplished by children of all ages.

- Stretch a rubber surgical glove or a large piece of rubber balloon over a tin can and secure with a strong rubber band. Pluck, tap, or hit with a stick. Or just hit the tin can itself.
  - Strike two smooth rocks together.
  - Find a hollow log, or a whole one, and strike it with sticks.
  - Collect a few cardboard tubes of different sizes. Experiment with striking these against the log or some other inanimate object.
  - Fill an empty soda can with pebbles or dried beans, tape the opening closed, and shake. Small film canisters will also work for this.
- Older children may want to try filling glasses of water to different levels and striking gently.
- Glass bottles of different sizes, including the traditional jug, may be filled partway with water. Blow gently across the top opening; little ones may have to practice quite a bit before they can produce a sound, but the results are well worth it.
- Dry a few gourds, then cut off the tops, fill with pebbles or dried beans, and glue the tops back on—primitive and delicious-sounding rattles. These may be painted and decorated with magical symbols if desired.
- Stretch rubber bands of different lengths and thicknesses across a dinner plate and experiment with plucking them.
- If you've had to replace any plumbing lately, save those lengths of copper pipe! They make lovely windchime sounds when struck with a drumstick.

Your children will become adept at discovering new and wonderful sources of musical noise; just about anything can be used to produce sound if given a chance. Flowerpots, pie tins, old toys—anything goes. Rummage around and see what marvels you can unearth to bang on.

When you have made or collected a variety of instruments to play, have a family jam session. At first, don't even try to reproduce any specific song; just keep a beat together. This is an ancient technique for entraining the participants and often leads to states of gently altered consciousness during which magic-making can take place.

With continued practice, it becomes possible to improvise and embellish, and to sing simple songs and chants along with the beat; or you can make up songs by taking turns chanting whatever word comes to each person's mind. But the primitive power of a simple heartbeat rhythm has a special magic all its own.

Try doing this heartbeat music before family discussions or before festival celebrations. Everyone will be more relaxed and receptive after a few minutes of making some good, wild noise, and the energy raised by your group will feel like a harbinger of spring.

MAKE A RAINSTICK

Soon the spring rains will come, washing the last traces of dirty snow away and nourishing the seeds in their dark womb of earth so that they can burst forth into the light.

To encourage the coming of spring and its nurturing rain, you and your children can make beautiful, magical, and inexpensive rainsticks like those traditionally used in South and Central America; these are currently popular among people everywhere for use in relaxation and ceremony.

All you need is a cardboard mailing tube with two end pieces and a pound of nails for each rainstick you want to make—the nails should be the same length as the diameter of the tube. Each child hammers the pound of nails into the tube, as far as they will go; these can be patterned evenly or unevenly down the length of the tube, as desired. Glue or tape one of the end pieces on the tube and then pour in a cup or two of dried beans or rice—different varieties of beans will give a different quality of sound to each stick. Now glue or tape on the other end piece.

Rainsticks may be covered with duct tape or contact paper, or you can glue brown paper on them—the covering keeps the nails in place. Then paint or decorate. Your children will come up with vibrant and beautiful ways to personalize their sticks.

To use your rainstick, hold it with one end up and then slowly tilt it completely upside down. The mysterious and soothing rainlike sound will be sure to inspire you. You can incorporate the rainstick's music into your family jam sessions, or use it before guided meditations—its gentle magic makes it easy to relax and journey.

CREATING THE IMBOLC ALTAR
LIGHT GARDEN, SPECIAL CANDLES,
SEEDS AND SPROUTS, GODDESS FIGURE

The Lady of Light is with us, bringing longer days and the promise of spring. In her honor, we like to include a statue of the Goddess on our Imbolc altar. You may want to drape a string of small holiday lights around the altar and wreathe her head with a few; the faery twinkle of the Lady's halo will charm all beholders.

You will want to set your light garden in a prominent place, and many of us like to include a small bowl of seeds and sprouts to nibble together. A light green or pale yellow scarf draped on the altar brings the fresh hues of new spring growth indoors and reminds us that, underneath the still cold earth, seeds are stirring into life.

Be sure to give a few of your handmade candles a special place on the altar. If you can find anything green growing outdoors (hardy chickweed and garlic mustard are usually about, even in the colder regions), pluck a few sprigs to place in an earthenware jug or vase.

SPECIAL IMBOLC FOOD
EARTHY, DARK FOODS; SURPRISE FOODS; SPROUTS; SEEDS

Imbolc food can teach our children of the amazing potential hidden in the earth's darkness, the interesting things waiting just out of sight for us to discover in nature and in ourselves. Dark bran muffins filled with a "surprise" of jam or fruit, or the treat-filled carob brownies described below, are ways to make this idea visual (and edible).

You could make individual pies in a muffin tin and stuff them with savory goodies before fitting on the top crust, or make traditional pasties with an onion and potato filling, or pizza pockets with lots of sun-dried tomato, spinach, and cheese—anything that opens to reveal its inner surprise.

You may want to include a salad with lots of sprouts as a reminder that seeds will soon be sending their own sprouts aboveground, and toasted seeds, such as sunflower or pumpkin, to honor their magic of death and resurrection.

Beverages for Imbolc might include digestive herbal bitters (for the brave) or any dandelion cordial left over from the previous summer, as well as herbal teas to nourish and tonify our winter-sluggish systems. Children might enjoy a traditional posset of warmed milk, honey, and a soothing herb such as chamomile, strained and served in mugs.

For dessert, you may want to make a pan of rich carob brownies and "plant" them with a few special surprises—coins, rings, crystals—for everyone to find. Decorate the brownies with lit-up birthday candles on top to echo the light garden. Be sure to warn your family, though, so that nobody chips a tooth or chokes on their lucky find; if your household includes very young children, omit the surprises and just light the candles instead. Or you could make individual cups of dark, earthy-looking carob pudding and hide pieces of honey candy inside.

THE FAMILY IMBOLC

Today is the traditional day to do some magical spring cleaning. If you haven't already done so, all of your faded, dried, and dusty Yule greens may be removed now and either burned in your Imbolc fire (carefully, and only adding a little at a time) or put outside in your compost. If you don't have a fireplace, burn a few small sprigs of your dusty greens carefully in a heat-proof container. By getting rid of the old, we make room for new things to sprout and grow, and it becomes a ritual way of banishing winter and inviting in the spring to burn, sweep, and dust all the grime away.

If you have a special family shrine in addition to your altar, Imbolc is a good time to dust and clean it. Cait's small son spent one entire Imbolc morning removing the accumulations of beeswax from the family shrine and candleholder and apparently enjoyed every minute of it. Get your children some small sponges and scouring pads, and let them have fun. Young ones love to be given this kind of responsibility and will beam with pride when they're finished.

Dead leaves and snow may be cleared away from any outdoor altars or shrines as well; soon there will be wild things popping up around them, so we need to give them room to breathe and reach the sun. And you may want to scoop up a bowl of snow to bring inside and set on your Imbolc altar. Watching it melt throughout the day becomes a happy reminder that the big thaw is approaching.

Imbolc is an ancient fire festival, so it is traditional to burn a few of your new candles today, in honor of the brightness of the sun and the visibly longer days. After dark, you will want to light the small candles on your light garden as a lovely way to encourage and cheer each other during these last cold days of winter. And your Imbolc fire (indoors if possible, not only because of the outdoor cold and damp but because this is the traditional day to celebrate the hearth fire) may be the focus for the following simple ritual activity.

After you have lit your fire and thrown in a few dusty Yule greens, encourage your children to think of anything in the past year that they wish they had done differently—a hurtful word said to someone in anger, a half-hearted job done on an important project—anything that has accumulated some psychic "dust" in their minds. Have them draw or write it out on a piece of paper, keeping the contents strictly private unless they wish to share. Then crumple the papers and throw them in the fire, releasing all regret. Sprinkle a few grains of salt or some homemade smudge herbs in afterward to cleanse and purify the atmosphere. What's gone is gone. Now encourage each child to visualize shining new opportunities for joy in the months ahead.

When the fire has burned down and bedtime draws near, open a window and take a moment to stand beside it all together. Smell the newness in the air, the green earthy energy that is reawakening after its long, cold slumber. Know that, after the window is closed and we are all asleep, the seeds will still be stirring in their dark beds, and that soon the dawn light will show us their brave green shoots rising from the last traces of snow.

SPRING

By the end of February, the winter stillness that was such a blessing in December has begun to feel constricting. Most of us find ourselves longing for some warmth and sunshine after endless bleak days when the earth seems locked in a coffin of ice. And then the spring miracle occurs. After months of immobility, the earth begins to dance again. The return of light and warmth is a return to movement, sound, and activity.

Spring has held out its message of hope and renewal to generation after generation: after seeming death comes rebirth. Every year the sheer beauty of spring fills us with delight; we rediscover, as if for the first time, the tenderness of eggs and hatchlings, fields dotted with wobbly colts and calves, and the grace—the incredible, colorful display— of the green, growing world released from its casing of white.

Spring is easy to love—and easy to share with our children. It's one thing to bundle up in endless layers to brave the subzero windchill at Yule, and quite another to run carelessly outside in our shirtsleeves to romp in the sunshine at Beltane. And our children are themselves a manifestation of the spring principle; of all the seasons, this is the one that pays homage to life's eternal power of regeneration. The children we have brought into the cycle are our own contribution to the cosmic dance of life renewing itself.

Any celebration of spring is a celebration of renewal, of life force rising when all seemed dead and hopeless. It is a rebirth to the possibilities inherent in the world—and to our power to achieve great and stirring things in that world. It is the traditional time to hatch new ideas, plans, and projects, infused with the freshness of the season.

The primary symbol of spring in popular culture is the egg. Clearly a holdover from ancient pagan fertility magic, eggs also remind us of a central inner truth. Many of us, toward the end of winter, feel as if we are trapped inside a small cramped space with energy so low and vision so darkened that positive action becomes a terrible effort, too much to even attempt.

Spring's return gives us the vitality to push our way out of that psychic egg. Spring becomes a dawning of possibility, a discovery of the transformative new vision that waited for us all along. Imagine hatching for the first time, seeing light and space and all the myriad wonders of the earth when you thought only darkness existed. The inconceivable becomes reality. We are fortunate that our lives offer so many opportunities for hatching, for personal metamorphosis.

Exploring the outside world takes on a special magic in spring. There is a treasure seeker in every child, and our own wild selves still remember the pleasures of gathering edible goodies very well. (In fact, the eggs in baskets, so plentiful around this time, are reminders of our ancestors' penchant for wild birds' eggs after a long winter on short rations.) Looking for signs of spring together can be a wondrous thing. If we can echo our children's willing-ness to be amazed, to be thrilled, then we will have truly entered into the spirit of spring.

OSTARA

Spring Equinox
March 20-23

In our calendar, spring officially begins on Ostara, but in some regions, it's hard to believe that spring is even remotely around the corner in March. In a recent year, we were hopefully dyeing Ostara eggs with eighteen inches of snow on the ground outside! We had to take the beginning of spring on faith.

The ancients also called this festival Eostara or Eostre, after an Anglo-Saxon spring goddess of that name. The word for the Christian festival of Easter has nothing to do with Christ at all; it harks back to this ancient goddess, and the eggs and bunnies and baby chicks that feature so prominently in our culture's Easter celebrations are all Ostara fertility images. In imagery even more graphic, white "Easter" lilies were once revered as representations of Eostre's miraculous, self-generating vulva. For those of us who are actively working to reclaim the sacredness of our female sexuality, this can be a powerful and healing image.

This is the time of year when we celebrate Persephone's return. As described earlier in the autumn celebration of Mabon, according to ancient Greek myth Persephone is a young maiden abducted by Hades, God of the underworld. Her mother, Demeter, an earth and grain goddess, is so grief-stricken over the loss of her daughter that she causes winter and death to cover the earth. Persephone eventually was restored to her mother, but because she ate six pomegranate seeds in the underworld, she must return to it for six months out of every year, the months of autumn and winter. Her yearly reemergence in spring brings such joy to her mother that the earth blooms once more.

The vernal equinox celebrates the balance of light and dark: this is one of two days in the year when the day and night are of equal length. At this equinox, a shift takes place from the earth energy of winter to the airiness of spring. From the cold darkness of earth and stone and the roots of trees, sap begins to rise; the breeze begins to warm and soothe us; and the skies become thickly inhabited once again.

Air is spring's element and is linked in our collective unconscious with birds. People have been watching their effortless grace wistfully for centuries and associating it with soaring thought, the ease of mental as well as physical flight. To celebrate the birds, we have included an activity in their honor.

Making and burning special incense is another uniquely air-related activity; we watch the curls and eddies of incense smoke rising in the air and the sweet, powerful scent reaches both nose and consciousness by way of that same element.

Many of us share our lives with companion animals who are just as ready for spring to return as we are. A winter-weary, housebound cat or dog often craves a nibble of something fresh and green, and our grass pots activity gives your family a way to respond to that need in a direct and loving way.

Finally, no talk of spring is complete without mention of its central image: that of the seed that dies, falls into the dark ground, and is reborn as the sprout, the seedling. The ritualized action of planting intention is the focus for our first activity.

OSTARA ACTIVITIES

PLANT YOUR BEAN RUNES

There is nothing as magical to a child (or to an adult, when you stop to think about it) as the metamorphosis from dead and dried-up little seed to living sprout, leafy seedling, lush green plant. The central mystery for earth-burying cultures was this image of death and planting and rebirth. And because we are offered so many opportunities throughout life for death/rebirth transformational experiences, any conscious engagement in this parallel activity touches a deep chord.

Besides, children love to plant things and wait breathlessly for them to grow. As well as sharing the sense of the miraculous, this rune-planting activity encourages children to give some real thought to the quality they wish to increase for themselves in the following months. Then it empowers them to manifest that quality. Physicalizing their desire in this way becomes the first step toward achieving that desire.

So—using the set of bean runes you made for Samhain, choose a rune, or two or three, that most closely sums up what it is you wish to grow in your life. (You will want to make bean runes to replace these so you always have a complete set.) Prepare a pot of soil by stirring it with your finger, visualizing your good energy entering into the soil. Smooth the surface of the soil and then make shallow holes for the beans, about the depth of a pencil eraser. Hold the runes in your hand and breathe into them, infusing them with your hopes. Plant them as you visualize concrete things you intend to do during the next few weeks to make your wish become reality. Then water them well, cover the pot with plastic wrap, and put it on top of the refrigerator (the warmth will help the sprouting process). In a couple of days, check to see if anything has come up. If the soil is dry, water it. Soon your rune will sprout. If you plant your runes a few days before Ostara you can choose to eat the sprouts as part of the family feast; ingestion is powerful magic, literally incorporating the energy of the rune into yourself. Or you can nurture your sprout—with proper care (water, warmth, and sunlight) it will become a green plant. After the danger of frost is past, you can plant it in your garden. If for some reason your rune fails to sprout, you may want to rethink your goals and try a different rune, or try the same one again. This can be a good measure of your level of commitment.

MAKE YOUR OWN INCENSE

This is a favorite activity—children love it. First of all, there is something intrinsically magical about grinding away with a mortar and pestle; then, too, the strong scents of the ingredients stir deep feelings (as any aromatherapist will tell you) and children are highly susceptible. Knowing that they are doing something important and being given real magical responsibility is part of the charm, as well. And the results are satisfying.

Because the process can be lengthy, lots of the pure, sweet energy of the child goes into the blend. Nothing smells as special as the incense your children have made; whenever you use it outside the home, you bring your warmth for its makers with you.

The recipes included here are simple and effective, but once you get the hang of them, you will want to experiment with more exotic ingredients and complex formulas; ideas may be found in Suggested Reading at the back of the book.

These incenses may be burned on little self-igniting charcoal rounds available at occult, herbal, or religious supply stores or through alternative catalogues. (You will need a good amount of earth, clay kitty litter, or ash underneath your charcoal to prevent cracking of your container from the heat. We use a small cast-iron cauldron filled with earth from the garden.) Or you can throw pinches (or handfuls, if you're in a generous mood) of incense on a fire. This works better on an open fire outdoors; indoors, the smoke goes up the chimney. Or you can make a mound of it in a heat-proof container—a heavy ashtray on a trivet, for instance—and light a portion of it with a match. It won't burn completely and you'll have to keep relighting it, but this is a useful method if you've run out of charcoals. In any case, incense should be burned only under adult supervision.

Ordinary store-bought ground cinnamon makes a great base for many blends. The smell of burning cinnamon has the effect of making people feel safe and at home, but if cinnamon's associations are too autumnal or wintry for you, try using simple sawdust from untreated wood, or sandalwood chips or powder available at herbal supply stores. If you use sandalwood chips, you'll need to grind them for a long time to make the blend fine enough.

Ostara Incense

3 parts base (ground cinnamon, sawdust, or sandalwood powder or chips)
1 part dried lavender or jasmine petals
$1/2$ part dried sage

Grind well with mortar and pestle. Store in a glass bottle or jar with a label. (You can buy pretty, decorative ones if you want.)

Safe and Loving Home Incense

3 parts ground cinnamon
2 parts sandalwood powder or chips
$1/2$ part dried bay leaf
$1/2$ part dried angelica
$1/2$ part dried marjoram

Grind well with mortar and pestle. As you do this, visualize your home glowing with warm and loving energy (see "How to Visualize" on page 58). Store in a labeled glass bottle or jar with a tonka bean for good luck (available at herbal supply stores or through witchy catalogs), and burn it whenever you feel the need.

Protection Power Incense

This incense is good for making children feel safe and secure at bedtime. Little ones will call it PP Incense for laughs.

3 parts ground cinnamon
1 part dried vervain
$1/2$ part ground cloves

Grind with mortar and pestle, visualizing feeling strong and safe and empowered. Store in a labeled glass bottle or jar.

True Love Incense

This incense is especially nice to burn for Beltane; it makes you feel more loved and loving.

> *2 parts sandalwood powder or chips*
> *1 part dried rose petals*
> *¹/₂ part dried lavender flowers*
> *13 drops of essential oil of rose per ¹/₂ cup of mixture*

Grind dry ingredients in mortar until fine. Then, using your fingers, mix in the rose oil. Children will enjoy smearing themselves with their resultant rosy-smelling fingers. Store in labeled bottle or jar.

Essential oil is madly expensive but don't be tempted to use synthetics: they smell awful when burned. You can also use rose oil in a homemade aromatherapy pot with great results—just float a few drops of oil on some water in a heat-proof pot and simmer atop a stove or candle.

HONORING THE BIRDS

We often don't realize how we missed the sound all through the winter until spring brings birdsong back to us. To celebrate the birds' homecoming, it can be fun to take a trip to the local bookstore or library and get a good field guide: make friends with your birds by learning their names and habits, the shapes of their nests, and the colors of their jewel-like eggs.

On Ostara (or anytime in March), you may want to clean the hair out of the family hairbrushes and put it out for the birds to use as nesting material. When you do, send loving thoughts to the birds who will use your hair to make their homes.

Another way to honor the birds is to dye regular chicken eggs with natural food-stuffs. We find that using the small-size eggs gives the best results. Even though it takes a little more time to dye eggs this way, rather than using the commercial tablets sold at Easter in every grocery store, the results are so charming that it's well worth it. What you end up with, in most cases, is something that closely resembles the speckled and delicately colored eggs of the wild birds. (But because the never-seen-in-nature neons are also—we have to admit it—fun, we've solved this dilemma by using natural dyes at Ostara and celebrating the cultural holiday of Easter by using one of the box dyes from the supermarket.)

It is a lovely gesture at Ostara to forge this visual link to the wild birds that are beginning to show up in your backyard around this time. Here is our recipe, but you can experiment with other foods and dried herbs.

Collect all the dropped-off papery outer skins from the onions that live in your cupboard or refrigerator. Put the skins and the raw eggs in a stainless steel or enamel pot with enough water to cover them. More skin means darker color—tidy housekeepers will get yellow or peach-tinted eggs from this process. If you only clean out the onion skins once a year, like some of us, your eggs will turn a rich dark terra-cotta. Bring the water to a boil and continue boiling until the eggs are hard-cooked and then some—about twenty minutes or so. Remove your pot from the heat and cool the eggs by running cold water on them.

That's the basic method. You can vary it by using a chopped head of red cabbage, or a bunch of chopped beets, greens and stems and all.

But both of these coloring materials require an extra step. After removing the now-cooked eggs from the pot you will notice that they are depressingly lacking in color. Don't despair—strain the chopped cooked veggies and then pack the eggs in a bowl and cover them with the chopped-up stuff. When cool, rub bits of the softened cabbage or beets on your eggs. This is what gives them that charming speckled wild look. The beet-dyed eggs will be pink to maroon and the cabbage-dyed ones will be gray to lavender to bluish. And children love to smash those bits of slimy stuff onto the eggs.

You can place the eggs in baskets, many of which are available with a natural wild nestlike look, or you can buy a bag of dried Spanish moss from a craft store or florist supply and shape handfuls of it into nests; children enjoy doing this and are charmed by the realistic effect. If you leave the eggs out for longer than an hour or two, don't eat them—you may want to refrigerate a few for snacking and put the rest out. One is always placed on the Ostara altar. And after the celebration, you can plant it in the garden for luck and fertility.

GRASS POTS

This simple, satisfying activity becomes a welcome gift to any companion animal. First, find a medium-sized flowerpot, preferably earthenware or ceramic. You can decorate it with paint or ribbons to make it really special. Fill the pot with earth and then plant it with grass seeds, or with catnip seeds if you have a cat. Water it well and put it in a sunny windowsill. In a few days, your animal friend will have something fresh and green to chew on. As a variation on this idea, you may put the pot inside a nest or basket and present the sprouted greens to your pet as her or his Ostara basket. You may want to hide a biscuit or two among the greens for a dog, or small sachet bags stuffed with dried catnip for a cat.

Children may want to include companion animals in your family celebrations in other ways as well. Let the animals themselves decide how much of the festival they want to bless with their presence—and how much they'll put up with for the sake of their human friends. (Dogs are often willing to wear flower garlands, and we know a cat who meows piteously unless he's allowed to attend the family bonfire.)

CREATING THE OSTARA ALTAR
FLOWERS, NESTS AND EGGS, SPROUTS OR GREEN WILD PLANTS, FEATHERS

What a great excuse to buy some flowering bulbs from your grocery store or florist! Flame-colored tulips with yellow tips, paperwhite narcissus, hyacinths, sunny daffodils—there are so many possibilities, and many of them add a heavenly fragrance to their visual appeal.

You can also include real birds' nests on your altar if you found any blown down by the wind in autumn, but any nestlike basket or bunch of Spanish moss will do. In it, you can place a few of your home-dyed eggs.

If you planted your bean runes early, the pot containing the sprouts could be included, and children will enjoy searching outdoors for some sprouted seeds, or for handfuls of onion grass, which they can put in a small vase or glass filled with water.

If you collect bird feathers, now is the time to display them on the altar. You will also want to include a safe container in which to burn your incense. Children will enjoy adding spring-related artwork and any outdoor treasures they've found, as well as gemstones, crystals, rocks, or other special objects that have meaning for them. If you want to include a candle, any pastel color will be pleasing.

SPECIAL OSTARA FOOD
SPROUTS, GREENS, EGG DISHES

Sprouts, including those from your bean runes, are a great choice for your Ostara celebration. Children enjoy making nests out of alfalfa sprouts to hold the eggs you've dyed, or you can make cups with radicchio, as one friend did for a Full Moon celebration around this time—it's expensive, but the deep pink color is lovely and the leaf holds a cup shape perfectly. Fill the radicchio cups with sprouts (especially fun if your family grew them, via the wide-mouth bottle method) and serve with homemade dressing. Mayonnaise is a cinch to make, and children are fascinated to see the color transformation as they add ingredients to the blender; some children even enjoy beating the mixture by hand with a wooden spoon, which is time-consuming but much more traditional. Mayonnaise is a logical choice because of its egg content (eggs being the other traditional Ostara food), but considering the number of hard-boiled eggs your family will now have on hand, a simple oil and wine vinegar dressing might be a healthier alternative.

If you're lucky enough to live in a region where wild greens, such as dandelion or garlic mustard, are growing this early, pick some to make a wonderful, energizing addition to the meal, served either raw as a salad, lightly steamed, or stir-fried.

An eggy idea for a main dish is quiche; an oval baking pan will add to the effect. For those who don't eat dairy or eggs, garbanzo or millet patties are a good golden color and can be made in an egg shape.

For dessert, egg-shaped cookies are perennial favorites, since decorating them is so much fun. Use your favorite cookie recipe and either use a cookie cutter to make the eggs or cut the shapes freehand. After baking, frost them with a cream cheese frosting. The addition of mashed strawberries or some of your beet-cooking water will make a pleasing pink, or you can use food coloring to make icing in an array of colors. You can serve your cookies in small baskets, one for each family member.

THE FAMILY OSTARA

Spring is associated with the dawn, with new beginnings, so one traditional thing that some of us manage to do for Ostara is to wake up early enough to watch the dawn (usually, it's not the children who have trouble getting out of bed for this). If you try to watch in silence, you will find that the experience goes from eerie to inspiring; quietly watching the world turn from a dark and colorless place into brightness and glory is a great way to start the day. Children love to point out the early birds in flight against the lightening sky, and the first appearance of the sun's bold disc. Then you can toast the sun with juice.

If you do a traditional nest-hunt, you may want to fill the nests with crystals and small toys, as well as sweets of the healthiest variety you can find. Your local health food store will probably have a supply of these. And you can also include a big unhealthy chocolate bunny, because you just can't be healthy *all* the time.

One friend tried an amusing variation on the traditional Ostara egg-hunt, placing a note saying "Follow my trail" next to her child's pillow—and in the morning he had to follow a trail of raisin bunny-droppings to find the treat-filled nests tucked here and there.

You may want to forgo the sweet-treat nest-finding altogether and go on an outdoor search for signs of spring. The only drawback to this plan is that there may be precious few signs of spring in your region at this time—but children will ferret out whatever there is to find. And they get just as excited finding a newly risen tulip or a budded branch as they do with their jelly beans and chocolate stuff.

Looking for and finding real birds' nests (as long as everyone is careful not to touch or disturb them in any way) is deeply magical, and you don't have to climb trees to find them—some nests are built in touchingly vulnerable, low-to-the-ground places. A neighbor reports seeing one in a forsythia bush right next to the road, so close to the earth that she could peer right in, and house wrens have built their nests in Cait's living room window for generations.

After dawn-watching and nest-finding, you may want to take some time to dress in clothes that feel special to you. Little girls may want to dress as Eostre or Persephone, with store-bought real or artificial flowers in their hair. Vibrant spring greens and pastels are the logical color choices for Ostara clothing, but anything goes; it's how you feel that really matters here, not the costume, and if your child hates pastels but feels energized in denim, then denim it is.

Because of the associations with Persephone and Demeter, this is a perfect time to invent some special activity for mothers and daughters to celebrate the deep, unique bond that you share. You could try washing each other's hair, for instance, or feeding each other some finger foods by hand—this can be fun, encouraging not only a lot of silliness but a sense of real closeness as well. Or you can simply spend some time alone together reading, taking a walk, or playing a favorite game.

Consult a *Farmer's Almanac* or astrological calendar to determine the exact time of equinox: rumor has it that a raw egg can be made to balance on its end at that moment. We tried it and it worked—but the egg was still standing there two hours later, so we concluded that it must have been a trick egg (it had little bumps on the bottom). Anyway, children love trying this one.

Put aside some special time to burn your homemade incense. You may want to say something about the new beginning given to us year after year by the Earth Mother or sing little made-up songs about the spring. You may want to hold your celebration outside. One memorable year, a group of us went outdoors on a damp, cool Ostara, holding hands in a circle and dancing, singing, and stomping with glee. And we discovered that the earthworms were awakened by the energy we raised; all over the circle they came wriggling out of the earth like the triumphant dead bursting from their coffins in the Judgment Tarot card. Events like these will become special family memories for years to come.

Here is a guided meditation that you can try with your family. Children as young as eight or nine can enjoy it, and it puts everyone in a lovely, vernal frame of mind. First, be sure to help everyone relax and feel safe and protected (see "Preparing for Guided Meditation" on page 60).

Spring Maiden Meditation

You are walking in a meadow, high up on a hillside. The sun is shining brightly, and the sky is a joyous blue. You feel the warm breeze ruffling your hair, whispering in your ears, and the sun feels warm and gentle on your skin. You breathe deeply with delight. There are wildflowers growing in the meadow all around you and their sweet honeylike fragrance fills you with pleasure. As you continue to walk on the springy green grass that carpets the meadow, and breathe in the fresh flower smells, you notice a grove of trees in the distance, a circle of slender young saplings with young, vibrant green leaves that toss joyously in the wind, shiny and new.

You walk toward the grove, noticing how the trees seem to be dancing together in the breeze. Now you can see that someone is standing in the center of the grove, a young maiden crowned with a circlet of flowers. As you near the grove, she holds out her hands toward you and you walk into the circle of trees and take her hands, and you both laugh and twirl each other in a circle with your joined hands. When you stop, you both sit down and face each other, and you know that this Spring Maiden has something important to tell you, something for you alone to hear. It may be a new idea that will inspire you this spring, or a word of comfort or advice. (Pause for about a minute to allow time for the message to be given.)

You smile and thank her, and you reach into your pocket and find a special small treasure to give her. You both stand up and she hugs you. Then you walk out of the circle, away from the trees, walking back across the meadow, walking slowly back to this room and your ordinary awareness. Wiggle your fingers and toes, stretch, and open your eyes.

Now it's time for the feast that everyone has helped to make. You can take turns, after you sit down, saying what it is you would like to see blossom and grow for the family, the community, and the world in the coming months. Then you can make plans and send some energy to help those wishes manifest. And we always like to remind the children that they are the incarnation of spring and the ongoing renewal of life.

After the feast, there may be storytelling or amateur theatrics, an outdoor walk or an indoor cuddle—whatever feels right to your family.

We like to leave the window open a little in the bedroom at night starting on Ostara. The fresh air helps us to sleep better and, besides, that way we can be sure to hear the first spring peepers and smell all the delicious damp green smells that let us know spring is really here.

BELTANE

Flowering
May 1

To our ancient ancestors, sex was sacred. It was the force that brought forth new life and made life worth living, and so they celebrated the ancient Beltane festival to honor fertile sexual energy, dancing their dances around phallic maypoles that recalled the World Tree, making love in the newly planted fields, and generally having a wonderful time.

But our culture and our attitudes toward sex have undergone some big shifts since those days. Many of us were teens in the permissive 1960s and 1970s: we're no strangers to the idea of happy, carefree sex and openness about lovemaking. But the shadow of herpes and the full blown nightmare of AIDS have changed our feelings about sex forever.

And there's another very real thorn among the roses: childhood sexual abuse, once inconceivable except to its victims (estimated to be a staggering one out of three among girls, one out of seven among boys), is now recognized, openly discussed—and we are getting hyperconscious. A friend recently took some snapshots of her little boy, playing without his diaper on, by the lakeside at her parents' home in Florida. When her mother strolled down to the beach and saw the camera, she gasped and said, "Don't let anybody see you doing that! You can get arrested here for taking nude photos of children!"

This is not an easy time. Once, no one spoke out. Now we live in an atmosphere of constant suspicion and accusation. Want to get back at your ex-spouse? Accuse her or him of child abuse. Substantiated or not, the horror sticks.

Add to all this another factor. Children are intensely physical beings, very firmly "in their bodies." And what does our culture tell them? Madison Avenue makes money by feeding our physical insecurities, pushing everything from acne medicines to feminine hygiene deodorant sprays to diet pills to mouthwashes. Everywhere the message is blared that we are not good enough; that our bodies look bad and smell bad; and that the only way to be okay is to spray, rub, drink, and gargle our humanness away.

So what can we do to encourage a positive, responsible, joyous attitude toward sex for our children? We offer this Beltane section as a way to begin the healing process for all of us. To find a balanced and heart-centered way to feel about sensuality, which will someday be the basis for our children's emerging sexuality. Because while we want to warn them about the very real dangers of unprotected sex, we also want them to feel wonderful about their bodies, about themselves. We want to let our children know how perfect they are *just as they are,* without the intervention of countless carcinogenic chemicals and "beauty aids." We want to celebrate their healthy physicality.

We gave a lot of thought to our activities for Beltane and chose these precisely because they allow all of us to feel good in our bodies—and proud of them. The first activity has a very important function: it makes a connection between ourselves and the Goddess, the Earth Mother who gives us such bounty, year after year. We all can use a reminder that we are a part of her sacred body. If children grow up knowing that their bodies are sacred manifestations of a powerful and magical force—not objects or commodities or instruments of power over others—they will make wiser choices about what they do with those bodies. The ancients called Beltane a fire festival and celebrated it with huge bonfires. Sexuality is a fiery power; never before have we seen more clearly the devastation it can cause. But it is also one of the chief makers of warmth and light in our world, a real way to oneness with another and with our concept of deity.

BELTANE ACTIVITIES

CREATE A GARDEN GODDESS

Beltane honors the earth in her time of flowering. There is nothing stingy or self-effacing about this season, and we make our own link to this spirit of cosmic generosity by making small images of the Earth Mother to place in our gardens or window boxes.

First, choose materials with weather in mind. If you don't mind your goddess suffering a sea-change, you can use just about anything and then enjoy watching her transformation after repeated rain showers and bakings in the sun: beeswax, feathers, metals (such as coat hangers), water-based paints, and paper will all do interesting things after being exposed to the weather. If you want your goddess to stay the same, your choices are more limited. If you have access to a kiln, making your image out of clay and then firing it is a great solution. Or you can buy one of the oven-baked varieties of clay at your local craft store. A hand-carved wooden goddess will last a while, especially if you oil her or coat her with beeswax. Or you can find a rock that says "goddess" to you and then paint or otherwise adorn her, or simply leave her as is. Once you start looking, you'll be amazed at the infinite number of goddess-rocks there are. (In our home, we have at least a dozen owl-rocks. We find owls everywhere. Next time you take a walk, look and you'll see.) Children will enjoy the search for materials as much as the process of making the images. They'll find seashells, twigs, nutshells, buttons, string, ribbons—empty out your old junk drawers and sewing boxes and go crazy, or take a special walk, on the lookout for things to use.

The form each goddess takes will be as unique as the child who makes it. What does the Earth Mother look like to your children? It's fascinating to see what they come up with. Some will make goddesses that are the traditional large-breasted, large-bellied, large-hipped variety, a clear parallel between the fertile earth and the primary sex characteristics of a fertile, childbearing woman. But other goddesses may be more ethereal; one of our personal favorites was a bare tree branch hung with wispy bits of fabric that floated in the breeze.

There are no rules here (and you can't have too many goddesses). The only thing to keep in mind is that these images are being made to bless and protect the family garden, a sort of calling down of the great universal fertile energy into your own piece of land.

While you are making your images, you can sing songs to link with each other and with the earth. There are a number of Native American–inspired songs that will work perfectly here.

> *The earth is our mother*
> *We must take care of her*
> *The earth is our mother*
> *We must take care of her*
> *Hey and a ho and a hey yan yan*
> *Hey and a ho and a hey yan yan*
>
> *We walk upon her sacred ground*
> *With every step we take*
> *We walk upon her sacred ground*
> *With every step we take*
> *Hey and a ho and a hey yan yan*
> *Hey and a ho and a hey yan yan*

After the goddesses are completed, you may want to have a family ritual to consecrate them. Smudging them with special incense smoke, sprinkling them with salt water, singing them a special song, and then carrying them out to the garden in a procession will all add to your sense of the special. And none of this needs to be solemn: kazoos make a welcome addition to the processional music.

MAKE SCENTED MASSAGE OILS

The Beltane season is perfect for pampering one another with a relaxing massage. Touch is our first language, a way to communicate our love and caring in a direct and uncomplicated way, and children will love both giving and receiving a soothing, sweet-smelling massage with oils that they have scented and prepared themselves.

You can buy the base (or carrier) for your scented oils at any natural-foods store: sweet almond, jojoba, grapeseed, calendula, sesame, even sunflower or olive oil all work well. Some are more expensive than others, and many have a heavier feel and scent. Experiment with blends that feel good to your skin and are pleasant to your nose.

Once you've chosen a carrier oil, you're ready to play. Everyone will need a clean bottle or jar that corks or has a screw-on lid, enough carrier oil to fill it, and some goodies with which to scent the oil. Essential oils can be expensive, but they are certainly worth it; we discourage using synthetics. Or you can try some of the thriftier alternatives listed below.

Essential oils, available through catalogs or from health and natural-foods shops. The scents of essential oils have different effects on people (see Suggested Reading at the back of the book if you decide to learn more about aromatherapy). With just a little study, you can experiment with blends that relax and soothe, or that invigorate; each family member will have different needs and preferences.

Dried materials, such as spices (allspice is nice) or pieces of scented wood (sandalwood, cedar, juniper). Tonka beans may also be added to oil and will give it a wonderful spicy/vanilla scent.

Fresh flowers and herbs. Dandelion flowers, for example, are a wonderful addition to your oil and are usually plentiful around this time. Pick them when the dew has dried and stuff them, unwashed, into a widemouthed bottle or jar (fill almost to the top), then fill the jar again with your carrier oil. You can keep this mixture for about six weeks in a cool place. After that, strain out the flowers: you can use them for a poultice or return them to the earth. The strained oil should be refrigerated or at least kept in a cool place. This oil is great for skin complaints, sore muscles, and headaches.

Violet flowers are another lovely idea. They don't give your oil much of a scent, but they'll turn it a beautiful color. Follow the same procedure as with dandelion flowers.

Be careful when you use certain herbs, spices, or essential oils in your blend: cloves and thyme both smell wonderful, but more than a couple of drops can burn the skin.

Gemstones may be kept in your oil bottle. They not only look mysterious and beautiful, but they are said to impart their particular qualities to the blend. If you want to know more about the spiritual properties of gems and minerals, see Suggested Reading.

Here are two recipes to get you started, but you will want to come up with your own concoctions.

Beltane Massage Oil

patchouli oil
rose oil (if you can't afford it, substitute rose geranium, or simply omit)
lavender oil
ylang-ylang oil
ginger oil

To a small bottle of carrier oil, add a few drops of each of the essential oils in proportions that feel right to you. Mix well, then add a small rose quartz stone to the blend (rose quartz has traditional associations with love).

Essence of Spring Massage Oil

This refreshing, energizing blend has citrus notes that really wake you up, and a solar warmth that soothes as well as invigorates.

patchouli oil
tangerine oil
lemon verbena oil

To a small bottle of carrier oil, add a few drops of each of the essential oils. Mix well and add a piece of jade to the bottle—because of its vibrant green color, jade is associated with the earth and was often buried in gardens to promote growth and fertility. You can sprinkle a few drops of this oil on your garden.

Because some oils may stain and all can be a little messy, you will want to put a towel underneath the person receiving the massage. Consult one of the many books available on the subject or just dive right in; if you're firm yet gentle, you can't go too far wrong.

You may find you have started a family tradition. Whenever our children are tense or tired, they ask us to massage their feet.

And your scented oils don't have to be used exclusively for massage; a few drops in the bath are great, and they make terrific skin moisturizers. Use your blends in a homemade aromatherapy pot, add to potpourris, or use to anoint candles or light bulbs. Before you know it, your family and your home will smell delicious.

FLOWER CHILD

Fun and inspiring, this activity helps us to visualize ourselves as directly involved in the blooming of Beltane. First, to help each participant sidestep the inner critic that blocks so much of our creativity, set the mood with dreamy or rhythmic music (there are numerous flute, dulcimer, or drum tapes that will work wonderfully.) Next, burn some of your home-made incense; this is another way to bring yourselves into a sense of sacred time and space.

Once you have established a relaxed and special atmosphere, give each participant a sheet of paper, some crayons or paints or markers, and a mirror. Each person then makes a simple self-portrait—it doesn't have to be great art, or even look like its subject, as long as the artist is having fun. After the basic portrait is complete, have the participants draw or paint a flower garland on the head of the figure in the picture. Title it _____ of the May (Queen, Prince, King, Princess—or some other title that feels powerful and ap-propriate) and have a grand procession with each artist carrying her or his portrait to a designated display area. Offerings of flowers may be placed before each one. Then the entire royal family may toast each other with special tea or juice.

MAGICAL BATHS

Besides the massage mentioned earlier, another way to be kind to our bodies is to take special baths. We include recipes for making your own bath preparations, and some ideas for making bathtime a time for magic and fun that the whole family will enjoy.

First of all, preparing the bathing area and creating a special atmosphere is essential. This is not just a bath to wash off the grime—this is a magical activity that will make you all feel renewed, purified, and inspired. Besides, it's fun. So, with the addition of some burning incense and candles, perhaps a few gemstones and flowers, you can turn your bathroom into a place of mystery and beauty that will appeal to the Wild Child in all of you. Let the children decorate: you may end up with festoons of vines and flowers draped over the mirror, seashells adorning the toilet tank, and potted plants in a jungle all over the floor, but it will be great.

Music also makes a great addition to the mood. Many bewitching tapes are available these days that add special magic to the proceedings; or you can make your own sounds. You haven't lived until you've been serenaded in the bath.

Once the stage is set, you have a number of options. We'll start with the easiest and least expensive ideas and work our way up to the things that take more time and money.

Both oats and honey, traditional at Beltane, are great additions to the bath as well as to the diet. Honey is a natural humectant, which means it is kind to dry skin, and its undeniable gloppiness makes this idea a favorite with children everywhere.

Honey Bath

Do this one while sitting in a tub of warm water, using a honey bear or a widemouthed container filled with honey. Participants either squeeze honey onto their hands or dip into the cup and pat the sweet and sticky stuff on their faces, necks, arms, or whatever. Then, using both hands, continue to pat until the honey gets *very* sticky indeed. If you do this long enough, you will actually be pulling the skin up with every pat, which is terrific for the circulation. Everyone will end up with a wonderful pink glow. When you've had enough, simply rinse off the honey.

Oatmeal Bath

We discovered the miraculous soothing properties of oatmeal when we had poison ivy and, later, chicken pox. But why wait until you're itching to play with this wonderful slimy stuff?

We have found that a muslin teabag (available at natural-foods stores or through herbal catalogues) makes an ideal container for your oats, but any cotton cloth will do, as long as the oats are tied or knotted firmly within; escapees will clog the plumbing.

So—fill your cloth or bag with plain old-fashioned oats and tie firmly shut. Participants may hold this oat bag underneath the running water as the tub fills (they'll love the way it makes the water milky looking). Then use the oat bag as a washcloth, rubbing the soothing slime all over. Your children will enjoy shaking hands with the unwary after they've done this.

Other Easy Baths

Cleopatra used asses' milk in her bath, but regular cow's milk (or goat's milk if you like the smell) makes a pleasing addition to the bath. For added fun, float a few violet flowers on top of the water. Just be sure to pick all the flowers out before you drain the tub.

Or you can have the bather lie in the tub and gently toss blossoms of any variety at her or him. Make it a magical game: be the child's good fairy and send wishes along with the blossoms.

Ever try adding a large liter bottle of seltzer to the tub? Children love fizz.

Squeeze a lemon into the tub and add a handful of sea salt. This is a traditional purification bath.

Make a strong herbal tea and add it to the bath. Chamomile is soothing, peppermint is refreshing, and mugwort will relax you and give you deep dreams. You can experiment. Dried lavender flowers or rose petals are especially nice at Beltane and can be placed in a cloth just like the oats—a big tea bag for the tub.

Add some of your massage oil to the bath, or mix a few drops of the essential oils that appeal to each person, to make a unique, personalized scent.

You can easily make your own bath salts by adding a few drops of the appropriate essential oils to the bath-salt base. You can either buy expensive unscented mineral salts for this, or you can mix your own. Once you have learned to make the bath-salt base, you can make your own bath salts. You can use the same ingredients listed above in the massage oil recipes, or you can try the following (and then experiment on your own).

Bath-Salt Base

3 parts Epsom salts
2 parts baking soda
1 part sea salt

You may also add 1 to 2 parts powdered mineral clay (available from herbal catalogs or natural-foods stores) to help absorb impurities.

Magical Feel-Good Bath Salts

rosemary oil
lavender oil
sandalwood oil

To the bath-salt base, add a few drops of the essential oils in the proportions that feel right to you. Mix well with a spoon until all the base has been moistened with oils.

Green Lady Bath Salts

This recipe is in honor of the Queen of the May, the Forest Goddess, the Lady of the Greenwood.

> *patchouli oil*
> *cedarwood oil*
> *rosemary oil*

Add drops of the essential oils to your bath-salt base. You may add a few drops of green food coloring to this blend along with the oils.

You can store your bath salts in glass jars or bottles with pretty labels—and it's a lot of fun to invent your own names for original blends.

CREATING THE BELTANE ALTAR
FLOWERS, FIRE, GODDESS IMAGES, REPRESENTATIONS OF THE SEX ORGANS

This is the time for flowers, lots of them. Some regions are lucky enough to have lilacs blooming at this time; they are a wonderful addition to the altar, but any flower will do. Wild ones that you pick yourselves are especially meaningful. After they wither, you may want to bury them in your garden plot.

Since Beltane was originally one of the great solar fire festivals, you will want to include a container for a small blaze or arrange several candles in warm colors such as pink, red, or peach—or you can make a real bonfire outside and place the altar near it.

Your garden goddesses will feel right at home on the altar; the energy they absorb from the festivities will be a good addition to the garden after you place them there.

Many earth-based cultures include images of the sex organs in their spiritual observances, and Beltane is certainly the time for us to consider this. Treating the sex organs as holy does good things for our inner selves—particularly for women, who were often raised to think that "down there" (since most of us were never even taught a name for this) was something shameful, disgusting, and smelly. We can do our little girls a great favor and supersede the culture's messages. Get them used to the idea that their female parts are beautiful, flowerlike, and sacred.

For your altar, you don't have to be literal (unless you want to be); a vaguely phallic rock and a creviced stone or bowl (or the flowers you have already included) will do just as well as a graphic depiction. Or you can make a special place for a bell, symbol of the union of male and female (male clapper inside female shell), or a yin-yang symbol, which shows how masculine and feminine values interpenetrate and complete each other, both necessary parts of the circle of life and self. Or you can make a small circlet of green stalks and flowers with which to crown your phallic rock—this is another centuries-old image for the union of male and female.

Don't forget to include the Flower Child self-portraits: you can frame them and make garlands of fresh blossoms to loop over the frames.

SPECIAL BELTANE FOOD

EDIBLE FLOWERS, DAIRY PRODUCTS, OATS, HONEY

Now is the time to enjoy edible flowers such as dandelion and violet. Put a handful of blossoms in your fresh-picked wild greens salad, and the result will be both beautiful and tasty.

May wine has been associated with Beltane for centuries; you can make your own by infusing any white wine with sweet-smelling dried woodruff (or use fresh woodruff if you can get it). Children can make their own special drink by infusing their favorite juice with this lovely herb. Both drinks may be served with sliced strawberries.

Main dishes for Beltane often include dairy products, since this is the time of great abundance on the dairy farm: new calves mean lots of milk. If you don't want to support the often inhumane dairy industry, or if you simply don't eat dairy products, then you might enjoy a meal made with oats, another traditional Beltane food (oats have long been associated with sexuality, as in "sowing your wild oats"). You can make oats into loaves or special cakes, either pan-fried or baked.

Asparagus, with its phallic shape reminiscent of the maypole and its vibrant green color, is another perfect choice for the Beltane meal. Lightly steamed and served in a bundle tied with ribbon or wild onion greens, asparagus adds vitamins and visual appeal to the feast.

Beltane desserts are often made with honey, a traditional favorite of the Goddess, and may be decorated with crystallized violets or rose petals, or with colored sugar-coated almonds. It can be fun to bake a special cake and wreath it with garlands of fresh flowers as well.

THE FAMILY BELTANE

The first thing you may want to do, following an old tradition, is to waken while there is still dew on the grass. Bathing your face in the dew of May Morning is said to bestow beauty all year long. More sedate children will use their hands to gather the dew. Others will wallow.

If it's a nice day, you can set your altar space up outside. You may want to make flower wreaths for those who will wear them; pick flowers with long, flexible stems and simply braid them together. Forsythia is about the thickest stem you'll want to try; unless it's thin and flexible, it will break. Searching for flowers to use is a good way to pay attention to the amazing energy all around us at this time of year.

Then you can stand or sit around your altar and talk about the things that are flowering for your family right now. Maybe one of you is involved in a creative project or has been newly promoted. Another may be making new friends or discovering new interests. Whatever you choose to celebrate now will echo nature's activity.

Even if you don't do a traditional maypole, Beltane is a perfect day for the whole family to hold hands in a circle and dance. Outside is the preferred place for this, but indoors works fine if the weather is disagreeable. You can simply skip around, or you can learn traditional circle-dance steps like the grapevine. All dancers hold hands in circle and move continually to the left. First, move left foot one step to the left. Next, bring right foot behind left foot. Then step left with left foot again. Now bring right foot in front of left foot. Continue until dizzy or exhausted.

After you've raised some energy with dancing (and singing if you feel like it), you can plant your garden goddesses in your garden. Beltane is a good time to do a garden blessing, which can include making small offerings of beverages (May wine is good, or juice), sprinkling the garden with special oil, and burying small gifts in the earth. Crystals and gemstones are ideal for this, or you can leave a piece of fingernail or hair from each family member.

Making a bonfire is satisfying and exciting and makes a direct connection with our pagan ancestors. You will need to use very careful supervision to avoid accidents, and be sure to check the fire codes in your neighborhood—in ours, for example, uncontained fires are not allowed, so we have to use a hibachi or grill.

Everyone can get in on gathering fallen twigs and branches for the fire and placing them in a circular sun-shaped mound. You can throw in some incense once it's lit, and a bunch or two of wildflowers tied with ribbon. If it's rainy, try making a miniature bonfire in a safe container on your altar indoors; though matchstick-sized twigs burn quickly, there is still magic in a tiny blaze. You can even decorate it with small flowers, such as baby's breath.

After everyone has danced up an appetite, it can be fun to decorate the table for the feast with vines and flowers wreathing each plate, and bunches of ribbon-tied flowers for each family member; bringing nature indoors is an activity that brings out the Wild Child in all of us. After the feast, as you digest, you may want to take turns giving each other a massage with your scented oils.

If the weather permits, Beltane is a wonderful time to sit quietly outdoors and simply look at and listen to the incredible hubbub going on. Children will enjoy pointing out birds and insects, squirrels and other wildlife as they go about their business. Nature spirits are very strongly felt at this time: there is an age-old tradition of seeing faeries at Beltane. See how quiet you can be, and you may sense something nearby.

A special bath before bed is a good way to wind down after the excitement of the day. After preparing the bathroom and the bath, you can help the participants visualize all their cares and tension gently leaving their bodies, being drawn out by the warm, scented water. You can plant the idea that this special bath will purify and strengthen them to face the tasks of spring.

After the children are asleep, you and your partner may want to have some special time together; decorate your bedroom with flowers and candles, or make love outdoors. Forces much larger than our individual selves flow through us at Beltane and every act of love and pleasure becomes a celebration of the life force in all of us.

SUMMER

Summer is a celebration of the earth's incredible bounty. Just like the song says, in summertime the livin' is easy: a few steps from our back door are bushes heavy with ripe raspberries, and across the yard is the mulberry tree simply dripping with sweet, soft fruit. Tomatoes ripen and zucchini appear magically overnight in the garden; flowers in all the colors of the sun and sky grace the fields and highways. A gentle chorus of insects sings us to sleep at night as we lie stretched out in bed, our skin smelling sweet and sun-warmed after a long day outdoors. And the scent of smoke from neighboring barbecues and bonfires—and the faery lights of fireflies off for a night on the town—remind us of fire, summer's element.

Summer is a festival of this inner fire-power, the power that makes abundance and nourishment grow from tiny seeds. The power that brings things to fulfillment, that expands and brightens our lives, that makes good things come from seed-ideas and plans. And the warmth of the sun and the long, hot days continually remind us of how good it is to find a balance between intense activity and lazy, idle hours doing nothing.

Summer teaches us patience. The fruit is green until it's ripe and you just can't rush it. Something of the slow, sure rhythm of the time will enter into us if we let it; no, we can't hurry things, but if we just relax and let go, things will reach their fullness without effort or ego-striving on our part. And as we watch the ripening and flowering and fruiting all around us, we can't help but be moved by and grateful for the generosity of the Earth Mother, who gives us what we need so unstintingly. Summer is a perfect time to discover our earth connection: by receiving her gifts with respect, taking only what we need, and doing what we can to minimize our impact on the delicate balance of the planet, we strengthen and nourish the bond we were given at birth with the great parent who sustains us all.

Many of us take vacations in summer; we can use this time to create whole days of celebration around the ancient festivals that honor the earth's life-giving relationship with the sun. By entering into activities that teach respect for and connection with these great powers—vital sun and nourishing earth—we align ourselves with those powers in a very deep and real way.

And as we watch the fields baking in the heat—as we feel the sun's power to burn as well as to bless—we can feel our own gifts, our own special abilities as they ripen and swell, and know that we, too, have the power to make a difference for growth or for destruction in the world. The great festivals of summer teach us how to use our power wisely for the good of all.

LITHA

Summer Solstice
June 20-23

Litha, the solstice, marks the zenith of the sun, the longest day of the year, when the sun's power is at its peak. It is a time to mark peak moments, moments of warmth and growth. Our ancestors built huge bonfires on this day to celebrate their tangible connection to the vital power of the immense burning star that keeps our planet bright, warm, and alive. It's a good time to remember that we, like the sun, contain the power to nurture and sustain, and that we have a responsibility to burn as brightly as we can.

Z. Budapest, witchy feminist author of *The Grandmother of Time,* tells us that this festival, also known as Midsummer Day, is named for the goddess Litha, known in Europe and North Africa as a goddess of fertility, power, and order. In Celtic countries there were torchlight processions through the fields on this day, and cattle were driven between two bonfires to purify and protect them.

Litha is the time to invite fire into our lives—fire to burn away all that we have outgrown and all that no longer serves us; fire that makes the wild things grow in us, for which our inner selves have longed. We are not in this alone: that, more than any other, is the primary lesson of the festivals, and of this book. We are all connected—people, planet, and sun. If we align ourselves with the power in others and in the natural forces around us, what we are unable to do with our own puny ego-selves can be made to happen—if it is attuned to the needs of the inner self and of those with whom we are connected. By gently sharing this basic truth with our children, we will save them a lifetime of alienation and futility.

The activities we have chosen for Litha are simple ways for children to show their respect for the earth and to make a tangible connection with the sun, to invite solar power into their lives. Making round, golden shapes that mimic the sun is as time-honored and old as memory, and having a visible reminder of warmth hanging nearby when the days begin to shorten and the winds grow chilly can be wonderfully heartening. The moment of peak power is very, very brief. Honoring and acknowledging this empowers us to seize the moment—and to prepare for the inevitable future.

Making special wands is magical indeed; when made by young hands, they are not only full of very real power, they teach some important truths as well. Real magic doesn't go "poof" and happen dramatically; it has a rhythm as slow as the berries ripening on the vine. But it is real. And we are all magic wands, in a sense: our very bodies become channels for forces larger than ourselves. Guiding our children to explore their powerful energies and to use them for the greater good, as well as for their own safety and comfort, becomes a gift to the planet and all who share it.

And there is nothing as sweet as watching our children dance in the sun, faces shining, dazzling and splendid in the Sun Child crowns they made. This warm and enchanting way to end the Litha activities encourages our sons and daughters to celebrate and empower themselves by reminding them of their likeness to the sun, and creates a little extra brightness on this longest day of all.

LITHA ACTIVITIES

HONORING THE EARTH

It is difficult to teach our children respect for the earth if they see us wasting its resources on a daily basis. Litha is a perfect time to clean up our act, if we haven't already done so. Take a good look at the amount of garbage your family produces and see where you can cut back. Make a trip to the recycling center part of your yearly ritual: if your community has curbside recycling, then incorporate a park or other community-site clean-up as part of your celebration. Write eco-minded letters to government officials today; the sun's power, like a great spotlight, will help you to focus on what needs to change, and its fiery warmth will give your words strength and passion. Speaking from the heart is a tremendous force for good.

Litha is also a good day to take a hard look at the products you use around the house and on your person. Enlist the help of the whole family to scout out toxins where they may be hiding in your home; read the labels on your detergents and cleansers, on your shampoo bottles and tubes of antiperspirant—and then work together to find healthier alternatives. Explore your local natural-foods store for low-impact cleaning and personal care products, or make your own using the recipes in Annie Berthold-Bond's book *Clean and Green*—she gives hundreds of ideas for natural ways to keep you and your home smelling and feeling clean and sweet. (For example, why use nasty chlorine bleach–based cleansers when baking soda works just as well? Make a paste with water and let it sit on your stained sink for a few minutes, then scrub. Citrus-based cleaners are amazingly effective against odors and grease, or you can try plain old pumice-based Lava soap to scrub away really serious grime. Pure castile soap can be used for everything from toothpaste to bath soap to shampoo, and you can add a few drops of your favorite essential oil to scent it.)

Try to use paper products that have been recycled without chlorine bleaching—your local grocery store probably carries Marcal paper towels and tissues, and the Seventh Generation catalogue offers excellent toilet paper and lots of other wonderful products to help you become more eco-conscious. Feel good about helping to save the trees that are our planet's lungs.

The sun's power today helps us to shake off the fog of helplessness or habit that keeps us locked in patterns that are destructive to our planet and to one another (see Suggested Reading for books that will help you get started). After a little initial effort, you will find that it's just as easy to use natural, harmless products as it was to use the other kind, and you can feel so much better about your earth-loving choice.

The following simple activity will help remind us of our commitment to sustain and protect the life of this planet.

Salvaged Planet

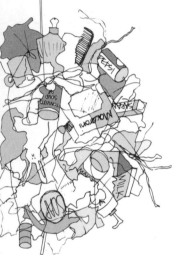

Go through the household wastebaskets and gather things that aren't food items, or potentially germy or decomposed; children love to ransack the trash for treasures, and now's their chance to turn their finds into a visual reminder of our responsibility to the Great Mother.

Have the family sit in a circle around this pile of salvaged stuff. Now each family member closes their eyes and grabs something from the pile. Open your eyes. What is it? Where did it come from? Who used it? How could its trip to the trash can have been avoided? How could it have been reused?

Next, with everyone working together, using string, twist-ties, or some other item from the trash, crumple and bind the salvaged items together in the rough shape of a ball or globe. Hang this masterpiece somewhere to remind yourselves that this is what could happen to the earth if we don't change our habits.

Then, to show how we can help to nourish the earth, take some of the soil from the bottom of your compost heap, if you have one, and strew it around your garden as fertilizer. If you don't compost, take some leftover vegetable food scraps and bury them in the earth. Make a commitment to start composting now, if you can; it's surprisingly simple and very satisfying.

Composting: Giving Back to the Mother

You can pay for a fancy composter—or you can make your own with a metal drum or simply allocate a corner of your yard for compost. Many people cover their open compost piles periodically with grass clippings to keep down flies and odor, and some stir it occasionally to keep it well aerated. Only eggshells and vegetable material should go into your pile, but this can include tea bags, coffee grounds, dead flowers, and Yuletide evergreens as well as the usual food scraps. Many of us keep a small pail on our kitchen countertops that we fill with kitchen waste; when it's full, our children take a trip to the compost heap.

As they fling your contribution onto the pile (and most children love to do this), they can visualize giving energy back to the earth. Talk to them about the rich soil your refuse will help to create; gardens love it, and when it's time to transplant pot-bound houseplants, a cup or so of well-rotted compost in the bottom of the pot will make your plant's new home a nutritious and happy one.

MAKE A SOLAR IMAGE

Hundreds of years ago today, our ancestors sat in sun-drenched fields or on stones as warm as living flesh, fashioning small round suns from straw or vines, decorating them with sun-colored flowers, honoring the mysterious, fiery light that warmed and brightened their days and made the plants grow that fed them.

The human response to anything round and golden or warmly colored is immediate, primal, and positive. If you have made your image while sitting in the strongest sunlight of the year, allowing it to shine on and infuse your creation, you bring that strong, life-promoting energy indoors with you when you are done. After Litha the days begin to shorten; in the knowledge that cold and dark surely lie ahead, it can be comforting to have this visual image where we can see it and be reminded of our connection to this vastly powerful life-giver, remembering that the sun will not forsake us, that life will continue.

Children love to create their own small suns to hang above their beds or over their doors, and the possibilities for creative play here are endless: there are as many different ways to make solar images as there are children's personalities. The only prerequisites are that it be round and that its colors evoke the sun's warmth and passionate splendor.

Here are just a few ideas for possible materials to get your youngsters going. Chances are that they will come up with their own marvelous and surprising inventions that will work just as well. If you can, make your images outdoors in the sunshine.

- Grapevine wreaths make excellent bases, which may then be decorated with fresh or dried flowers and yarn or ribbons. You can home-dye your yarn and ribbon using onion skins (just as you did with your Ostara eggs) to achieve a rich terra-cotta or golden yellow, depending on how long you boil them in the pot with the skins.
- Modeling clay comes in many types, some self-hardening or bakeable. Get out the toothpicks, chopsticks, and other carving implements, and make suns with jolly faces.

- Your older children may want to make a mold out of bakeable clay and experiment with handmade paper pressed into it, allowed to dry, and then painted gold—many catalogs sell similar solar ornaments at Christmas. Recycled handmade paper is easy and fun to make. Here are some simple instructions. Rip several sheets of used paper—office paper, construction paper, or newspaper—into bite-size pieces. Toss into a bucket of water and allow to soften, at least ten minutes or more. Then take a few handfuls of this paper sludge, draining off some of the water between your fingers (this part is messy—your children will love it), and whiz in a blender. Press the resulting paper pulp into your mold, using folded towels to press out excess moisture, and then air-dry (in the sun.) You can also buy pottery cookie molds that will work well with your homemade paper.

- Modeling beeswax, which you warm with your hands and then use as you would playdough or clay, is another good choice for a solar image. Or you can pour melted beeswax into your baked clay mold (you may want to lightly grease it first) and allow it to harden partially, then remove it. Beeswax is golden already, and you also end up with a sun that smells sweet. Just be careful not to let it sit too long in strong sunlight or it will revert to a bloblike state.

- Very young children may want to crumple bright tissue paper into balls or use blunt scissors to cut gilt paper into solar shapes with rays they can stick on with paste afterward.

- Crayon shavings can be grated onto wax paper and carefully melted with an iron between two sheets of brown paper bag—adult supervision required—and then cut into a round shape to hang in a window as a stained-glass sun-catcher. Older children may want to try their hand at making more elaborate stained-glass creations using one of the kits available at craft or hobby shops.

- Help your children to cut oranges into quarter-inch round slices: they can be strung and hung in a sunny window or placed on a cookie sheet in a low oven to dry. The result is beautiful, sweet-smelling, and very solar-looking.

- Older children can recycle a tin can bottom and either punch or tin-snip a pleasing pattern on it. Or they can stretch fabric in an embroidery hoop and paint with fabric paint or embroider: the result is hung, hoop and all.

- Wood-carvers will want to whittle and paint a sun out of wood. Younger children can color or paint on cardboard and then cut out their sun with sturdy scissors, punch a hole, string, and hang.
- Children of all ages enjoy finding four slender sticks from the yard, crossing them to make an asterisk shape with eight spokes—reminiscent of the eight festivals of the year—and winding brightly colored yarns and ribbons around and around to make a round solar variation on the ancient "God's Eye" shape. If four sticks are too bulky for small fingers to manage, use only three—the solar shape is more hexagonal but still appealing. Poke in a flower or two for an especially pleasing result—marigolds and daisies are the classic sunny favorites.

When the images are finished, your children may want to hold them up to the sky for a few moments so that the sun shines on them. They can be used to decorate the family Litha altar, then hung in the house (or in a tree outdoors, if your little ones prefer) and displayed with pride.

MAKE A MAGIC WAND

The wise women and men in our ancestors' villages knew how to make magic wands. And how to use them. A magic wand is a way to amplify and send our personal energy out into the world, so that it can manifest to benefit us all. But, unlike cartoons that make this kind of magic look both intensely dramatic and instantaneous, real wands are not showy or made for instant gratification; real magic often takes time to happen. But a magic wand can help to get things going—it starts the user thinking in the right direction and sends a positive message to the universe—and it will enchant your children. Just be sure to stress the importance of using the wand only for good, never with the intention of harming another.

First, have your child find a natural tree branch (some prefer to cut it live from the tree, but we find that fallen limbs are less painful to the tree and work just as well) that can be broken or cut to measure the exact length of your child's forearm from fingertip to inner crook of elbow. (Wands do get outgrown; in time, she'll have to make another, longer wand.) The bark may be peeled off or left on; if your branch looks scaly, you will want to peel it now to avoid flaking later.

Next, choose a special crystal, about an inch or so in length. Crystals are transmitters, and unpolished, natural quartz points are recommended, but you may want to use a rose quartz, amethyst, or other stone that is special to your child. Attach the point to the stick, allowing half of the pointed end of the crystal or more to extend beyond the end of the stick, using a rubber band or glue or a thin, wet leather thong (when the leather dries, it will tighten). Then wrap this juncture of crystal and tip of stick with thin copper wire, available at craft and hobby shops or electronics stores. (Copper is a conductor; energy travels through it.)

Then your child can decorate the wand to personalize it, using ribbons, feathers, shells, small gemstones glued into hollows carved into the stick, and symbols or runes, also carved into the wood.

When everyone's wand is completed, you may want to hold a wand blessing, which could include purifying the new wands with salt and water, or smudging them with sage or sweetgrass. Then you can consecrate the wands by visualizing them glowing with power and energy, and each child can say a few words to cement her relationship with this beautiful and powerful new tool: "This is my wand and I will use it to make things better." You can devise simple or elaborate rituals to empower your wands and your children—twirling around three times, holding the wand up to the sky and then down to the earth, doing a wand dance, singing a wand song—whatever appeals to your children and feels right to you. Then they can make a first wish, picturing the desired result as if it were already an accomplished fact, and sending energy to make it happen down the wand and out into the world. Visualization is helpful here: some children see energy as lightning bolts, as bluish rays, or as a golden glow. Yours may imagine something completely different. When the wishes have been made, know that the sun's power at this time of year will help to bring many of them to fruition.

MAKE A SUN CHILD CROWN

As part of this season's solar focus, you can help boost self-esteem by making a visual and physical connection between your child and the sun's vivid, bright energy. Children need to feel a sense of their own brilliance, and one way to achieve this is by having your child make and wear a special crown, so that she or he becomes an embodiment of the growth-promoting and magical sun. In a culture rife with violence and negativity, encouraging your child to become one with this healthy and life-affirming image becomes a positive step for our world. And by honoring our little ones for their incredible power to grow and change and become ever more deeply themselves, we teach them to shine brightly.

The crown should be comfortable, wearable, and as flashy as possible: the point is for the child's head to radiate and shine as brilliantly as the sun. Most children adore sparkling stuff, so this is a chance for them to indulge their taste for glitter and glitz.

Some ideas for good crown bases include grapevine or flower wreaths, either purchased or homemade, or the twisted paper sold in craft and hobby shops, untwisted and braided if desired. Raffia or straw and wide ribbon also make good bases, twisted or braided, and there are some great metallic crowns available at party or costume shops that work well. You can also cut basic crown shapes from cardboard or construction paper. Check the fit before decorating.

Trim can include live flowers and dried flowers, and ribbons, cord, or metallic ric-rac for streamers. Then comes the shiny stuff: costume jewelry, sequins, gilt paint, crystals, rhinestones, tiny mirrors, glitter, glow-in-the-dark paint, even battery-pack lights for the technically inclined are all great additions to a basic crown. Get out the glue and stand back. (If you're using a hot-glue gun, though, supervise carefully.)

After the crowns are complete, you may want to have a grand coronation ceremony, invoking the sun's positive energy and praising your children as manifestations of its power. If it is a sunny day, place each child with the sun behind her head, and then, after she has been crowned, hold up a mirror so she can see herself shining. If you are indoors, set up a lamp so that you will get a similar effect. Some children will want to wear their crowns all day as proud reminders. Some will be loathe to take them off at bedtime. If glow-in-the-dark paint or battery-pack lights were used, you can let your child see the effect after the lights go out.

CREATING THE LITHA ALTAR
SUN IMAGES, FLAME, FRUITS, FLOWERS

Bring down the round warmth of the sun to bless your altar by including the solar images your children made—or do a group project and paint a picture of the sun all together to display. Or you can make the altar itself in the sun's shape, using a round table or large log set on end.

It is important to have some sort of fire on your altar. Depending on the ages of your children and the resulting possible safety hazard, you may want to use a warm-colored votive candle in glass rather than an open flame.

With so much wonderful fresh fruit available at this time of year, it is easy to have a few mouthwatering reminders of the earth's bounty on your altar; if your altar is outdoors, it is especially lovely to eat the fruit after it has been warmed by the sun. If you are lucky enough to have berries growing in your yard, your children will want to gather some to arrange in a circle on the altar. It is a special, satisfying ritual activity to make round solar patterns today, so if there are no berries at hand, your children could use small pebbles instead.

There is usually a profusion of sunlike flowers growing wild at Litha and many of them, in shades of gold and orange and yellow, or because of the rayed effect of petals surrounding a glowing center, make perfect sunlike offerings: daisies, black-eyed Susans, chamomile, Saint-John's-wort, marigolds, zinnias, and dandelions are fun to gather and arrange. Sunflowers make the perfect altar decoration, but, alas, they don't bloom in most regions until later in the season. Try your local craft shop for a beautiful fake in paper or silk. Roses are a traditional flower for Litha as well.

If you have a Polaroid camera, you may want to include pictures of your children wearing their crowns. And many of us choose to place a representation of the earth—a small globe or one of the famous photos taken from the moon—on the altar as a gentle reminder to honor her.

SPECIAL LITHA FOOD
FRUIT, AND ANYTHING SPICY, GRILLED OVER A FIRE, OR FLAMING

There are multiple possibilities for creating special Litha meals. Caribbean sauces or Cajun blackened dishes, golden curries, Mexican peppers, and Szechuan spices are all perfect reminders of the sun's blazing heat. If your children dislike hot foods, simply marinating some vegetables in a mildly spicy sauce and grilling them over the traditional Litha bonfire or the family barbecue grill will do. You can also marinate fresh raw onions (a mild variety, such as Vidalia, will work best) and tomatoes cut into rounds as a special salad, or make a more usual tossed salad with the unusual addition of a few fresh marigold flowers or nasturtium blossoms.

Zucchini blossoms are often available fresh from the garden at this time of year; sautéed, they make a beautiful sun-colored side dish, or you can make them into fritters with a little flour and egg. Dandelion flowers are an interesting base for fritters, as well; some children look askance at these, but if you can persuade them to taste one, the fritters will disappear in no time.

Dandelion wine, or herbal iced tea with lemon slices, make appealing adult beverages for Litha, and sunny yellow lemonade is a favorite with children. Make your own the old-fashioned way with a lemon-reamer, elbow grease, and the sweetener of your choice.

Litha Lemonade
One serving

1 1/2 Tbs. lemon juice
3 Tbs. sugar, honey, or rice syrup

Add the ingredients to one cup of warm water. Stir well until sweetener has dissolved. Then ice well and serve with lemon rounds.

If the weather cooperates, this can be the perfect day to picnic together in a beautiful, natural spot or in your own backyard. Sharing your Litha food outdoors in a conscious way, while enjoying the sun's warmth and one another's company, will make a special memory, and cleaning up the area after your feast is a quiet way to show respect for the planet.

For dessert, there is nothing as spectacular as a flambé: make a simple seasonal fruit salad, using the fruits from your altar, warm it, and pour some good-quality brandy over it. Light it with a match (the alcohol will burn off) and serve. This is especially bewitching after dark.

THE FAMILY LITHA

This is the sun's peak day. One way to weave the significance of this into your family's lives is to share memories of peak experiences with one another: the time you laughed the hardest, ran the fastest, felt the happiest. Know that the sun will take a year to return to this time of greatest strength. This festival has much to teach us about living in the present moment, appreciating the peaks while realizing that they don't last forever and honoring the time it takes to build back up again.

Spend the day becoming aware of the sun. Being mindful of its position in the sky throughout the day is a simple and powerful way to honor it. Notice the shadows and how they shift, and how different things reflect the sun's brilliance—if you can visit a river, lake, or other body of water, celebrate the shimmer and gleam of light on ripples. Watch the leaves on the trees around you. Catch the reflection of the sun in a mirror or a pan of water. Then ask each other how *you* shine. What are your special gifts? How do you make life brighter for each other? Join hands in a circle and raise your faces to the sun. Feel your feet firmly standing on the earth.

You may want to wear special clothes in colors that make you feel festive and sunny. If you enjoy making costumes, you can sew soft collars and skirts from strips of old clothing, which will be reminiscent of flower petals or sun rays.

Litha is the traditional day to gather many varieties of wild herbs to hang and dry indoors. Consult a pocket field guide to find out what you have growing in your yard, or take a weed walk with a local herbalist. There are many pretty weeds available in most regions now: red clover, smartweed, Saint-John's-wort, Queen Anne's lace, and tansy are all beautiful when dried. Vervain has been gathered at Litha for centuries to protect the home and banish negativity from it, and if you have mugwort in your garden, today is the traditional day to harvest its leaves and dry them for use in dream pillows and teas. Experiment to see which flowers dry well; some are lovely when they're alive but lose their color when dried—chicory's vibrant blue blossoms, for instance, quickly turn a faded brownish lavender.

You will need to caution your children about nettles, which sting, and about poison ivy and oak. And don't eat anything unless you're sure it's safe: lamb's-quarters, purslane, and wood sorrel are all delicious, but poison hemlock and the berries of deadly nightshade will kill you.

Cut your herbs, keeping the leaves on, after the dew has dried, and hang them upside down in small bunches in a warm, dry location. Many of us favor the kitchen for this, since the herbs make it look magical and children love to have the results of their labors displayed for all to see. Besides, it creates an intimate connection with the wild plants thriving near you.

Families may want to bring representations of projects or creative endeavors to the Litha gathering; these can certainly use some of the sun's empowering energy to help them ripen, or, if a project is already finished, the maker can bask in the rays of the sun and enjoy her empowering kinship with it.

Show how the sun translates into flame by experimenting (carefully) with a magnifying glass and bits of paper. You may be able to light your bonfire—an important traditional part of the Litha celebration—using this magical method.

If you are able to have bonfires in your neighborhood, you can make a special fire that will often form the shape of the sun, rays and all, as it burns: place the tips of your branches or small logs with their ends all raised and touching in the center—like a tepee—with the kindling material inside. There is usually a fiery crash at some point in the fire and all the logs fall, making the blazing rays. (As always, be especially careful to keep your young ones at a safe distance.) You can achieve the same effect in a round grill or hibachi, using smaller branches. If any kind of open fire is out of the question, light an oil lamp or candle: many votive holders are decorated so that the light from them forms rays. It is traditional to light your Litha flame so that it continues to burn after the sun has set.

One traditional use for the Litha bonfire is to ritualize the shedding of things that no longer serve us, consigning to the purifying flames what does not promote life and growth. Each family member takes a small piece of paper and writes down or draws a picture of what she or he would like to get rid of: a self-limiting habit, a fear, a negative attitude. Then, either silently or aloud, each person asks the fire to help destroy it, burn it away, freeing them to become stronger and more empowered. One friend's daughter asked the fire to help her overcome her paralyzing shyness; now she carries a small sunflower in her knapsack to remind her that she is a Sun Child. Another reports that her son's bedwetting decreased markedly after he "burned it" in the Litha fire.

After everyone has burned their papers—watching the mysterious transformation into smoke and ash—hold your hands out toward the fire and feel the heat. You may want to dance around the fire until you feel hot, too—and know that the energy inside you can make changes just as intense and mysterious.

It becomes especially important on Litha to mark the passing of the sun at sunset; there won't be another day this long for a year. Some children will want to wave as the sun goes down or sing a little song. Then you will have the fire or flame still with you as a reminder. As you gather around its glow, hold one another close and feel the warmth in your bodies; see the fire dancing in one another's eyes.

As the darkness deepens, many of us remember chasing the fireflies of dusk with out-stretched hands, and it can be both sweet and satisfying to watch our children do the same. As they chase the elusive, tiny lights back and forth, gently capture them, and then release them back into the night sky, your little ones can send messages of love to fly along with the fireflies. Let their elfish gleam, and that of the fiery stars blazing far away, light your way to bed. And as you drift off to sleep, know that the sun is still shining on the other side of the world.

LUGHNASAD

First Harvest

August 1

Slowly the burgeoning energy of summer has shifted, and at Lughnasad we begin to see signs of the wheel's turning. The earth ripens and grows mellow—we can smell the warm and heavy difference in the air. All around us, plants once stiff with juice are softening, drying, going to seed. Everywhere are the signs of early harvest, with roadside stands and farm markets overflowing with produce. The light at sunset grows hazy and golden, and the nighttime insect lullabies outside our windows are softer and less strident, weaving through our dreams. Summer has passed its prime.

This festival is named for the ancient Celtic sun god, Lugh, one of several gods that must die to be reborn; Lughnasad becomes a feast of mourning for his passing. Old songs such as "John Barleycorn" echo the idea of the grain personified, who willingly allows his body to be sacrificed so that the people will be fed. Our ancestors understood this great drama in their very bones; some fashioned huge figures made of grain with bread dough in their bellies. Then, at the height of the Lughnasad celebration, these figures were thrown into the bonfire and consumed. When the ashes had cooled, the dough, now magically transformed into bread, was shared and eaten in token of the grain's great sacrifice of love. To even earlier people, this was the time to honor the loving Earth Mother, who blesses the fields with grain from her endless bounty in order for her children to thrive.

The sacred grain is the central symbol for this festival, especially in the form of bread baked with reverent consciousness of the earth that provides our nourishment; this festival is also known as Lammas, or "Loaf-mass."

The harvest was literally a matter of life or death to our ancestors: a poor harvest would mean starvation, and the knowledge that many would not live to see another spring. A good harvest at Lughnasad was cause for rejoicing, but there was also some uncertainty; after all, there was still the second, main harvest to come. Lughnasad is an in-between time, and our early ancestors baked their special, magical loaves of bread from this first harvest partly in hopes of pleasing the Goddess, to ensure even greater abundance later on. They also braided elaborate wheat goddesses to hang in their homes, in reverence for her great and generous spirit. Our first activity combines the idea of honoring the Earth Mother with making a harvest figure: we can teach our children to make simple green goddess shapes from the grasses and weeds close at hand, honoring the cycle of sprouting, growing, fruiting, decaying, and seeding again.

Like the early people who made offerings of wine, oil, beer, or mead to the first sheaves in the fields, we can foster respect for growing things by encouraging deep relationship with the trees on the land we share—and by leaving them offerings with thanks and love, our second activity for this special season.

Lughnasad celebrates transformation: the seed that grows, flowers, and fruits finally becomes the food that sustains us. The grain that stands tall and ripe in the fields is cut down, separated from the chaff, ground into flour, and baked into life-giving bread. Our third activity honors transformation by slowing us down and giving us a focused way to pay attention. Out of the mindful participation in a common miracle can come a profound appreciation of change on many levels.

Perhaps, above all, Lughnasad marks the seed time, when everything begins its gradual descent. No longer growing, blooming, or fruiting, the plants turn their energies to seed, preparing for the inevitable winter, but holding the promise of new life in spring. The seeds give us an imperious command to pay attention: in the dying body of the old is contained the mystery of renewal. By encouraging our children to discover and honor the seeds, we remind them of this mystery. And when we really notice the plants that surround us, we grow into a very deep respect for their cycles and rhythms, and an understanding of the patterns in our own lives.

LUGHNASAD ACTIVITIES

MAKE A HARVEST FIGURE

Bringing the green indoors in the form of a special goddess shape or harvest figure to bless the home and remind us of the earth's bounty is a satisfying activity that makes living connections to our planet and to our ancestors who originated this lovely way to honor the Earth Mother.

There are a number of craft books now available with instructions for braiding beautiful and elaborate wheat straw figures, but unless you grew the wheat yourself, you can make a stronger link with the land you live on by making a simple shape from things found on your particular spot of earth.

First, look at your garden or at the wild things growing nearby. If you are growing corn this year, the shucks and more slender stalks will work beautifully to make corn goddesses. (One year a single stalk of corn magically appeared among our tomatoes—from a seed dropped by some passing crow, perhaps. The little earth goddess we carved from its dried and stunted ear was a truly special one.) Or you may have leftover bean vines or other long, flexible plants that can be fashioned into harvest figures. If you don't have a garden, a handful of long grass, wild grapevine, or any pliable weed will give pleasing results that even the youngest child can master.

Gathering the plants for your figure is half the fun. Make a party of it. You can give each of the children a basket for carrying their finds, and, if they like the idea, a small trove of gifts to place on the ground next to the plants they pick, as a thank-you or give-back to the earth. Native peoples on this continent used pinches of cornmeal or tobacco to thank the plant spirits. You may want to use tiny crystals or a spoonful of compost.

Once you have gathered your green treasures, choose a comfortable spot to sit, and begin. Although there are countless ways to create a harvest figure, here is our favorite method:

Double a handful of stalks to form the head, tying with string or a twist-tie about two inches from the loop for the neck. Tie another piece of string a few inches down for the waist, and insert a bunch of stalks crosswise between neck and waist for arms, tying with string at the wrists. The stalks hanging below the waist can be a female figure's skirt, or you can separate the stalks into two bunches and tie them both at the ankle for a male figure—harvest figures can be male or female, depending on the preference of your child, since both vegetation gods and earth goddesses are honored at this time. Leaves clinging to the stalks make graceful additions to your figure, and you may want to add a few finishing touches: a tiny clover crown, or a necklace or belt made of some contrasting weed or plant.

You can place the figures on your family altar for your Lughnasad celebration. Afterwards, have a grand procession as you bring the harvest figures indoors and hang them in a special place.

HONOR THE TREES: MAKE OFFERINGS

Trees give us so much: shade; fresh air; nesting places for the wild creatures; branches for kindling, wands, or craft projects; leaves for decoration; nuts or fruit to eat or admire. They have such generous and kindly spirits—we've never met a tree we didn't like. Children love to hang out with them; those who are sensitive to such things will begin to feel their different personalities and will see each one as a special and valuable friend.

You can encourage this relationship by trying the following activity from Joseph Cornell's *Sharing the Joy of Nature*. Blindfold your children and lead them to a tree. Allow each child to touch and smell and listen. Little fingers love to explore the deep grooves and rough shagginess of a hickory or to stroke the smooth, papery birch; and evergreens are easy to recognize, with their fresh, sharp scent and sharper needles. After the children have had several minutes to explore, lead them away, remove the blindfolds, and see if they can figure out which one was "their" tree.

Or try this as a family: sit with your backs against a tree trunk and quiet your minds, breathing deeply and fully for a few moments. Watch the patterns of light and shade formed by the sun on the tree's leaves. Listen to the sounds made by the wind through its branches. Feel the roughness or smoothness of its bark, and smell its unique smell—some trees smell spicy, others nutlike or earthy. Then close your eyes and allow the tree to "talk" to you in its own language. What feelings come to you? What do you perceive as the tree's mood? What does it have to teach you? Many of us have found that, when we are tense or unhappy, we can go and sit beside a tree in this way and something of the tree's grounded energy and quiet wisdom will enter into us, soothing and comforting our troubles away.

With all that trees are, with all that they give us, it becomes a sweet gesture of thanks and respect at this season to give little gifts (like those we left as thank-you offerings for the harvest figure plants) to the trees that live nearby.

You can give your trees ceremonial pinches of cornmeal or tobacco, or small crystals, pennies, or seashells, or something more personal, like a fingernail clipping or strand of hair. Get a field guide and learn the names of your trees. Then find out what fertilizer each type needs and invest in some plant-food spikes from your neighborhood nursery. Talk to your trees, and listen to them. Soon they will be sending their energy deep underground to sleep through the long, cold winter. Celebrate their powerful presence in our lives during these warm, waning days of summer.

HERBAL ICE-CUBE CIRCLE

By focusing our attention on things that shift and change in obvious but deeply magical ways, we encourage our children (and ourselves) to slow down, pause, and take notice. This activity celebrates the sun's power to make change occur. A simple, powerful way to take time out and to focus the self toward a specific feeling or purpose, the ice-cube circle is a way for all of us to deepen in new respect for the many transformations that go on around us all the time.

First, choose an herb to make into tea, depending on what it is each child wants to honor or invoke today. If you want more friendship, try lavender; for more mental energy, try peppermint or rosemary. Borage is a traditional herb for courage; chamomile brings relaxation; and mugwort encourages us to hear our wise inner wisdom. Take a look at Correspondences on page 204 for information, or consult one of the herb books from Suggested Reading to find out the properties of the plants you have readily available.

Now make a strong tea, using about one-quarter cup of the dried herb to a quart of boiled water. Allow to steep until the tea has reached room temperature, then strain and refrigerate. When the tea has cooled, put aside a cup of it in a special glass or mug (many children will not want to drink unadulterated herb tea; for them, mix the tea half-and-half with fruit juice), and pour the rest into ice-cube trays. Children will enjoy poking a few sprigs of dried herb into each compartment of the tray before the cubes have frozen solid.

Now go outside and sit in a comfortable place with your glass of tea and your cubes. If it is a hot day, a shady spot will work fine; or you can sit in the sun, as long as you are wearing plenty of sunscreen.

First, take a little time to open and become receptive to your surroundings. What does the ground feel like under your seat? What green things are growing around you? Can you see any small creatures—bees, gnats, spiders—busy in the grass or the air? Notice the scents and sounds that wrap themselves around you. This will be your sacred spot, your power circle.

Now, carefully place the ice cubes from your tray in a circle around you, as you think about the quality you are inviting into your life. You may want to make up a little rhyme or song and say it aloud as you place the cubes on the ground. This Native American–inspired chant is a warm ally:

Where we sit is holy, holy is the ground
Forest, mountain, river, listen to the sound
Great Spirit circling all around us
Oh yay yay yay yay yay yay

Then, when your circle is complete, slowly sip your tea and pay close attention to the cubes. Watch carefully as the sun and the warmth make them change. As they melt, imagine that the energy of the herb is releasing itself into your life, making a strong and powerful circle around you. Smaller children, who may find it difficult to sit still for long periods of time, may want to sing and dance inside the circle to help the ice cubes melt. And if the tea is too weird for them to drink even when mixed with juice, they can simply dip their fingers into the glass and splash some about.

When you have finished drinking (or splashing) the tea, and the cubes have been completely transformed, take another moment to feel the power of the sun and the herbs, the solid shapes that have shifted and flowed and become one with the earth. Then touch the moisture remaining on the ground around you and place a little on your forehead or "third eye," to make a physical link with the energies of your tea.

DISCOVER SEEDS

At this seeding time of year, it becomes a special way of appreciating the season to really notice and admire the tiny packets of potential that are silently forming all around you. Take a leisurely walk as a family and see how many different kinds of seeds you can find. Graceful unmowed grass, mullein with its stiff brown heads, tenacious burdock's clinging burrs—all are part of the great dance of preparation and life's continuing.

Blow away the dandelion's airy puffs and make a wish. Open a bell pepper and eat the seeds inside rather than putting them in the compost pail. Harvest some dock seeds, sprinkle them on your salad, and enjoy the crunch, knowing you are eating nature's concentrated nourishment. Enjoy the pattern of the sunflower's seeds as they grow in their perfect spiral shape. Make yourselves a seed snack with pumpkin seeds, sesame seeds, and sunflower seeds to munch—leftovers make great gifts for the birds. And if you gardened this year, gather some seeds to save for next year's planting and store them, labeled, in a safe dark drawer.

As a final way to mark the seeding, collect several of as many different kinds of seeds from your yard and pantry as you can, and use them to make a mosaic with craft glue on wood or cardboard. Suns, spirals, or earth goddesses, made with all the myriad colors and shapes of your special seeds, will make beautiful and meaningful additions to your Lughnasad altar and, later, to your home; children love to make patterns in this way.

CREATING THE LUGHNASAD ALTAR
HARVEST FIGURE, BREAD, SEASONAL PRODUCE, SEEDS

A loaf of bread that the entire family had a hand in making is often at the center of the Lughnasad altar, flanked by the harvest figures made by our children. Many of us include a wooden bowl heaped with seasonal fruits and vegetables; if you have a garden, it will feel very satisfying to include a few of everything that you've grown—the jewel-like colors of bell peppers, eggplant, and tomatoes are beautiful reminders of the earth's bounty.

As well as displaying the seed mosaics they have created, children love to make simple or complicated patterns with loose seeds directly on the altar itself. Gather as many as you can find and let them sprinkle away to their hearts' content. If your altar is outdoors, these can be left out for the birds when your celebration is over.

An earthenware pot or vase filled with a handful of seeded weeds that our children have gathered is fitting, and beeswax candles, with their golden color and sweet scent that reminds us of the bees' harvest, are a lovely addition to the altar, as well. We sometimes carve little bees into the wax or stick on small metal or enameled pins in their shape, to honor and thank these marvelous creatures.

SPECIAL LUGHNASAD FOOD
BREAD, GRAINS, FRESH VEGETABLES AND FRUITS

What a mystery it must have been to our early ancestors to discover that dough could puff up and change! Combining this idea of magical transformation with the grain that is the central image for Lughnasad, baking a special loaf of bread becomes a ritual offering that aligns us with the earth and with the spirit of the festival.

This is the perfect opportunity to share the special pleasures of yeast-baking with your children, if you haven't already. Children love to hear that yeast is alive, little critters that feed on the milk and sweet stuff. You can explain that the yeast will die if the milk is too hot, and that if it's too cold, they'll be sluggish. After this, one friend's little boy insisted on keeping some of the yeast as pets.

If you just don't have enough time to make whole-grain yeasted bread, with its hours of rising, punching down, and rising again, then make a simple corn bread. What matters is that the entire process is undertaken with a special kind of consciousness. Imagine what this bread would mean to you if you depended upon it for survival; think how precious every grain of wheat or kernel of corn would be to you if it were your main source of nourishment. Imagine how connected to it you would be if you had planted the seeds yourselves, weeded, harvested, winnowed, and ground it. Imagine how you would feel about the flour if you knew in your hearts that it was the body of the Goddess or the sacrificial God.

Allow everyone to take a turn kneading the dough, if you can. You may want to make several small loaves—one for each family member—as well as the large one for the altar. These small loaves may be decorated with the maker's handprint (although the shape disappears in baking, the energy remains) or with patterns cut gently into the dough with a knife. We love to make round loaves with spirals or pentacles cut into the top, sprinkled with seeds.

As your special bread bakes, really savor the aroma. When it is done, take time to appreciate its warmth, color, and texture. After making your own delicious breads, you will never feel quite the same about the tasteless stuff sold in supermarkets.

The following recipe (see page 198) is adapted from Pauline Campanelli's *Wheel of the Year*.

Lughnasad Loaves

2 cups warm milk
2 packages active dry yeast
1 tsp. salt
¹/₂ cup honey
¹/₄ cup dark brown sugar
3 Tbs. softened butter
2 cups unbleached white flour
1 cup rye flour
2 cups stone-ground whole-wheat flour

Combine the milk, yeast, salt, honey, and sugar in a bowl, cover, and put in a warm place to rise for about thirty minutes, until doubled in volume.

Add the butter and unbleached white flour and stir until bubbly. Children enjoy scraping off the flour from the top of a full measuring cup with a knife, and dumping in the ingredients is always sure to please.

Mix in the rye flour and whole-wheat flour. Give everybody a chance to stir. Then put a little flour on all hands and turn the dough out onto a floured board. Take turns kneading, adding in more unbleached white flour, just a little at a time, until the dough is smooth and elastic and doesn't stick to your fingers anymore. This is one of the most delightful parts of bread-making: a good dough feels yummy to the touch, soothing and reminiscent of skin. Early people made their Lughnasad loaves in the shape of human bodies and, when you feel the dough at this stage, it makes perfect sense.

Grease a large bowl and place the dough in it, turning it so that the dough is greased as well. Cover the bowl with a clean cloth and put it in a warm place to rise until doubled. This will take about an hour, depending on how often someone peeks at it to see how it's doing.

Punch the dough down and divide it in half. Form it into two round balls, slightly flattened, or into one large and several smaller ones, and place on greased baking sheets. Cover and put back into the warm place to rise and double again.

When the dough has risen again, cut your designs into the top of the loaves with a knife, or allow each child to press her or his hand gently onto the dough. Then brush the loaves with an egg beaten with a tablespoon of water, sprinkle with whole rolled oats or seeds if you like, and bake for about an hour in a preheated 350°F oven. The smaller loaves will take less time. When the loaves are done, they will sound hollow when tapped.

Along with the home-baked bread, Lughnasad foods include fresh vegetables and fruit from the garden; a ratatouille of onions, garlic, peppers, eggplant, and tomatoes all stewed in olive oil and their own natural juices makes a delicious Lughnasad supper. Children love to examine the garden for the most perfect vegetables they can find.

Ratatouille   Makes 4–6 servings

1 large eggplant, diced into 1-inch cubes
2 medium zucchini, sliced into 1/2-inch rounds
1 green pepper, cut into squares
1 large onion, chopped coarsely
2 cloves fresh garlic, chopped
2 Tbs. olive oil
3 fresh tomatoes, chopped
1 tsp. salt
1/2 tsp. dried basil
1/2 tsp. dried oregano
1/8 tsp. black or cayenne pepper (or to taste)

Using a heavy stockpot, sauté the garlic, onion, and green pepper in oil until soft. Stir in the eggplant and zucchini and continue to sauté for a few more minutes. Add the remaining ingredients, cover, and simmer about 30 minutes. Then uncover and increase the heat to evaporate some of the cooking juices, stirring occasionally.

Other Lughnasad meal ideas could include mushroom-barley pilaf or a stir-fry of garden vegetables served over bulghur wheat.

Adults may enjoy beer with the meal, traditional because of its grain-based ingredients. For the children, orchard cherry or pear juice, pure and organic from the natural-foods store, makes a special seasonal drink.

For dessert, try making a pear tart: arrange the slices of fruit in an overlapping spiral and glaze with honey. This sweet and sunlike wheel makes a fitting end to the Lughnasad meal.

THE FAMILY LUGHNASAD

Many of us like to wear grainlike or earthy colors today—green, gold, and brown make a direct connection with the Great Mother. Some children may enjoy making a belt or necklace from wild grapevine to wear, as well.

Baking your bread, time-consuming and deeply satisfying as it is, is often the central activity for the day. Like a magnet, it draws us back into the kitchen again and again to oversee the mystery of its transformation. Cutting and eating this special bread, while standing around the family altar, becomes a shared spiritual experience that awakens some very deep ancestral memories. And nothing tastes as good to children as the bread they have helped to mix, knead, and shape themselves. (See the recipe above, or feel free to invent family variations that will become a tradition. One Irish friend makes only oatmeal soda bread for Lughnasad, while another's daughter is partial to blue corn bread made with bits of hot pepper.)

It is traditional to burn a bit of bread from the family loaf in the Lughnasad bonfire, as well as the old harvest figures from last year. Anytime we do this kind of magical housecleaning, we are preparing the way for new blessings to come, and each family member can voice wishes for her or his own personal harvest.

After the bread has been eaten, and your special burning has been done, you may want to sit for a few minutes near the fire, listening to the birds and insects all around you and feeling the difference in the air and in the earth as the sun's energy goes deeper, glowing now from the plants that share our planet. As the fire dies, feel the warmth that lingers in the air and know that it will soon be growing chilly.

When the fire has cooled, it is time to bring the new harvest figures indoors. We like to do this with a great deal of hoopla and celebration, singing and clashing the lids of pots and pans, ringing small bells, and sometimes throwing bread crumbs colored with food coloring instead of confetti (nicer to both the earth and the birds) or a handful of birdseed.

Before bed, we often take a bat walk, looking expectantly up at the dusking sky in hopes of seeing these wonderful winged and furry creatures before colder weather drives them to barns and caves for their winter sleep. As they swoop and flitter around us, we are reminded that Halloween will be here before too long.

Then, as a fitting end to the day, we invite the cats to knead our tummies with their paws, in echo of the bread-making we did together. If yours is a catless household, you can play pat-a-cake with your youngest children and gently rub the backs or tummies of your older ones, feeling the smoothness of their skin like the silky dough you kneaded earlier and sending loving energy for bright harvests in their lives. Smell the dusty golden smells coming in the windows and begin to welcome back the fall.

PART 3

Magical Allies

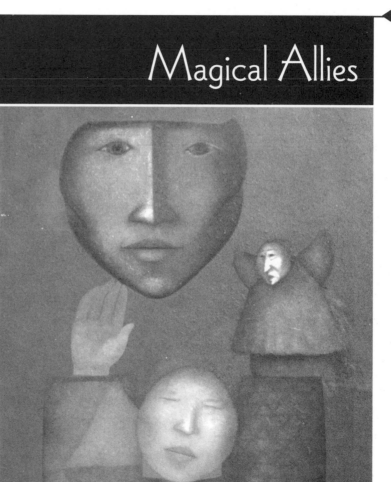

CORRESPONDENCES

The following allies may be consulted, combined, or otherwise enlisted for support whenever you have a specific need—talismans, rituals, and other focused activities can be helpful when your children are dealing with emotionally charged issues. Chapter 7 will give you some ideas on how to put a talisman together, and you might want to try some of the correspondence activities listed under the appropriate section. Or you may simply want to invite certain energies into your lives and homes and celebrate them; feel free to experiment and play. As always with any kind of magical work, be sure to back it up with concrete, practical action: talismans to protect your home, for example, will do their work more effectively if you remember to lock the front door.

CLEAR THINKING

If you have an important test or a big exam coming up, the following will help you study, memorize, and analyze. Use these allies anytime you need to have an especially clear head.

Animals: birds, especially hawks and eagles, winged insects
Colors: pastels, peach, turquoise blue, white, yellow
Direction: East
Foods, herbs, and plants: caraway, dill, lavender, parsley, peppermint, rosemary, sage, spearmint, celery, lentils, nuts, sprouts
Gems, minerals, and gifts of nature: agate, aventurine, feathers, fluorite, mica, rhodochrosite, topaz, turquoise
Goddesses: Aradia, Arianrhod, Athena
Incense or essential oil: frankincense, lavender, neroli, thyme
Tarot cards: Magician, Ace of Swords, Four of Swords

CLEAR-THINKING ACTIVITIES

Anoint a yellow candle with some lavender and frankincense oils, then dab a drop of each oil on your temples. Put a blue, yellow, or white feather in your hair. Visualize your mind growing wings that will help you to soar, to see clearly. Make a cup of rosemary and lavender tea, and bring it and the candle with you to your work or study space; then, with your books or papers spread out in front of you, light the candle (carefully, so that you don't start a fire) and sip the tea slowly as you think about the project at hand, gathering your thoughts and ideas together. Light a sage smudge and pass your pencil or pen through the smoke. Then close your eyes for a moment and invoke the goddess of your choice to help you in this endeavor—or make one up (try the goddess Midtermia, for instance, or the goddess Facta Remembra). Open your eyes and get to work. Use the candle as a focus for your resolve: will your mind to burn as clearly and brightly as its flame.

COMMUNICATION

If you are writing an important letter or paper, giving a speech, or preparing to speak your mind to someone, these correspondences will help you get your ideas across as clearly and successfully as possible.

Animals: bee, frog, hawk, whale, wolf
Colors: rainbow, violet
Foods, herbs, and plants: dill, fennel, horehound, lavender, licorice, valerian, black tea, carrots, coffee, hazelnuts, mushrooms, olives
Gems, minerals, and metals: agate, amber, citrine, copper, opal, sodalite, yellow fluorite
Goddesses: Athena, Maat, Metis
Incense or essential oil: cedar, honeysuckle, lavender, lily of the valley, sage, sweetgrass
Planets or celestial bodies: Mercury

COMMUNICATION ACTIVITIES

Burn a sweetgrass braid while you drink a cup of black tea with honey. Ask Whale to help you speak from the heart, say clearly what it is you need to say for the good of the group. Invoke the energies of the planet Mercury and think of the fluidity of quicksilver and its likeness to our amazing minds that move so swiftly. Remember the magical power of words. Become like Frog and speak out. Hold a hazelnut, traditional giver of wisdom, in your hand as you talk. Make yourself a communication talisman in a violet pouch with some of the herbal ingredients listed above. Pour a tablespoon of dried lavender onto your letter or paper after it is completed; spread the sweet-smelling flowers around so that they touch all the words, then pour them off and save the flowers in a special place until the letter has been received or the paper delivered: this is a traditional spell for successful communication.

CONFIDENCE, STRENGTH, SUCCESS

Use these correspondences whenever you need a little extra boost in the right direction, to help you feel brave, strong, and ready for anything, or to ensure the positive outcome of a situation.

Animals: bear, elk, horse, mountain lion, ox

Colors: gold, yellow, purple

Foods, herbs, and plants: bay, borage, catnip, cinnamon, clove, clover, dandelion, ginger, oak, sunflower

Gems and minerals: agate, amazonite, amber, bloodstone, carnelian, diamond, garnet, hematite, marble, ruby, rutilated quartz, smoky quartz, tiger's eye, tourmaline, turquoise

Goddesses: Bast, Brigid, Hera, Hestia, Isis, Juno

Incense or essential oil: cinnamon, clove, frankincense

Planets or celestial bodies: Jupiter, Sun

Tarot cards: Chariot, Strength, Wheel of Fortune, Sun, Six of Wands, Seven of Wands, Three of Cups, Nine of Cups

CONFIDENCE AND STRENGTH ACTIVITIES

Do a creative visualization and picture yourself riding fearlessly on the back of a horse or a mountain lion, bounding smoothly over all obstacles, tirelessly approaching your goal. Draw a picture of a sunflower and carry it with you; remind yourself that the warmth and power of the sun is always within you. Make a magic wand (see page 183 in the Litha section of Summer) and use it to focus your will toward your desired outcome. Paint a small sun or a spiral or a simple goddess shape on your chest, using face paints or clay. No one will know it's there except you—but its strength and power will help to charge you up. Make a strength talisman: rub some frankincense oil on a small piece of tiger's eye and wear it in a purple pouch around your neck. Or wear a purple shirt—purple is the traditional color of power and authority. If it's energizing sun strength that you need, wear something golden yellow. Drink some borage tea: the old saying, "Borage for courage," points to its traditional use of promoting bravery.

CREATIVITY

These magical allies will help you to unlock your creativity, loosen up your inner artist-self, and inspire you.

Animals: birds, spider

Colors: gold, silver, violet, yellow

Foods, herbs, and plants: acorns, bay, beech tree leaves or wood, cinnamon, ginseng, horehound, lavender, mace, seeds, valerian

Gems, minerals, and metals: agate, aventurine, carnelian, citrine, clear quartz crystals, gold, pyrite, sapphire, silver

Goddesses: Athena, Brigid, Cerridwen

Incense: bay laurel, cinnamon

Planets or celestial bodies: Earth, Mercury, Moon, Sun

Tarot cards: Magician, High Priestess, Empress, Star, Sun, Ace of Wands, Ace of Cups, Queen cards

CREATIVITY ACTIVITIES

Keep a small piece of citrine in your mouth, tucked in your cheek (be careful—don't choke; this is recommended for older children only). Or suck on an old-fashioned horehound drop—horehound is traditionally used to dissolve any blocks to creativity. Burn some bay laurel leaves on charcoal and think of the Delphic priestesses who breathed in the same smoke and were filled with divine inspiration. Call on Brigid, the Goddess of poetry and inspiration (among other things), and ask for her help. Draw a small spider on the back of your hand with a washable marker, and remember how the spider creates all she needs out of her own body. Do a creative visualization and become the Queen of Cups Tarot card: look deep within the chalice that you hold and see what there is to see. Carry some beech leaves or acorns in your pocket. Write down the first word that comes into your mind, and then the next, and the next, and the next. Continue simply writing down your thoughts for ten minutes. Read what you have written, dedicate it to Cerridwen, then crumple up the paper and burn it in a cauldron-shaped bowl (carefully, to avoid a fire). Ask Cerridwen to transform your words.

FRIENDSHIP, LOVE

The following correspondences will make you feel more lovable and help you to attract a friend or romantic interest. Please be sure not to attempt to force anyone else's will: trust that the right person will be called to you, and don't try to work manipulative magic on anyone.

Animals: dog, dove, swan, wolf

Colors: green, orange, pink, rose red

Foods, herbs, and plants: basil, coriander, honey, jasmine, lavender, marjoram, meadow-sweet, myrrh, orris root, rose, rosemary, violet, apples, strawberries

Gems, minerals, and metals: amber, beryl, calcite, copper, emerald, jade, malachite, rose quartz, silver, topaz, tourmaline, turquoise

Goddesses: Aphrodite, Artemis (especially for friendships between girls or women), Astarte, Diana, Freya, Hathor, Isis, Oshun, Venus

Incense: benzoin, jasmine, lavender, patchouli, rose, violet

Planets or celestial bodies: Venus

Tarot cards: Lovers, Temperance, Ace of Cups, Two of Cups, Three of Cups, Six of Cups

FRIENDSHIP OR LOVE ACTIVITIES

Dust yourself with orris root, traditional to make yourself feel attractive. Burn some lavender incense. Carry a piece of rose quartz in your pocket to encourage yourself to feel open-hearted, loving, and receptive. If you are shy and wish to become more outgoing, carry a piece of turquoise. Make a copy of the Two of Cups or the Lovers, if a romantic relationship is desired, or the Six of Cups for friendship, and place it where you will see it often. Invoke your favorite Goddess and tell her what you're looking for in a relationship. Do you want a friend with whom to share your interests? Someone to have fun with? A serious relationship? Be as specific as you can and then work on allowing yourself to be authentic and open with the people you meet. Bake an apple pie or an apple cake with lots of cinnamon and share it with your classmates.

HAPPY HOME

Use these correspondences to promote harmony and happiness at home. No home can be happy all the time, but these allies will help.

Colors: *brown, green, yellow*
Foods, herbs, and plants: *allspice, basil, cinnamon, clove, honey, marjoram, nutmeg, rose, vanilla, apple*
Gems and minerals: *amethyst, chrysoprase, copper, yellow zircon*
Goddesses: *Heartha, Hera, Hestia, Isis, Juno*
Incense: *benzoin, cinnamon, vanilla*
Tarot cards: *Four of Wands, Ten of Cups, Nine of Pentacles*

HAPPY-HOME ACTIVITIES

Make some special sachets from cinnamon and just enough applesauce to make a stiff dough (yes, it really works). Roll out and cut with heart-shaped cookie cutters and dry the shapes on top of the refrigerator or radiator, then place one in every room of the house. Invest in a large amethyst cluster and put it where all family members will see it often. Sprinkle a little dried marjoram in the corners of the house to help everyone feel more loving. Invoke Hestia and invite her to share your happy home. Make an altar just to honor her in a special place and bring her little gifts of home-baked goodies or flowers picked from the garden. Plant a green plant in an earthenware pot and bury a tiny piece of cinnamon stick in the soil. Put it in a special spot and care for it well.

HEALING, HEALTH

These magical allies can be used to bolster the immune system and increase optimism and serenity—all of which are helpful in gaining better health—or may be used in combination with the healing method of your choice.

Animals: *butterfly, snake*
Colors: *blue, brown (for healing animals), green, gold*
Foods, herbs, and plants: *all healing herbs, bay, eucalyptus, garlic, thyme*
Gems and minerals: *agate, amber, amethyst, aventurine, azurite, citrine, clear quartz crystals, emerald, fluorite, jasper, lapis lazuli, peridot, rhodochrosite, tourmaline*
Goddesses: *Artemis, earth goddesses, Hygeia, Isis, moon goddesses*
Incense or essential oils: *frankincense, sandalwood, thyme*
Planets or celestial bodies: *Earth, Moon, Sun*
Tarot cards: *Star, Sun, Nine of Cups*

HEALING ACTIVITIES

If you are sick, picture yourself surrounded by a warm, safe cocoon of healing energy. Ask yourself what you will be when you emerge from this "time-out" of illness. What will it have taught you? How can you better love and nourish yourself while you are in your cocoon? Place special healing stones in the four corners of your bed. Invoke a healing goddess. Take a bath with a few drops of sandalwood and one or two drops of thyme oil (not too much—thyme can burn). If you want to help heal someone else and you have their permission, charge a special stone or crystal with healing energy—visualize it glowing with healing light—and then give it to the person to be healed. If your companion animal is ill, place the charged crystal near or underneath its sleeping place. Do a hands-on healing. Invoke your favorite Goddess and make the sickroom a temple to the Inner Healer. (See chapter 9 for more information on healing and wellness.)

INNER WISDOM

For use whenever you want to encourage your intuitive self; these magical helpers work well for deeper dreaming, divination, and psychic work of all kinds.

Animals: bear, owl

Colors: black, deep blue, silver, white

Foods, herbs, and plants: bay, chamomile, galangal, lovage, mugwort, star anise, valerian, vervain, wormwood

Gems and minerals: amethyst, crystal balls, Herkimer diamonds (double-terminated quartz points), jet, lapis lazuli, mica, milky quartz, moonstone, obsidian, selenite

Goddesses: Hecate, Cerridwen, all moon goddesses: Selena, Artemis, Diana, Hathor, Isis

Incense and essential oil: nutmeg, patchouli, sandalwood

Planets or celestial bodies: Moon

Tarot cards: High Priestess, Crone (Motherpeace deck), Moon

ACTIVITIES TO ENCOURAGE YOUR INNER WISDOM

Take a bath with a few drops each of nutmeg, patchouli, and sandalwood oils. Place the Crone card from the Motherpeace Tarot deck (or the High Priestess or Moon) near your workspace before doing any kind of divination or intuitive work, or underneath your pillow for deeper dreaming. Drink a cup of mugwort tea or place a few drops of mugwort tincture underneath your tongue. If you want to try scrying (see "The Family Samhain" on page 123 of Autumn), drop a little mugwort tincture into the bowl of water first, or rub a small mirror—or a crystal or crystal ball—with dried mugwort before you gaze into it. Light a dark blue or silver candle. Sleep with a Herkimer diamond near the bed (see chapter 5 for more information on dreaming). Ask for Bear to accompany you as you hibernate for the night.

PROTECTION

These magical allies help to dispel fear and anxiety and make you feel secure, safe, and protected.

Animals: badger, porcupine, wolf

Colors: blue, gray, silver, white

Foods, herbs, and plants: basil, bay, burdock, garlic, High Joan the Conqueress root, motherwort, nutmeg, purslane, rosemary, salt, vervain

Gems, minerals, and metals: agate, alexandrine, citrine, coral, crystal clusters, flint, fluorite, jet, malachite, sardonyx, silver, tiger's eye, turquoise

Goddesses: Artemis, Hera

Incense: cinnamon, sandalwood

Planets or celestial bodies: Moon, Sun

Tarot cards: Star, Sun, World

PROTECTION ACTIVITIES

Place a dried bay leaf above every window and door in the house, along with a pinch of salt. Walk around your space with a burning stick of sandalwood incense. Make a strong tea of dried vervain and use it to wash the doors, inside and out. Hang a bunch of fresh or dried rosemary branches in your room. Make a protection talisman with any of the ingredients above, and hide it in a safe place in your home or put it in your pocket. Visualize your ability to protect yourself, like porcupine with her quills or badger with her fierceness. Carry the bean rune for protection with you (see the bean rune activity on page 115 in the Samhain section of Autumn).

PURIFICATION, CLEANSING

We all have times of crabby moods, quarreling, tension, or simple "bad vibes" that could use some attention. These correspondences act as psychic housecleaners to restore balance and freshness to your home and your self. They are also useful to help you prepare for inner work when you need to feel clear of unwanted energies.

Colors: white

Foods, herbs, and plants: angelica, basil, bay, cedar, copal, lavender, lemon, lemon verbena, nutmeg, parsley, peppermint, rosemary, sage, salt, sweetgrass, thyme, tobacco, vervain

Gems and minerals: amber, aquamarine, azurite, bloodstone, clear quartz crystals, emerald, fluorite, lapis lazuli, malachite, obsidian, peridot, selenite

Goddesses: all of them will help

Incense and essential oil: copal, lavender, lemon, sage, sweetgrass, sandalwood, thyme

Tarot cards: Star

PURIFICATION ACTIVITIES

When the atmosphere is negative or tense, light a smudge stick (homemade, if possible— see the activity on page 129 in the Yule section of Winter) and give the entire house a going-over. Mix salt and water and sprinkle a little as you walk around the house clockwise. Hide a whole nutmeg in the drawers or cabinets of every room, or place a dish of them where they are most needed. Make a strong tea of angelica and use it to dust the furniture. Put the leftovers in your bucket, add soap and water, and mop the floors. Carry a clear quartz crystal with you and purify it periodically by allowing it to bathe in the light of the sun and the moon, soaking it in salt water overnight or burying it in salt for three days. Take a bath with the juice of a whole lemon (peel and all thrown in after juicing) and a handful of sea salt. Light a white candle. Take plenty of deep, cleansing breaths.

GATHERING LISTS

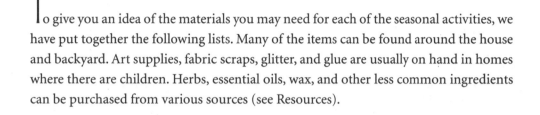

To give you an idea of the materials you may need for each of the seasonal activities, we have put together the following lists. Many of the items can be found around the house and backyard. Art supplies, fabric scraps, glitter, and glue are usually on hand in homes where there are children. Herbs, essential oils, wax, and other less common ingredients can be purchased from various sources (see Resources).

AUTUMN
MABON

Talking Stick

A special, found stick
Any or all of the following for trim and
    decoration:
    paint
    feathers
    gemstones
    cord or thong
Optional beeswax or beeswax-based
    polish

Dream Pillow

Fabric (all-natural if possible), approxi-
    mately ½ yard to ¾ yard for each
    pillow
Two cups of dried herbs in any combina-
    tion: mugwort, hops, lavender,
    rosemary, rose petals, etc.
Scissors
Pins, needles, and thread

Native American Corn Necklace

Ears of dried Native American corn in
    different colors
Needles and thread

Door Blessing

Base:
    three ears of Native American corn
    wreath (grapevine, straw, raffia,
        willow, etc.)
    tree branch
Any of the following decorations:
    Native American corn necklace
    dried apple slices
    Earth Goddess made of clay, corn
        shucks, carved apple, or weeds
    feathers
    crystals or gemstones
    nuts or seed-pods
    dried flowers or weeds from the yard
    symbols of personal harvests made
        from basic art supplies and
        cardboard or wood
Glue (hot-melt preferred, but only with
    careful supervision)

SAMHAIN

Bean Runes

Twenty-five large dried lima beans for
    each set of runes
Sharpie or other permanent marker

Samhain Cauldron

One or more Tarot decks
Cooking pot, large bowl, or cauldron
    (plastic ones are readily available at
    party supply stores)

Spirit Guide

Large turnip or rutabaga
Knife (supervision required)
Spoon for scooping
Instruments for etching the design:
    toothpicks, kabob skewers, chopsticks
Votive candles or tea-lights

WINTER

YULE

Smudge Stick

Several cedar branches, approximately
    one foot in length
Embroidery floss or thread

Sacred Cave

Rocks
Handmade figures from any of the
    following:
    modeling beeswax
    papier-mâché
    Sculpey or self-hardening clay
    assorted trims
    recycled materials
Votive candles or tea-lights

Handmade Yule Ornaments

Any or all of the following:
- fresh cranberries and popcorn for stringing
- gingerbread mix
- icing, paint, or trim
- flour/salt/water dough or yeast dough
- Sculpey or self-hardening clay
- solar images from Litha
- small grapevine wreaths
- gilded nuts or acorns
- sprigs of holly and ivy
- pomander balls
  - lemons, oranges, or apples
  - large needle
  - whole cloves
  - ground cinnamon, allspice, cloves, and orris root
- small paintings on cardboard or wood
- crystal points
- small bells
- dried pomegranates
- winter figures from dried weeds
- ribbon, braid, or trim
- small wrapped gifts

IMBOLC

Light Garden

- Baking or lasagna pan
- Soil
- Slips of paper
- Birthday candles

Music with Heart

Any or all of the following:
- rubber surgical gloves or large balloons
- sticks
- tin cans
- cardboard tubes, various sizes
- rocks
- hollow logs
- dried gourds
- empty soda cans or film canisters
- dried beans or pebbles
- glasses of water filled to different levels
- glass bottles
- copper pipe
- rubber bands
- flowerpots, pie tins, old toys, etc.

Handmade Candles

- Bulk beeswax, or paraffin wax and hardener (available at craft shops)
- Candle wicking
- Double-boiler or heavy pot for melting wax
- Large tin can
- Optional:
  - sand for sand candles
  - milk cartons
  - tin cans for pillar candles
  - leaves or pressed flowers for trim
  - small magical gifts (crystals, charms, etc.) to embed in wax
  - essential oils

Rainstick

Sturdy cardboard mailing tube with two
  end-pieces
One pound of nails for each rainstick, the
  same length as the diameter of the
  mailing tube

Hammer
Glue or tape
One or two cups of dried beans, lentils,
  seeds, or rice
Duct tape, contact paper, or brown paper
  and glue
Paints for decorating

SPRING

OSTARA

Plant Your Bean Runes

Bean runes from Samhain
Small flowerpot
Potting soil
Plastic wrap

Incense

Base (may use any of the following):
  ground cinnamon
  sawdust
  sandalwood powder or chips
Assorted dried herbs and essential oils
Mortar and pestle
Self-igniting charcoal
Heat-proof container filled with soil, ash,
  or clean kitty litter
Glass jars and labels for storing the
  finished incense

Dyeing Eggs Naturally

Eggs
Separate cooking pots for each color
Any of the following:
  onion skins
  fresh or canned beets
  red cabbage

Grass Pots

Medium-sized flowerpot
Potting soil
Paint or ribbon for decoration
Grass seed or catnip seeds

BELTANE

Garden Goddess

Any of the following:
  Sculpey or self-hardening clay
  modeling beeswax
  recycled materials
  wood
  fabric

twigs, rocks, and feathers
seashells
nuts, seeds, fresh or dried flowers and
  weeds
buttons, ribbons, string, costume
  jewelry
paints and other art supplies
varnish (optional)

MAGICAL
ALLIES

Massage Oils

Base or carrier oil: sweet almond, jojoba,
grapeseed, calendula, sesame,
sunflower, or olive oils
Any of the following:
essential oils
fresh or dried flowers
dried seeds and spices
gemstones

Flower Child

Mirror
Paper
Art supplies such as paints, markers, or
crayons

Magical Baths

Any of the following:
honey
oats
milk
fresh or dried flowers
seltzer
herbal teas
fresh lemon
sea salt
essential oils
Bath-salt base:
Epsom salts
baking soda
sea salt
powdered mineral clay (optional)

SUMMER
LITHA

Salvaged Planet

Salvage from family wastebaskets
String, glue, or twist-ties

Magic Wand

Natural tree branch cut to appropriate
length
Crystal point, approximately one inch
long
Rubber bands
Copper wire
Assorted decorations:
ribbons, braid, or trim
feathers
leather thongs
gemstones
carving knife

Solar Image

Any or all of the following:
modeling beeswax
bulk beeswax to pour into molds
handmade paper in molded shapes
clay
assorted papers: gilt, tissue, construction
grapevine wreaths
ribbons, braid, and trim
fresh or dried flowers
sticks and yarn
orange slices
crayon and wax paper "stained-glass"
embroidery frame, cloth, fabric paints
or embroidery threads
tin can bottoms and tools to punch or
snip
wood for carving
assorted art supplies

Sun Child Crown

Any of the following for the base:
  grapevine wreath
  twisted paper ribbon
  raffia, straw, or hay
  wide fabric ribbon
  costume crown
  cardboard or construction paper

Assorted trims, including:
  fresh or dried flowers
  ribbons, metallic braid or trim
  costume jewelry
  glitter
  paint
  glow-in-the-dark paint or putty
  battery-pack lights
Mirror

LUGHNASAD

Harvest Figure

Weeds, vines, or other green garden
  leftovers
String or twist-ties

Herbal Ice-Cube Circle

Dried herbs for tea
Ice-cube tray

Discover Seeds

Cardboard or wood for mosaic backing
Assorted seeds
Glue

SUGGESTED READING

The following listings are by no means exhaustive or definitive, but they will give you a place to start if you would like to learn more about the Goddess, women's spirituality, Wise Woman healing ways, dreams, herbs, gemstones, green housekeeping, Tarot, food, astrology, rituals, and more. See pages 226–227 for a list of references by subject areas.

Achterberg, Jeanne, Barbara Dossey, and Leslie Kolkmeier. *Rituals of Healing: Using Imagery for Health and Wellness*. New York: Bantam, 1994.

Adler, Margot. *Drawing Down the Moon: Witches, Druids, Goddess-Worshippers, and Other Pagans in America Today*. NewYork: Viking, 1979.

American Indian Society. *American Indian Society Cookbook*. Forestville, MD: Anaconda Press, 1984.

Arrien, Angeles. *The Tarot Handbook: Practical Applications of Ancient Visual Symbols*. Sonoma, CA: Arcus, 1987.

Ban Breathnach, Sarah. *Victorian Family Celebrations*. New York: Simon and Schuster, 1990.

Beck, Renee, and Sydney Barbara Metrick. *The Art of Ritual*. Berkeley: Celestial Arts, 1990.

Bernath, Stefen. *Common Weeds Coloring Book*. Mineola, NY: Dover, 1976.

Berthold-Bond, Annie. *Clean and Green: The Complete Guide to Nontoxic and Environmentally Safe Housekeeping*. Woodstock, NY: Ceres Press, 1990.

Bettelheim, Bruno. *The Uses of Enchantment: The Meaning and Importance of Fairy Tales*. New York: Alfred A. Knopf, 1976.

Beyerl, Paul. *The Master Book of Herbalism*. Custer, WA: Phoenix, 1984.

Blair, Nancy. *Amulets of the Goddess*. Oakland, CA: Wingbow Press, 1993.

Blum, Ralph. *The Book of Runes.* New York: St. Martin's, 1987.

Bolen, Jean Shinoda. *Crossing to Avalon: A Woman's Midlife Pilgrimage.* San Francisco: HarperSanFrancisco, 1994.

————. *Goddesses in Everywoman.* San Francisco: Harper & Row, 1984.

Brown, Dee. *Bury My Heart at Wounded Knee.* New York: Holt, Rinehart, Winston, 1970.

Budapest, Z. *Grandmother Moon: Lunar Magic in Our Lives.* San Francisco: HarperSanFrancisco, 1991.

————. *The Goddess in the Office.* San Francisco: HarperSanFrancisco, 1993.

————. *The Grandmother of Time.* San Francisco: HarperSanFrancisco, 1989.

————. *The Holy Book of Women's Mysteries,* rev. ed.Vols. 1 and 2. Berkeley, CA: Wingbow Press, 1986.

Cahill, Sedonia, and Joshua Halpern. *The Ceremonial Circle: Practice, Ritual, and Renewal for Personal and Community Healing.* San Francisco: HarperSanFrancisco, 1992.

Callan, Ginny. *Horn of the Moon Cookbook.* New York: Harper & Row, 1987.

Campanelli, Pauline. *Ancient Ways: Reclaiming Pagan Traditions.* St. Paul, MN: Llewellyn, 1991.

————. *Wheel of the Year: Living the Magickal Life.* St. Paul, MN: Llewellyn, 1987.

Carlson, Laurie. *EcoArt! Earth-Friendly Art and Craft Experiences for 3- to 9-Year-Olds.* Charlotte, VT: Williamson, 1993.

Copage, Eric V. *Kwanzaa: An African-American Celebration of Culture and Cooking.* New York: William Morrow, 1991.

Cornell, Joseph. *Sharing the Joy of Nature: Nature Activities for All Ages.* Nevada City, CA: Dawn, 1989.

Cowan, Tom. *Fire in the Head: Shamanism and the Celtic Spirit.* San Francisco: HarperSanFrancisco, 1993.

Crow Dog, Mary. *Lakota Woman.* New York: HarperCollins, 1990.

Cunningham, Scott. *The Complete Book of Incense, Oils, and Brews.* St. Paul, MN: Llewellyn, 1992.

————. *Cunningham's Encyclopedia of Crystal, Gem, and Metal Magic.* St. Paul, MN: Llewellyn, 1988.

————. *Cunningham's Encyclopedia of Magical Herbs.* St. Paul, MN: Llewellyn, 1985.

_____. *Magical Herbalism*. St. Paul, MN: Llewellyn, 1983.

_____. *The Magic in Food*. St. Paul, MN: Llewellyn, 1991.

Dadd, Debra Lynn. *The Nontoxic Home: Protecting Yourself and Your Family from Everyday Toxics and Health Hazards*. Los Angeles: Jeremy P. Tarcher, 1986.

_____. *Nontoxic, Natural, and Earthwise: How to Protect Yourself and Your Family from Harmful Products and Live in Harmony with the Earth*. Los Angeles: Jeremy P. Tarcher, 1990.

_____. *Sustaining the Earth: Choosing Consumer Products That Are Safe for You, Your Family, and the Earth*. Los Angeles: Jeremy P. Tarcher, 1994.

Davis, Patricia. *Aromatherapy A-Z*. London: C.W. Daniel, 1988.

Delaney, Gayle. *Living Your Dreams*. New York: Harper & Row, 1979.

Dixon, Jo, and James Dixon. *The Color Book: Rituals, Charms and Enchantments from Castle Rising*. Denver, CO: J & J, 1978.

_____. *The Witches Jewels: A Traditional Witches' Treatise: The Nature of Stones and Other Gifts of Mother Nature*. Morgantown, WV: Magickal Days, 1989.

Dolfyn. *Crystal Wisdom: Spiritual Properties of Crystals and Gemstones*. Oakland, CA: Earthspirit, 1989.

Doore, Gary, ed. *Shaman's Path: Healing, Personal Growth, and Empowerment*. Boston: Shambhala, 1988.

Duerk, Judith. *Circle of Stones*. San Diego: LuraMedia, 1989.

Dye, Jane. *Aromatherapy for Women and Children*. London: C.W. Daniel, 1992.

Editors of Klutz Press. *Face Painting*. Palo Alto, CA: Klutz Press, 1990.

Edwards, Carolyn McVickar. *The Storyteller's Goddess: Tales of the Goddess and Her Wisdom from Around the World*. New York: Harper Collins, 1991.

Eisler, Riane. *The Chalice and the Blade: Our History, Our Future*. San Francisco: HarperSanFrancisco, 1986.

Eisler, Riane, and David Loye. *The Partnership Way: New Tools for Living and Learning, Healing Our Families, Our Communities, and Our World*. San Francisco: HarperSanFrancisco, 1990.

Elium, Jeanne, and Don Elium. *Raising a Daughter: Parents and the Awakening of a Healthy Woman*. Berkeley, CA: Celestial Arts, 1994.

Elium, Don, and Jeanne Elium. *Raising a Son: Parents and the Making of a Healthy Man.* Hillsboro, OR: Beyond Words, 1992.

Estés, Clarissa Pinkola. *Women Who Run with the Wolves: Myths and Stories of the Wild Woman Archetype.* New York: Ballantine, 1992.

Faber, Adele, and Elaine Mazlish. *How to Talk So Kids Will Listen and Listen So Kids Will Talk.* New York: Avon, 1980.

Farley, Ronnie. *Women of the Native Struggle: Portaits and Testimony of Native American Women.* New York: Orion, 1993.

Francia, Luisa. *Dragontime: Magic and Mystery of Menstruation.* Woodstock, NY: Ash Tree, 1988.

Gardner, Joy. *The New Healing Yourself: Natural Remedies for Adults and Children.* Freedom, CA: Crossing Press, 1989.

Garfield, Patricia. *Your Child's Dreams.* New York: Ballantine, 1984.

Gawain, Shakti. *Creative Visualization.* Mill Valley, CA: Whatever Publishing, 1978.

Gimbutas, Marija. *The Language of the Goddess.* San Francisco: HarperSanFrancisco, 1989.

Gitlin-Emmer, Susan. *Lady of the Northern Light: A Feminist Guide to the Runes.* Freedom, CA: Crossing Press, 1993.

Goodman, Felicitas D. *Where the Spirits Ride the Wind: Trance Journeys and Other Ecstatic Experiences.* Bloomington, IN: Indiana University Press, 1990.

Gray, Eden. *A Complete Guide to the Tarot.* New York: Bantam, 1972.

_____. *The Tarot Revealed: A Modern Guide to Reading the Tarot Cards,* rev. ed. New York: NAL-Dutton, 1988.

Greer, Mary K. *Tarot for Your Self: A Workbook for Personal Transformation.* San Bernardino, CA: Borgo Press, 1984.

Griggs, Barbara. *The Green Witch Herbal: Restoring Nature's Magic in Home, Health, and Beauty Care.* Rochester, VT: Healing Arts Press, 1994.

Halifax, Joan. *Shamanic Voices: A Survey of Visionary Narratives.* New York: Penguin, 1979.

Harner, Michael. *The Way of the Shaman.* New York: Bantam, 1980.

Howard, Michael. *The Magic of Runes: Their Origin and Occult Power.* London: Aquarian Press, 1980.

Jayanti, Amber. *Living the Tarot: Applying the Ancient Oracle to the Challenges of Modern Life*. San Bernardino, CA: Borgo Press, 1988.

Johnson, Cait. *Tarot for Every Day: Ideas and Activities for Bringing Tarot Wisdom into Your Daily Life*. Wappingers Falls, NY: Shawangunk Press, 1994.

Johnson, Cait, and Maura D. Shaw. *Tarot Games: 45 Playful Ways to Explore Tarot Cards Together: A New Vision for the Circle of Community*. San Francisco: HarperSanFrancisco, 1994.

Katzen, Mollie, and Ann Henderson. *Pretend Soup and Other Real Recipes: A Cookbook for Preschoolers and Up*. Berkeley: Tricycle Press, 1994.

Kelly, Marguerite, and Elia Parsons. *The Mother's Almanac*. Garden City, NY: Doubleday, 1975.

Kinscher, Jonni. *Dreams Can Help: A Journal Guide to Understanding Your Dreams and Making Them Work for You*. Minneapolis: Free Spirit Publishing, 1988.

Knight, Gareth. *Tarot and Magic: Images for Ritual and Pathworking*. Rochester, VT: Inner Traditions, 1991.

Kofalk, Harriet. *The Peaceful Cook*. Eugene, OR: Talking Leaves, 1991.

Lair, Cynthia. *Feeding the Whole Family: Down-to-Earth Cookbook and Whole Foods Guide*. San Diego: LuraMedia, 1994.

Lang, Jenifer. *Jenifer Lang Cooks for Kids*. New York: Crown, 1991.

Lorie, Peter. *Wonder Child: Rediscovering the Magical World of Innocence and Joy Within Ourselves and Our Children*. New York: Simon and Schuster, 1989.

Luxton, Leonora. *Astrology, Key to Self Understanding*. St. Paul, MN: Llewellyn, 1978.

Mariechild, Diane. *Mother Wit: A Guide to Healing and Psychic Development*. Freedom, CA: Crossing Press, 1988.

Matthiessen, Peter. *In the Spirit of Crazy Horse*. New York: Penguin, 1992.

McLeester, Dick. *Welcome to the Magic Theater: A Handbook for Exploring Dreams*. Amherst, MA: Food for Thought, 1977.

Milord, Susan. *The Kids' Nature Book*. Charlotte, VT: Williamson, 1989.

Monaghan, Patricia. *The Book of Goddesses and Heroines*. New York: E. P. Dutton, 1981.

Murdock, Maureen. *Spinning Inward: Using Guided Imagery with Children for Learning, Creativity, and Relaxation*. Boston: Shambhala, 1987.

Murphy, Joseph M. *Santeria: African Spirits in America*. Boston: Beacon Press, 1993.

Nabhan, Gary Paul, and Stephen Trimble. *The Geography of Childhood: Why Children Need Wild Places.* Boston: Beacon Press, 1994.

Noble, Vicki. *Motherpeace: A Way to the Goddess through Myth, Art and Tarot.* San Francisco: Harper & Row, 1983.

_____. *Shakti Woman: Feeling Our Fire, Healing Our World: The New Female Shamanism.* New York: Harper Collins, 1991.

_____. *Uncoiling the Snake: Ancient Patterns in Contemporary Women's Lives.* San Francisco: HarperSanFrancisco, 1993.

O'Gaea, Ashleen. *The Family Wicca Book.* St. Paul, MN: Llewellyn, 1993.

Pollack, Rachel. *Seventy-Eight Degrees of Wisdom: A Book of Tarot: An in-depth analysis of the symbolism and psychological resonances of the Tarot suit cards, including instructions on how to give readings. Parts 1 and 2.* London: Aquarian Press, 1983.

_____. *Tarot Readings and Meditations: How the Tarot can help us answer specific questions, act as a tool for psychological analysis and tell us how to overcome problems.* London: Aquarian Press, 1986.

Robertson, Laurel, Carol Flinders, and Brian Ruppenthal. *The New Laurel's Kitchen: A Handbook for Vegetarian Cookery and Nutrition.* Berkeley, CA: Ten Speed Press, 1986.

Sakoian, Frances, and Louis S. Acker. *The Astrologer's Handbook.* New York: Harper & Row, 1973.

Sams, Jamie, and David Carson. *Medicine Cards: The Discovery of Power through the Ways of Animals.* Santa Fe: Bear, 1988.

Serith, Ceisiwr. *The Pagan Family: Handing the Old Ways Down.* St. Paul, MN: Llewellyn, 1994.

Shanberg, Karen, and Stan Tekiela. *Plantworks: Field Guide, Recipes, Activities.* Cambridge, MN: Adventure, 1991.

Shaw, Maura D., and Sydna Altschuler Byrne. *Foods from Mother Earth: A Basic Cookbook for Young Vegetarians (and Anybody Else).* Wappingers Falls, NY: Shawangunk, 1994.

Sjöo, Monica, and Barbara Mor. *The Great Cosmic Mother: Rediscovering the Religion of the Earth.* San Francisco: HarperSanFrancisco, 1991.

Smith, Penelope. *Animals: Our Return to Wholeness.* Point Reyes, CA: Pegasus, 1993.

Starck, Marcia. *Earth Mother Astrology: Ancient Healing Wisdom.* St. Paul, MN: Llewellyn, 1989.

_____. *Women's Medicine Ways: Cross-Cultural Rites of Passage*. Freedom, CA: Crossing Press, 1993.

Starhawk. *Dreaming the Dark: Magic, Sex, and Politics*. Boston: Beacon Press, 1982.

_____. *The Spiral Dance: A Rebirth of the Ancient Religion of the Great Goddess: Rituals, Invocations, Exercises, Magic*. San Francisco: Harper & Row, 1989.

_____. *Truth or Dare*. San Francisco: Harper Collins, 1989.

Stein, Diane. *All Women Are Healers: A Comprehensive Guide to Natural Healing*. Freedom, CA: Crossing Press, 1990.

_____. *The Kwan Yin Book of Changes*. St. Paul, MN: Llewellyn, 1985.

_____. *The Women's Spirituality Book*. St. Paul, MN: Llewellyn, 1987.

Stone, Merlin. *Ancient Mirrors of Womanhood: Our Goddess and Heroine Heritage*. New York: New Sibylline, 1979.

_____. *When God Was a Woman*. New York: Harcourt Brace Jovanovich, 1978.

Teish, Luisa. *Jambalaya: The Natural Woman's Book of Personal Charms and Practical Rituals*. San Francisco: Harper & Row, 1985.

Tisserand, Maggie. *Aromatherapy for Women*. Rochester, VT: Healing Arts Press, 1988.

Walker, Barbara G. *The Crone*. San Francisco: Harper & Row, 1985.

_____. *The Woman's Dictionary of Symbols and Sacred Objects*. San Francisco: HarperSanFrancisco, 1988.

_____. *The Woman's Encyclopedia of Myths and Secrets*. San Francisco: Harper & Row, 1983.

_____. *Women's Rituals*. San Francisco: Harper & Row, 1990.

Weed, Susun. *Healing Wise*. Woodstock, NY: Ash Tree, 1989.

Weinstein, Marion. *Earth Magic: A Dianic Book of Shadows*. Custer, WA: Phoenix, 1986.

_____. *Positive Magic: Occult Self-Help*. Custer, WA: Phoenix, 1984.

Wilshire, Donna. *Virgin Mother Crone: Myths and Mysteries of the Triple Goddess*. Rochester, VT: Inner Traditions, 1994.

Wolfe, Amber. *In the Shadow of the Shaman: Connecting with Self, Nature, and Spirit*. St. Paul, MN: Llewellyn, 1993.

Woolger, Jennifer Barker, and Roger J. Woolger. *The Goddess Within: A Guide to the Eternal Myths That Shape Women's Lives*. New York: Ballantine, 1989.

Worth, Valerie. *The Crone's Book of Words*. St. Paul, MN: Llewellyn, 1986.

Aromatherapy

Cunningham, Scott
Davis, Patricia
Dye, Jane
Tisserand, Maggie

Astrology

Luxton, Leonora
Sakoian, Frances, and Louis S. Acker
Starck, Marcia

Children, Companion Animals, Family, Family Celebrations

Ban Breathnach, Sarah
Bettelheim, Bruno
Carlson, Laurie
Cornell, Joseph
Elium, Don, and Jeanne Elium
Faber, Adele, and Elaine Mazlish
Kelly, Marguerite, and Elia Parsons
Lorie, Peter
Milord, Susan
Nabhan, Gary Paul, and Stephen Trimble
O'Gaea, Ashleen
Serith, Ceisiwr
Smith, Penelope

Crystals and Gemstones, Divination (except Tarot)

Blum, Ralph
Cunningham, Scott
Dixon, Jo, and James Dixon
Dolfyn
Gitlin-Emmer, Susan
Howard, Michael
Stein, Diane

Dreams

Delaney, Gayle
Garfield, Patricia
Kinscher, Jonni
McLeester, Dick

Food, Cooking

American Indian Society
Callan, Ginny
Copage, Eric V.
Cunningham, Scott
Katzen, Mollie, and Ann Henderson
Kofalk, Harriet
Lair, Cynthia
Lang, Jenifer
Robertson, Laurel, Carol Flinders, and
    Brian Ruppenthal
Shanberg, Karen, and Stan Tekiela
Shaw, Maura D., and Sydna Altschuler
    Byrne

Goddess, Ritual, Women's Spirituality

Adler, Margot
Beck, Renee, and Sydney Barbara Metrick
Blair, Nancy
Bolen, Jean Shinoda
Budapest, Z.
Cahill, Sedonia, and Joshua Halpern
Campanelli, Pauline
Duerk, Judith
Edwards, Carolyn McVickar
Eisler, Riane
Estés, Clarissa Pinkola
Francia, Luisa
Gimbutas, Marija
Johnson, Cait
Monaghan, Patricia

Noble, Vicki
O'Gaea, Ashleen
Serith, Ceisiwr
Sjöo, Monica, and Barbara Mor
Starck, Marcia
Starhawk
Stein, Diane
Stone, Merlin
Teish, Luisa
Walker, Barbara G.
Weinstein, Marion
Woolger, Jennifer Barker, and Roger J.
    Woolger
Worth, Valerie

Green Housekeeping

Berthold-Bond, Annie
Dadd, Debra Lynn

Guided Meditation

Achterberg, Jeanne, Barbara Dossey, and
    Leslie Kolkmeier
Gawain, Shakti
Mariechild, Diane
Murdock, Maureen
Starhawk

Herbs, Healing, Weeds, Wise Woman Way

Berneth, Stefen
Beyerl, Paul
Cunningham, Scott
Gardner, Joy
Griggs, Barbara

Johnson, Cait
Shanberg, Karen, and Stan Tekiela
Stein, Diane
Weed, Susun

Native American Issues and Spirituality

Brown, Dee
Crow Dog, Mary
Farley, Ronnie
Matthiessen, Peter
Sams, Jamie, and David Carson

Shamanism

Cowan, Tom
Doore, Gary, ed.
Goodman, Felicitas D.
Halifax, Joan
Harner, Michael
Noble, Vicki
Wolfe, Amber

Tarot

Arrien, Angeles
Gray, Eden
Greer, Mary K.
Jayanti, Amber
Johnson, Cait
Johnson, Cait, and Maura D. Shaw
Knight, Gareth
Noble, Vicki
Pollack, Rachel
Sams, Jamie, and David Carson

RESOURCES

We have listed some of our own personal favorites here, just to give you a place to start. Any of these organizations will be happy to send catalogs or furnish subscription information.

Audiotapes

LADYSLIPPER, INC.
P.O. Box 3124-R
Durham, NC 27715
(800) 634-6044

LIBANA
P.O. Box 530
Cambridge, MA 02140

Books, Tapes, Gemstones, and Magical Stuff

PYRAMID BOOKS
P.O. Box 3333, Altid Park
Chelmsford, MA 01824-0933
(800) 333-4220

Earth-friendly Home Products

EARTH CARE
Ukiah, CA 95842-8507
(800) 347-0070

NATURAL CHOICE CATALOG
ECO Design Company
1365 Rufina Circle
Santa Fe, NM 87501-2965
(800) 621-2591

REAL GOODS
966 Mazzoni Street
Ukiah, CA 95482-3471
(800) 762-7325

SEVENTH GENERATION
49 Hercules Drive
Colchester, VT 05446-1672
(800) 456-1177

Earth-friendly Toys, Instruments, and Craft Supplies

HEARTH SONG
156 N. Main Street
Sebastopol, CA 95472
(800) 325-2502
(This is where we buy our modeling beeswax.)

MUSIC FOR LITTLE PEOPLE
P.O. Box 1460
Redway, CA 95560
(800) 727-2233

Great Goddess Goods

JANE IRIS DESIGNS, INC.
P.O. Box 608
Graton, CA 95444
(800) 828-5687

STAR RIVER PRODUCTIONS
P.O. Box 6254
North Brunswick, NJ 08902
(800) 232-1733

Herbs and Herbal Products

BLESSED HERBS
109 Barre Plains Road
Oakham, MA 01068
(800) 489-4372

GREEN TERRESTRIAL
P.O. Box 266
Milton, NY 12547
(914) 795-5238

JEAN'S GREENS
R.R. 1, Box 55J, Hale Road
Rensselaerville, NY 12147
(518) 239-8327

MOUNTAIN ROSE HERBS
P.O. Box 2000
Redway, CA 95560
(800) 879-3337
(A great source for bulk beeswax, self-igniting charcoal, glass jars, labels, essential oils, and much more—besides herbs)

Holistic Health Products

**AWARENESS AND HEALTH
  UNLIMITED**
3509 North High Street
Columbus, OH 43214
(800) 533-7087

Publications

MOTHERING
P.O. Box 1690
Santa Fe, NM 87504
(505) 984-8116

***SAGEWOMAN: CELEBRATING THE GODDESS
  IN EVERY WOMAN***
P.O. Box 641
Point Arena, CA 95468-0641
(707) 882-2052

INDEX